Child Life
Exam
SECRETS

Study Guide
Your Key to Exam Success

Child Life Test Review for the Child Life
Professional Certification Examination

Dear Future Exam Success Story:

Congratulations on your purchase of our study guide. Our goal in writing our study guide was to cover the content on the test, as well as provide insight into typical test taking mistakes and how to overcome them.

Standardized tests are a key component of being successful, which only increases the importance of doing well in the high-pressure high-stakes environment of test day. How well you do on this test will have a significant impact on your future, and we have the research and practical advice to help you execute on test day.

The product you're reading now is designed to exploit weaknesses in the test itself, and help you avoid the most common errors test takers frequently make.

How to use this study guide

We don't want to waste your time. Our study guide is fast-paced and fluff-free. We suggest going through it a number of times, as repetition is an important part of learning new information and concepts.

First, read through the study guide completely to get a feel for the content and organization. Read the general success strategies first, and then proceed to the content sections. Each tip has been carefully selected for its effectiveness.

Second, read through the study guide again, and take notes in the margins and highlight those sections where you may have a particular weakness.

Finally, bring the manual with you on test day and study it before the exam begins.

Your success is our success

We would be delighted to hear about your success. Send us an email and tell us your story. Thanks for your business and we wish you continued success.

Sincerely,

Mometrix Test Preparation Team

Need more help? Check out our flashcards at: http://MometrixFlashcards.com/ChildLife

TABLE OF CONTENTS

Top 20 Test Taking Tips... 1
Assessment... 2
Professional Responsibility 9
Intervention 41
    Play 44
    Child Life Programs and Issues... 58
    Postvention 78
    Grief 93
    Spirituality 102
Practice Test...109
    Practice Questions...109
    Answers and Explanations 117
Test Preparation Aids 128
    Practice Test Questions...128
    Case studies..147
Secret Key #1 - Time is Your Greatest Enemy 151
    Pace Yourself 151
Secret Key #2 - Guessing is not Guesswork..151
    Monkeys Take the Test..151
    $5 Challenge...152
Secret Key #3 - Practice Smarter, Not Harder 153
    Success Strategy 153
Secret Key #4 - Prepare, Don't Procrastinate 153
Secret Key #5 - Test Yourself...154
General Strategies..154
Special Report: How to Overcome Test Anxiety 160
    Lack of Preparation...160
    Physical Signals 161
    Nervousness 161
    Study Steps...163
    Helpful Techniques 164
Additional Bonus Material 169

Top 20 Test Taking Tips

1. Carefully follow all the test registration procedures
2. Know the test directions, duration, topics, question types, how many questions
3. Setup a flexible study schedule at least 3-4 weeks before test day
4. Study during the time of day you are most alert, relaxed, and stress free
5. Maximize your learning style; visual learner use visual study aids, auditory learner use auditory study aids
6. Focus on your weakest knowledge base
7. Find a study partner to review with and help clarify questions
8. Practice, practice, practice
9. Get a good night's sleep; don't try to cram the night before the test
10. Eat a well balanced meal
11. Know the exact physical location of the testing site; drive the route to the site prior to test day
12. Bring a set of ear plugs; the testing center could be noisy
13. Wear comfortable, loose fitting, layered clothing to the testing center; prepare for it to be either cold or hot during the test
14. Bring at least 2 current forms of ID to the testing center
15. Arrive to the test early; be prepared to wait and be patient
16. Eliminate the obviously wrong answer choices, then guess the first remaining choice
17. Pace yourself; don't rush, but keep working and move on if you get stuck
18. Maintain a positive attitude even if the test is going poorly
19. Keep your first answer unless you are positive it is wrong
20. Check your work, don't make a careless mistake

Assessment

Psychosocial assessment

When staff members are interacting with children, they will find that some knowledge about the key findings of a psychosocial assessment will be invaluable. Specific psychosocial understandings make it far easier to design successful activities, monitor children's needs, and resolve concerns. The essential elements of a psychosocial assessment include: 1) affect (range of emotional expression); 2) mood and temperament (depressed, withdrawn, angry, etc); 3) capacity for communication and interaction (verbal and physical willingness to interact with others, including family, staff, and peers); 4) prior physical health and medical history (including prior hospitalizations and burdensome treatments); 5) personal and family stressors; 6) coping skills and predisposed strategies and patterns; 7) preferred defense mechanisms and frequency and common situations of use; and 8) history of any self-esteem issues. Finally, knowledge of recent events is also important. Marked agitation, for example, would not be abnormal shortly after undergoing a difficult medical treatment.

Important theorists

James Robertson
In 1948 James Robertson was hired by the renowned child psychology theorist, John Bowlby, to observe and document the behaviors and reactions of hospitalized and institutionalized children who were separated from their parents. Robertson had previously been trained in techniques of Naturalistic Observation by Anna Freud in her Hampstead residential nursery for homeless children. In 1950, with Bowlby's assistance, Robertson began work on what was to become a pivotal film in the understanding of children's coping in medical settings: "A Two-Year-Old Goes to Hospital." A deeply moving film, it not only chronicled the experiences of a child going through the trauma of parental separation and serious health issues, but it also served to further enhance and validate much of Bowlby's own theories about children's coping.

Mary Salter Ainsworth
In her PhD dissertation ("An Evaluation of Adjustment Based upon the Concept of Security," 1940), Mary Salter Ainsworth proposed the idea that infants and children require what she termed a "secure base," i.e., an important attachment figure (ideally, parents) before they are able to venture into and cope well with unfamiliar circumstances. Where "familial security" is lacking, she concluded that all areas of infant development could be handicapped and diminished. In 1950, Ainsworth was hired by the child psychology theorist, John Bowlby, to analyze James Robertson's naturalistic observation data. Ainsworth's earlier thinking subsequently influenced Bowlby's, and she later went on to validate many of Bowlby's theories in research in Uganda and in subsequent clinical work in Baltimore, Maryland.

John Bowlby
In Bowlby's 1951 book, "Maternal Care and Mental Health" (later, "Child Care and the Growth of Love," 1965), he noted that children require a nurturing and uninterrupted relationship with a mother (or permanent substitute) in order to sustain emotional and

-2-

mental health. His theories were expounded in 3 classic papers: "The Nature of the Child's Tie to His Mother" (1958), "Separation Anxiety" (1959), and "Grief and Mourning in Infancy and Early Childhood" (1960). The first paper noted how instinctive behaviors such as sucking, clinging, and following (and maternal responses to "signaling behaviors" such as smiling and crying) produce an infant-maternal bond during the first year of life. The 1959 paper described infant/child-maternal separation responses as moving from "protest" to "despair," and then into "denial or detachment" (as defense mechanisms). Bowlby maintained that "separation anxiety" is activated when a child feels threatened, but finds no supportive attachment figure. The third paper contradicted traditional theory that infants and young children were too immature to experience grief and mourning, and proposed that recurring losses of attachment figures would result in a later inability to form intimate relationships.

Child life service model

Assessment
"Assessment" includes information gathering regarding the child, family, and health care situation. Relevant child issues include diagnosis and recommended treatment course, maturational status (chronological vs. developmental age), responses to prior and current health care issues, capacity for communication and independent function, fears and coping styles, cultural and religious issues, and the presence of any other related life stressors. Important family information includes primary family relationships, involved significant others, general family availability, and financial and home stability. Also included are cultural and religious issues, emotional issues and coping skills, prior health care experiences, understanding and expectations regarding current health problems, etc. Assessments must be ongoing and continuously affect later activities and strategies.

Plan
Care plans are predicated upon a quality assessment. Even with very limited information, it is still generally possible to construct a broad-based care plan. However, the greater and more detailed the background assessment, the more specific and effective the care plan becomes. Care plans must also target specific outcome goals. More plainly put, a specialist must be able to identify an anticipated benefit to the child and/or family through specific care plan criteria. An example might be a plan to increase a child's coping skills relative to a specific fearful procedure through training in relaxation techniques and the use of mental imagery. The expected outcome is greater coping capacity and increased tolerance for the particular procedure. With time constraints, care plans must always be prioritized so that more crucial issues are addressed first, while time allows. Further, it is often advantageous to coordinate care plans with other treating providers, as collaborative benefits can often be realized.

Adjusting programming

It is also important to tailor activities and interventions to varying settings. For example, children in a pre-surgical waiting area might use blank cloth dolls upon which they can draw their own features and rehearse "the medicine sleep" along with placing dressings, tubes, and other devices consistent with their postoperative understandings. An infant and toddler unit will have special activities designed to combat "vulnerable child syndrome" arising from limited expression and mobility while coping with inexplicable pain. An ICU may provide "vicarious play" and comfort activities to cope with immobility, discussions of poor prognosis, death, etc. An oncology unit may attempt to build good memories at stressful times, with things to look forward to during recurring visits. Dialysis units are also structured around a longer duration of recurring services and stressors. Other unique settings include:

- HIV clinics where children cope with complex treatments
- Child and adolescent psychiatry units where activities also assess behavioral and emotional issues
- Dental settings where children face transient painful procedures and intrusions around the face
- Burn units where disfigurement is common

Each setting requires specific interventions designed according to participant diagnosis, development, and age.

Identifying need

Virtually all program settings have limited resources and funds and thus all available services must be properly allocated and prioritized. To create a workable service allocation hierarchy, consider the following:

- Common group types along with their most challenging interventions and procedures
- The ranked severity of relevant group illnesses and the time demands of each
- Those illnesses and treatments which arise suddenly and are most unfamiliar – i.e., those most likely to traumatize or overwhelm patients and families
- The patients and families most likely to benefit from services
- The need for care consistency and continuity
- The obligation to give priority to services that reflect the mission and goals of the institution.

By using these criteria, those groups most common, most in need, most likely to benefit, and reflecting the primary mission of the facility will not be overlooked.

Upon determining the specific areas of greatest need, it remains crucial to identify specific individuals at greatest risk of untoward issues and outcomes. This is often done by producing "vulnerability ratings" or "risk potential scores." A few key elements in such ratings are:

- *Child age:* Research indicates children between the ages of 6 months and 4 years are particularly vulnerable to emotional trauma from hospitalization (particularly if also separated from family for significant periods)
- *Parent/family unavailability:* Whether physical absence or emotional detachment or neglect
- *Stress points:* Such as when newly diagnosed with chronic conditions, times of acute deterioration, lengthy or frequent readmissions, or when current events evoke difficult past memories
- *Illness severity* and treatment regimen burdensomeness

All these elements should be recognized in prioritizing and allocating services and time.

Common pediatric stressors

Numerous psychosocial factors, such as emotional and mental development, personality, culture, prior experience, and existing expectations will shape each health care experience. Physiological factors include illness severity, whether it is transient or chronic, the suddenness of onset, and the burdensomeness of related medical interventions. Situations where both psychosocial and physiological factors more fully converge include circumstances of debilitation, disfigurement, dismemberment, and other body image insults. For pediatric populations, there are other significant stressors including:
- Separation from loved ones
- Any use of needles
- Prolonged waiting times when fears and imagination run rampant
- Any procedure or treatment involving pain or unexpected sensations
- Any exposure or examination of private bodily areas
- Being the focus of large groups of adults (such as in an operating suite)
- The use of any large and imposing medical machinery, along with unfamiliar situations, treatments, equipment, and procedures

Such stressors, in combination with underlying psychosocial and physiological factors, will likely require greater attention through a "stress point care" approach.

Diversity

Family diversity
Every family has unique strengths, weaknesses, and needs. No family is issue- and concern-free, particularly at times of distress. The goal of the child life specialist is to optimize family function, with a particular focus on collaborative support of the ill child. Some families are large and extended, with a constant stream of relatives creating overstimulation. Child life staff must respond by reducing toys, activities, and fuss that may contribute to the problem. Some families are poorly expressive, or they may have difficulty containing overt expressions of sadness, depression, or mourning even around their children. Treatment milestone celebrations, special treats, meals, and other events may be useful to promote sharing and a more positive outlook. Other families may live far away or have work demands that prevent them from being together. The child life staff then needs to facilitate letters, cards, e-mails, daily diaries, and photographs, etc, to aid in family bond retention. Where necessary, staff-child bonds may need to serve in proxy. Finally, there are also reconstituted families with many stepsiblings, stepparents, etc, who may require special attention to reduce conflicts, competition, and time and visitation demands.

Cultural diversity
Every culture has expectations, rituals, and values related to health care. They may also have unique perspectives on the role of families, medical authority figures, and treatment decision making. Becoming aware of these varied perspectives is essential to providing quality child life services. Certain cultural practices may seem unsupportive or even obstructive of the process of diagnosis and treatment. This may be particularly distressing to medical providers who feel compelled to pursue optimal approaches. Nevertheless, it is essential for all involved to recognize the holistic nature of family-centered care, and to understand that anything that produces distress in parents and close family members will produce proportional distress in ill children. Child life specialists can be particularly helpful

at such times, seeking to understand the cultural values and goals implicit in any parental behaviors and looking for innovative ways to incorporate culture into optimum healing endeavors. Often this is accomplished by creative thinking and brokering information between providers and families until acceptable strategies can be secured. This advocacy and amelioration role is ideal for child life specialists.

Family systems theory

Family systems theory conceives of every individual as an interrelated part of many other broader social systems – i.e., the family, the community, and society as a whole. Consequently, all individuals are interdependent upon and influenced by all other individuals. Standards, norms, expectations, values, and beliefs clarify those interactions that are acceptable and those that are not. All interventions intended to be effective at the individual level must also be effective at the relevant family and health care system levels. Parents and others can most meaningfully enhance and promote the successful adjustment of an ill child and the siblings only if properly guided by holistic family goals and expectations. Therefore, in search of effective change, professionals must consider a wide range of ecological and environmental influences in order to produce effective and enduring interventions.

Concept of caring

It has been said, "I don't care how much you know, until I know how much you care." Caring is the essential catalyst for nearly every higher-order human interaction that is ultimately effective at its end-point. Caring attends to both feelings and the mind – not just information alone. It preserves human dignity, provides essential impetus towards compliance and change, and imbues individuals facing difficult experiences and burdens with a compelling reason for pressing on and through. Thus, developing true and honest empathy and care about others is vital to health care professionals. In recent years, cost constraints and system efficiencies have eroded the ethic of caring. It is essential that the concept of "care" be returned to a paramount position in health "care" systems and services.

Scientific/biomedical health model

The scientific or biomedical health model is based upon the following 4 values: 1) determinism – the belief that a cause-and-effect relationship exists for every natural event; 2) mechanism – that "life" arises from structures operating very much like a machine; 3) reductionism – that everything can be reduced and/or disassembled into its constituent parts; and 4) dualism – that the mind and the body are separate entities. Although treating the body as a collection of physiological organs and biochemical processes serves the process of scientific discovery well, there are certain weaknesses inherent in this perspective. These include: a) piecemeal health services (i.e., focused too narrowly on "specialist" health concerns to the exclusion of a holistic approach); b) preventative medicine neglect in both research and treatment; c) little or no consideration of the known linkages between health of the mind and health of the body; d) a focus on symptoms over root disease causes; and e) an over-dependence on "prescription-ism" (i.e., pushing pills for all ills).

Prevention and poverty

Preventative medicine continues to be much neglected, as compared with symptom-focused medical care. The Institute of Medicine (1994) has proposed a prevention hierarchy: a) targeting large at-risk populations for disorders of concern; b) identifying subpopulations with higher than average risk; and then c) expending specific efforts on "high-risk" groups who already have symptoms. Some progress has been seen in areas such as prenatal care and well-baby checks, but most remain neglected. Large segments of the population remain uninsured or sufficiently underinsured to preclude receipt of adequate health care – especially preventative care. Non-traditional families (i.e., single-parent and grandparent-headed homes) and those with lower education and skills often lack the resources and knowledge to seek out and receive the health care they need. Considerable change is needed for truly universal health care to be provided to all our citizens.

Information technology

The internet has become a potentially powerful tool in medicine, for both patients and physicians. However, this has produced a power-shift from physicians to patients, as patients and families seek out ever more information and interject it into physician's contacts. Doctors, accustomed to being in charge and inevitably unable to keep up in an age of "information explosion," are often threatened. New physician-patient paradigms are needed to normalize and integrate mutual sharing, and avoid adversarial relationships. One particularly prime area for new inroads is that of home care. As cost and resource limits and an increasingly information-skilled populace merge, home care is becoming an ever more viable nontraditional care setting. By use of e-mail, telephone monitoring, internet teaching, web cams, and home visits, better and more cost-effective medical care may become available. Researchers and innovators should target these emerging opportunities.

Change agents

Numerous gaps and deficiencies continue to exist in health care systems and services. As all health care professionals must practice within these limits and deficiencies, it is imperative for each to assume the role of "change agent." Whether targeting issues such as limited health care access, insurance coverage gaps, increasing awareness of the need for prevention, and new service innovations and options, health care providers have a responsibility to seek after continuous improvement. This can be done through many means, including: 1) becoming politically active; 2) participating in systems planning, evaluation, and problem-solving committees and groups; and 3) joining or starting grassroots movements and educational campaigns. By so doing, health care experiences can be improved for all, and with a greater potential for effective success.

Health facility design

The Center for Health Design completed a review of over 400 studies on hospital facility design and quality of care. They concluded that there is a direct link between quality design and quality care. In particular, it was found that facility-based psychosocial impacts can be high. Environments with high levels of "press" (i.e., complex and cognitively challenging – such as hospitals) undermine confidence and well-being (i.e., healing and stability, etc). To compensate, these settings must emphasize: 1) an individually-centered "locus of control" ("way finding" markers and signs, temperature and lighting options, disability access features, etc); 2) privacy (both visual and auditory); 3) social interaction options; 4) proper personal space (varying according to relationship –general public, social, personal, and intimate); 5) territoriality (a feeling of personalized space – personal pictures, comfort items, familiar things, etc); and 6) comfort and safety (rest spaces, quiet retreats, telephone and bathroom convenience, readily available nourishment, etc). As facilities are rarely designed with children in mind, child life specialists should endeavor to participate in and support environmentally effective designs whenever possible.

Professional Responsibility

Ethical dilemma

Ethical dilemmas occur in the absence of a clearly-defined course of action. They most typically involve various competing interests, obligations, duties, standards, policies, protocols, and/or interests, which cannot all be satisfied by any given course of action. In exploring and seeking after an appropriate solution, it becomes necessary to rank and prioritize these competing interests in an effort to secure a plan that ideally provides for the most ethical ("best") outcome in terms of a hierarchy of all competing demands. A hierarchy is necessary, as not all competing interests will have equal claim on an ethical outcome. The first step is taken when it is recognized that an ethical issue has arisen. This requires an ongoing awareness of ethical practice parameters and a substantive familiarity with ethical concepts in general.

Ethical awareness need

First, advances in medicine continue to greatly expand the range of diagnoses, interventions, and treatments that are available. They also proportionally increase the potential for highly variable outcomes. Controversial issues such as experimental versus standardized treatments, genetic defect testing, DNA engineering, stem cell studies, cloning, along with a variety of other fetal and postnatal interventions, have burgeoned dramatically. Each has ethical dilemmas that invariably accompany them. Second, existing laws, policies, and protocols may also produce ethical issues that require appropriate address. Finally, ever-expanding court rulings ("case law") and new and revised legislation such as the federal Child Abuse Prevention and Treatment and Adoption and Reform Act (1985), as well as continuing guidelines issued by governing bodies such as the American Academy of Pediatrics, Bioethics Section (est. 1988), must necessarily be followed and thus require enhanced practitioner ethical awareness.

Ways to improve your ethical awareness include:
- Regularly review the Child Life Council Code of Ethics and consistently apply it in your practice.
- Keep current on guidelines for continuing education, confidentiality, informed consent, advance directives, etc.
- Learn how your own Ethics Committee is accessed; differences between formal and informal consults, subcommittees, etc.
- Recommend that staff meetings include an ethics presentation or similar educational content.
- Seek out and read literature on ethics topics.
- Attend ethics presentations, grand rounds, symposia, etc .
- Propose presentations on topics of special concern.
- Encourage the identification and sharing of ethical concerns in daily practice.
- Consider volunteering to join the ethics committee or to be an *ad hoc* member available when special child life concerns arise.
- Share in ethical discussions and debates to sharpen your ethical thinking and skills.

Goal of ethics

The goal of "ethics" is to engage in a process of thinking about what "should" occur when faced with difficult situations. It is not possible for ethical decision making processes to produce absolute or unquestionably "right" answers. Rather, the primary goal is to ensure that appropriate and necessarily rigorous pondering, consideration, and discussion take place before decisions are made. This process should include a careful scrutiny of our own previously unexamined assumptions, cultural expectations, philosophies, and beliefs that may shape, constrain, or limit our own perspectives. It should also include an open and respectful acceptance and integration of other beliefs (where possible) to avoid potentially unwarranted judgments and actions that might damage essential relationships and trust. Finally, appropriate deliberations must also include an appraisal of necessary constraints, laws, policies, and required practices, and seek alternative strategies for meeting essential child and family needs. In this way, the likelihood that reliable, consistent and ethical choices will be made can be greatly increased.

Primary ethical roles

One ethical role is that of "advocate." The child life specialist must serve as an advocate not only for their own immediate clients (children and youth), but for involved families, caregivers, and guardians as well. In carrying out this advocacy role, child life specialists must be able to identify and respond to a variety of clinical dilemmas, whether they involve the client and family alone or stem from larger policy and procedural concerns. A second ethical role occurs as a direct service practitioner, wherein the child life specialist must be able to assess and respond to ethical issues and concerns relating to their own daily performance. The third role is encountered as a teacher, supervisor, or mentor, wherein the child life specialist must be able to teach others those elements necessary to identify and resolve ethical dilemmas, to establish necessary boundaries, and to otherwise meet all ethical obligations.

Professional and ethical principles

Beneficence
There are a number of principles and values that underlie ethical decision making and behavior. Primary among these is the principle of "beneficence." This principle refers to the duty to produce "benefit" and to act for the good and well-being of another. It is important to note that ideals of beneficence may vary according to an individual's goals, culture, religion, and customs. What may be viewed as good and desirable by one individual or family may not be seen in a similar light by other individuals or families with different perspectives. Of further note, an individual's concept of beneficence may also include social concerns and the interests and needs of humankind. For example, much of the medical research for which individuals volunteer may hold limited promise for them personally. Rather, the good they hope to achieve may be the well-being of subsequent individuals seeking treatment, or even their posterity.

Nonmaleficence
The earliest indirect reference to nonmaleficence is sometimes ascribed to Hippocrates, the ancient Greek physician who wrote, "First, do no harm." The "harm" to be avoided can be physical, such as disability, disfigurement, pain, suffering, and a multitude of other similar

corporeal burdens. It may be emotional or psychological, such as unremedied fear, stress, anxiety, or similar intrapsychic traumas. The reduction of emotional and psychological distress lies at the heart of the work of child life specialists. Not only do they attempt to aid and enhance the capacity of children and families to cope well with physical issues such as pain, but they also labor to relieve the distress that accompanies separation, fear of the unknown, and potential loss – along with any other stressors arising from institutional impediments, family disruption, and compromise of other supporting relationships. In carrying out their work, practitioners must "first, do no harm" by fully understanding and addressing the unique individual perspectives that underlie all forms of distress.

It is important to note that doing good and avoiding harm must nearly always be carefully balanced, one against another. For example, dental work nearly always involves some transient pain that can be seen as maleficent or "harmful." However, the expectation of long-term good (i.e., beneficence) typically far outweighs the temporary discomfort. Even so, in the broader medical arena proposed treatments may not always provide outcomes as certain as those derived by filling a dental cavity. Few treatments can guarantee 100% success and some may even be experimental and lacking in outcome-validity data. In such situations, the full burdens of treatment may not be entirely known. Ethically, it is essential that all involved achieve a mutual understanding and acceptance of all relevant uncertainties in order to strike a proper balance between unwanted maleficence and truly beneficent decisions. Child life specialists have an obligation to assist in these deliberations, supplying their unique understanding of child development, coping strategies, family dynamics, and available interventions and likely outcomes.

Respect for persons
This ethical principle demands that every living being be acknowledged as unique and singularly valuable, intrinsically possessed of substantive worth and potential. Consequently, all must be treated with dignity and respect. While children have not yet attained full maturity and understanding, they are no less entitled to respect and dignity. Thus, any proposed intervention, treatment, or care plan should always be evaluated in light of dignity and respect for the "whole child" – i.e., how the proposal will affect the child over the long term and in all domains of life. In close corollary, proposals must also be considered in the light of any burdens placed on extended family and other important support systems, as the principle of respect for persons is broader than the individual alone. It has been noted that the more proposed interventions are evaluated from the vantage point of the "total child" perspective, the greater the likelihood that ethical decisions will be made.

Autonomy
The principle of autonomy refers to self-determination, individual freedom, and self-actualization. However, the concept may also induce competing interests depending upon whether it is viewed from the vantage point of the child, the family, or other involved caregivers. It is further complicated by the fact that children are not yet fully autonomous beings and remain considerably reliant upon others. Even so, child life specialists must recognize that children possess certain rights and interests, and that incomplete competence in the legal sense does not mean that a child is entirely without decisional capacity. Further, the child's buy-in, acceptance, and increased internal sense of self-control can ultimately mean the difference between success and failure in many treatment plans and interventions. Determining how to reconcile competing interests, varying degrees of competence, protections of rights, and important freedoms (such as cultural and religious

practices) with "beneficence" (i.e., the actual intended benefit, which may be compromised by certain exercises of autonomy) requires careful ethical deliberation and mutual consideration.

Justice

The principle of justice requires one to be fair-minded, even-handed, and nondiscriminatory. Justice is confounded by acts of partiality or prejudice. However, justice is not without competing interests of its own. The term "distributive justice" specifically addresses these competing interests. For example, the allocation of resources (both financial and human) must always be carried out in an environment of limitations and restrictions. Health care dollars are limited, staff and their energies are not without boundaries, and insurers and government programs have explicit margins. Granting resources to one often means (potentially unjustly) depriving another of similar access to resources. Such competing concerns lie at the heart of many ethical debates, and child life specialists must not fail to lend voice to deliberative processes when needed.

Veracity

The word "veracity" is derived from the Latin "veracitas," meaning "truthfulness." Child life specialists share with other professionals the duty to be truthful with others. As with all ethical principles, a duty to be truthful should never be equated with a duty to be "brutally truthful" nor to force upon another more "truth" than they are willing or able to accept. Neither, however, would the principle of veracity be upheld if one paternalistically withheld information based solely upon a highly constrained "need to know" perspective. Generally, when someone specifically asks, they are prepared to hear any information that intimately involves their own life and the lives of their loved ones. This information should be offered.

Fidelity

The term "fidelity" refers to being "faithful" and devoted to any obligation. As used here, however, the term closely adheres to the concept of "promise keeping." Whether carried out directly by keeping explicit commitments previously made to others, or indirectly by keeping those obligations imposed by laws, policy, or protocol, fidelity is an important component of ethical behavior for child life specialists. Failing to keep the principle of fidelity can be described by words such as undependable, irresponsible, and neglectful. Keeping the principle requires that one be honest, faithful, and ethical in all interactions with others.

Fiduciary

A fiduciary is someone who holds something in trust for another. In its most common use, it involves finances, the custody of an incompetent adult, or the guardianship of a minor child, etc. However, it is also the term used in characterizing relationships of asymmetrical power and authority. A fiduciary has privileged standing, information, education, and/or understandings, and thus holds significant advantages over others. The individual lacking these privileges is therefore in a position of marked vulnerability. This vulnerability is more pronounced when the free exercise of autonomy is also compromised by illness and debilitation, and is most acute when the individual also lacks full competence due to cognitive infirmity or developmental status. A child life specialist invariably holds considerable advantages due to education, position, and privileged information; a child is incapable of full self-determination and may be physically or emotionally compromised. Consequently, child life specialists have an ethical obligation to serve as fiduciaries and to seek after the well-being of others by assisting them to fully secure their own interests and rights.

Competence
Competence, in the ethical sense, refers to the capacity to faithfully and skillfully carry out professional responsibilities and assignments. Child life specialists have an ongoing obligation to acquire, maintain, and continuously improve their skills. To this end, credentialing bodies, agencies, and institutions typically require certification and continuing education to ensure that they hire and retain only competent and capable staff. Individual professionals must also be capable of self-assessment and should defer assignments and responsibilities for which they lack adequate competence. Finally, professionals have an ethical duty to contribute enhanced knowledge and understanding to others in their field. This can be done through research, mentoring, or presentations and should remain an important part of a child life specialist's career.

Confidentiality
Professional practitioners have an ethical obligation to respect, secure, and maintain the privacy of others. They often have unprecedented access to private and intimate information, which comes to them only because of their professional role. However, the principle of confidentiality has been described as a "stringent, but not absolute" tenet. While child life specialists must not indiscriminately share privileged information without obtaining permission from the individual or their proper legal representative (i.e., a parent or guardian) there is, nevertheless, some latitude. It is generally acceptable to disclose specific information to other professionals if it is relevant to their involvement. There also exists a legal mandate to disclose situations of life-and-death danger to the individual or others as well as in situations of criminal abuse or neglect. Privileged information should be carefully and properly guarded. This includes the exercise of due caution to avoid any unintentional breach of confidentiality – such as being overheard talking in an elevator, cafeteria, etc. Maintaining confidentiality is central to maintaining trust, and is often key to having a full professional working relationship with others.

Informed consent
Derived from the principle of self-determination, informed consent refers to the sharing of information sufficient for an individual to become adequately informed to consent to a proposed treatment or intervention. Informed consent requires communication with an individual personally, or if decision making capacity is lacking then with a legally recognized decision making substitute (a "proxy" or "surrogate"). The information shared must include the precise nature of the proposed intervention or treatment and any reasonable alternatives. It must also include expectations regarding the ultimate prognosis (both with and without intervention or treatment) and the risks and benefits involved. Special emphasis must be given to any serious risks even if they are relatively remote. Professional communication, however, is only one-half of informed consent. The practitioner is also obliged to secure "understanding" on the part of the decision-maker, and to answer all reasonable questions as forthrightly as possible. Understanding is generally demonstrated by having the information recipient repeat and explain the proposed treatment, risks, and benefits in his or her own words.

The "age of consent" (usually a minimum of 16 to 18 years, depending upon the state of residence) may also vary according to the treatment being proposed (i.e., situations of abortion, sexually transmitted diseases, etc), and whether or not an individual has "decisional capacity." Decisional capacity refers to the ability to comprehend information sufficient to provide informed consent. The threshold is lower for treatments of lower risk and higher where information complexity and higher risks are involved. Parents typically make treatment decisions for their minor children. However, in some situations parents may fail to make decisions in the "best interest" of the child, which may require further review or even court adjudication. Of note, special care must be taken in situations of language and cultural barriers. Appropriately skilled interpreters may sometimes be needed, even when bilingual family members are present, when adequate clarity cannot otherwise be ensured. Interpreters may also be helpful in providing further cultural insights and context clarifications.

Emancipated versus mature minor

A minor child may be deemed legally "emancipated" and allowed to make its own treatment decisions under certain conditions. Generally, this occurs when:
- The child has become self-supporting and/or no longer lives in the home of his or her parents
- If the child is legally married
- If the child is pregnant or has become a parent
- If they are in the military
- If a court of proper jurisdiction has declared them to be emancipated

A "mature minor" is generally a child who has attained at least the age of 15 and who appears able to make well-deliberated judgments. However, the application of "mature minor" criteria varies in differing locales, and will require further area-specific legal exploration before being applied.

Common ethical debates

Some of the more common ethical debates of relevance include:
- Is the parent or the child the "primary patient" of services?
- What defines a "life worth living"?
- Should death be defined clinically or philosophically (i.e., cessation of pulse vs. brain death vs. irreversible coma, etc)?
- Should parents' rights or children's rights prevail when they conflict?
- When does treatment become futile?
- What guidelines should prevail in including children in medical research?
- How much weight should be accorded the assent or dissent of children to medical treatments?
- How much medical advice can be supplied before informed consent is no longer objective?
- How best to account for uncertainty of prognosis in informed consent
- How to best resolve conflicts between individual and public interests

All of these are ethical issues that child life specialists may encounter in their professional practice.

Child Life Council Code of Ethics

History and relevance

The first Child Life Council Code of Ethics was established in 1983. It was revised in 2000 to clarify certain language and to expand its scope to include the growing number of professionals practicing in nontraditional settings. It is important to note that a Code of Ethics is not a set of standards imposed upon an organization by a body of outside reviewers or by any governmental agency. Rather, it reflects the organization's own determination of those principles of moral and ethical conduct necessary for practitioners within its professional domain. It not only guides the performance of formally certified practitioners, but should be adhered to by assistants, interns, students, and volunteers as well. The Code reflects the ethical conduct and responsibilities due all clients and their families or guardians, as well as those receiving training and supervision, other professionals, and the practitioners themselves. Every professional performance of duty should conform to the guidelines set out in the Child Life Council Code of Ethics.

Principles 1-4

The first principle in the Code of Ethics stipulates that the primary aim of all Child Life Specialist practitioners (including volunteers, interns, students, administrators, etc) must be the welfare of those whom they serve. The second principle emphasizes the need for competence, objectivity, and the professional integrity necessary to support the underlying values, philosophy, goals, and intended purposes of the profession. The third principle requires that all services be provided without bias or prejudice to all people regardless of background, financial status, disability, or personal or family orientation. The fourth principle stipulates adherence to concepts of privacy and confidentiality, with special emphasis on keeping verbal and written information within employment and government standards as well as storing all written information under lock and key (including computer password protections).

Principles 5-9

The fifth principle in the Code of Ethics specifies that all practitioners must continuously strive to enhance the services they provide, with special emphasis on diverse settings and relevance to the greater community around them. The sixth principle requires practitioners to constantly update and improve their skills and professional knowledge, and practice understanding to better aid those they serve. The seventh principle specifies that any practitioner involved in research must be guided by all applicable standards for ethical inquiry. The eighth principle stipulates that practitioners must make proper referrals to other professionals for services beyond their skills and competencies, with particular awareness of the competencies of other involved health care and community professionals. The ninth principle underscores the need for integrity toward employers and employing entities (organizations, facilities, etc), along with respect for other professionals and their needs and involvement constraints.

Principles 10-13

The tenth principle in the Code of Ethics specifies that practitioners must assess, maintain, and remedy any relationship or situation that prevents the effective practice of the profession, and that at least 2 years must elapse before any personal relationship can be allowed to develop with any client or related family member(s). The eleventh principle declares that monetary gain should never be primary over the delivery of services. The twelfth principle notes that practitioners who supervise or train others are personally responsible for providing proper learning opportunities and teaching the professional and ethical values needed in future practice. The thirteenth principle explicitly requires that practitioners engage in no illegal activities in the performance of their profession.

Ethical analysis

In order to consistently and appropriately resolve ethical dilemmas, it is recommended that practitioners follow a specific process:
- Confirm that the issue is actually ethical in nature (i.e., not one of regulation, law, or policy, requiring address elsewhere).
- Specify the related ethical principles.
- Identify all competing principles.
- Prioritize/rank the relevant principles.
- Identify the individuals involved, along with their unique values and perspectives, and where they agree and/or disagree.
- Seek after and obtain any missing information or professional clarifications.
- Using the Code of Ethics, identify all related professional obligations.
- Examine all governing laws and policies, and determine if they resolve or neglect the ethical issue.
- Clarify your response options.
- Explore the potential consequences of each response option.
- Consult with available resource persons.
- Seek proper discussion forums.
- Determine how to defend a proper ethical choice.
- Build consensus for an ethical response option.

Ethics committees

Formal ethics committees have been established in virtually all hospitals and similar related health care facilities. A primary purpose is to provide a standing forum in which to address ethical issues and reduce conflicts. The makeup of each committee is intended to be diverse and representative of key groups, including health care professionals, administrators, religious and philosophical specialists, trained advocates and social representatives, legal experts, and community members – all who share an expressed interest and who undergo specialized ethics training. Concern may be received from patients, families, staff, and others. After convening to hear relevant concerns, the committee is to offer well-considered feedback, options, and recommendations. Committees may also assist in program and educational materials development, and may provide presentations and educational experiences by which to increase the levels of ethical awareness and competence among staff in their respective facility settings. They provide an invaluable service, both in problem solving, avoidance of errant decisions, and in minimizing the need for painful and unnecessary litigation.

An ethics committee model for deliberation and response
One model (Mokrohisky, 1993) includes 4 basic steps. *FIRST*, establish a mutually acceptable meeting time and place. Preparations include: 1) operating from an assumption of good faith and trust; 2) keeping what is shared private and confidential; 3) keeping patient well-being paramount; 4) contributing a safe and supportive atmosphere; and, 5) allowing time for all to share. *SECOND*, identify the primary issue. Ideally, this would

- 16 -

include a summary of relevant facts and events and time for clarification and information exchange. *THIRD*, address major conflict(s) by: 1) reviewing patient status along with patient desires; 2) requesting family/caregiver perspectives; 3) requesting staff perspectives; 4) reviewing relevant social considerations; and 5) reviewing legal concerns, policy, professional protocols, and guidelines. *FOURTH*, conclude with consensus building. This involves: 1) identifying relevant principles and values; 2) prioritizing competing concerns; 3) selecting ideal responses; 4) offering suggestions and recommendations; 5) producing an outcomes-based plan; and 6) identifying follow-up expectations. Note: Ethics Committee recommendations are nonbinding. They are intended only to be advisory and supportive of all participants – although recommendations should be in harmony with existing standards and requirements.

Case background examples

Girl, age 9; 2 days preoperative for chronic reflux. You are called by the urology nurse who notes in passing, "the girl had a difficult time with the exam, glad you're here." Introducing yourself to the mother and child, the girl shows interest in a Zaadi doll you are holding. Mom, however, refuses your services and prepares to leave.

- *Key issues*: Teaching pre-surgical coping skills is beneficent and avoids maleficence by reducing stress and fear; duty includes keeping the welfare of those served the primary purpose (see Code Principle #1); preparation is standard policy.
- *Conflicts:* The child has shown interest (in the doll), but mother refuses, leaving respect for both persons and autonomy issues unclear.
- *Information Gap*: Why mother refused (running late? protecting daughter? cultural issues? misunderstands purpose?).
- *Options*: Problem solve time; explain your role, explore culture; clarify purpose.
- *Recommendations:* Consult urology team members familiar with the family; approach mother separately; defer to the mother if she remains adamant (see AAP policy), but remain available.

Administration proposes charging for services to preserve the child life program. A six-month pilot program, limiting services to patients with insurance or Medicaid, will provide data regarding which third-party payers will reimburse for services. On average, 65% of patients have some coverage. Patients without coverage will be diverted to volunteers.

- *Key issue:* Justice demands that you be fair minded, even- handed, and nondiscriminatory.
- *Conflicts:* Code Principle #3 specifically directs that you serve all, regardless of economic status. Code Principle #11 prohibits considerations of financial gain in providing services.
- *Ethical view:* The pilot program is unethical.
- *Options:* Defer to administration, or advocate for offering services without discrimination.
- *Recommendations:* Pursue objective service referral criteria to see those in greatest need and who will receive the most enduring benefits within cost constraint parameters. If pressures continue, consult the hospital ethics committee.

During a hospital-based group playroom session, numerous children begin sharing with each other why they are hospitalized, etc. One 6-year-old asks you to share for her because she feels it is difficult to explain. You know sharing could be helpful, but you also know her parents value their privacy and would likely not approve.

- *Key issues:* Code principle #1 urges beneficence, but principle #4 requires confidentiality.
- *Conflicts:* Beneficence vs. confidentiality and parental rights.
- *Ethical view:* Parental privacy is also important for well-being of the child. Further, the child could share in discussion of other common experiences (feelings and fears about IV needles, taking medicines, being separated from home and family, etc) without actually disclosing her specific diagnosis.
- *Options:* Reveal the diagnosis for the child; avoid actual diagnosis disclosure; seek parental permission.
- *Recommendations*: Meet with the parents; share the child's wishes; explore concerns; use the experience to learn how to handle other similar issues that may yet arise.

A 17-year-old cancer patient has had all available treatments, including radiation, chemotherapy, and surgery. Only a bone marrow transplant is left, but he is a "poor candidate." His parents are "talking up" the transplant and have given their approval. The teen tells you he doesn't want the treatment. He is tired of being a "lab experiment." He says he just wants to go home, sleep in his own bed, eat home cooking, see friends, etc. He adds, "You can't tell anyone, especially not my parents."

- *Key issues:* Code principle #4 requires confidentiality; fidelity requires promise keeping; beneficence requires doing "good."
- CONFLICT: Keeping the confidence may require him to suffer unwanted treatment.
- *Ethical view:* At 17, he may be a "mature minor." Regardless, he should be involved in decisions. Principles of Respect and Autonomy have been ignored.
- *Options:* Reveal his concerns, explore his communication fears, and work with the parents to talk more openly with him.
- *Recommendations*: Work with the teen regarding ways to share; work with the parents to explore his thoughts about transplant and share fully with the care team so no one thwarts the process.

A 4-year-old receives physical therapy twice a day after an auto accident. She screams and objects to the therapy. In a playroom session, she treats a doll very roughly, telling it "This is good for you!" She also tells it, "Don't yell! Mind me!" You voice concerns but therapy staff insist the treatments are routine. They want you to address her "behavior problems."

- *Key issues:* Code principle #1 requires that the "welfare" of the child be your first priority; principle #9 requires respect for other professionals and their needs.
- *Conflict:* Is the child the "problem" or are staff demands too high?
- *Ethical view*: Seeking the child's welfare is the priority.
- *Options:* Side with staff; enlist staff's help to mitigating the child's reactions; work with the child; press staff to change the therapy.
- *Recommendations*: Work with the child to reduce stress and negative reactions and to increase pain coping and tolerance. With supervisor approval, join in therapy sessions to observe and ease key issues. If rejected by therapy staff, examine issues further in a team meeting. If the situation appears abusive, pursue an ethics committee meeting and/or contact authorities.

You have diligently worked to develop a new relationship with the Juvenile Diabetic Clinic team, and finally received your first referral – a 10-year-old requiring insulin injections. However, both he and his mother are "needle phobic." You quickly accept the referral, only to realize that you've never dealt with this issue before. Your immediate thought is to research the literature.

- *Key issues:* There are questions about competency to respond to the referral.
- *Conflicts:* Beneficence requires that assistance be provided; nonmaleficence requires that no harm be done.
- *Ethical views:* Code principle #1 requires the welfare of the child be first priority; principle #5 requires practitioners to enhance the services they provide; but principle #8 requires practitioners not to engage in interventions beyond their skills and competencies.
- *Options:* Make a "good faith" effort; refer the patient to a colleague or other competent service (child psychiatry, etc).
- *Recommendations*: Observe another competent professional's intervention before independently attempting to intervene.

A patient with spina bifida needs a brace to walk. The parents cannot afford the brace. There is a foundation that can assist them, and you present it as a "service" rather than as a "charity." The foundation provides assistance and asks to photograph the presentation to the child. The parents don't like publicity but agree so as not to appear ungrateful. Later you learn that the family has been solicited to be filmed for a television feature and asked to attend a fundraiser.

- *Key issue:* Public relations staff from the foundation are pressuring the family.
- *Conflicts:* The family has received benefit from the foundation, but was not aware later solicitations might occur.
- *Ethical views:* Beneficence requires presentation of relevant resources; nonmaleficence requires proper understanding and presentation of all burdens.
- *Options:* Leave the family to cope alone; intervene.
- *Recommendations*: Contact the foundation and clarify their policy regarding family solicitation; clarify this family's concerns; share all information with colleagues to prevent future issues.

As a child life specialist you are to be a skilled observer, recording the "comfort-providing responses" of parents to their babies during placement of an IV. One group is left to their own devices to comfort their baby; another group has been coached and provided with aids (toys, musical devices, rattles, etc). The goal is to measure parental success with and without intervention. You find it frustrating to see parents without resources struggle with babies in preventable distress.

- *Key issue:* Should you violate the study to reduce genuine distress?
- *Conflicts:* Suffering is real; long-term benefits from the study are also real.
- *Ethical views:* Beneficence requires that you "do good"; nonmaleficence requires that you avoid harm; Code principle #1 requires that you seek the welfare of those you serve; principle #7 requires that research meet standards for ethical inquiry.
- *Options:* Follow the study; intervene to prevent suffering.
- *Recommendations*: Overall beneficence is expected; participants must be voluntary and informed and risks must be minimal. If so, you must either withdraw altogether or adhere to the guidelines of the study.

A practitioner in a small hospital, your inpatient census varies widely, 2 to 8 patients on average. You have accepted a variety of supplemental duties – in the employee childcare center, conducting hospital tours, in the migrant farmers' children's program – to maintain services. A student calls for an internship. You describe the situation and she has no reservations.

- *Key issue:* Should you accept the intern?
- *Conflicts:* Building the profession versus the limitations of a low census setting.
- *Ethical views:* Code principle #5 demands practitioners provide services to diverse communities, while principle 12 states internships must provide proper learning opportunities.
- *Options:* Accept the student; reject the student; try to augment the environment.
- *Recommendations*: Adhering to the ethics of Veracity (truthfulness) and Justice (fairness) is key – ensure the student is well informed. While pediatric hospital experience may be limited, other diverse opportunities remain. Leaving the student unsupervised is unethical and could result in harm; thus, she must accompany you in all tasks, or a divided internship with another nearby hospital may be permitted. Careful discussion and planning will be needed to ensure an ethical solution.

One of your patients has a deteriorative neurological condition and has gradually become comatose. The family values your interactions with the patient, seeing your services as hopeful and feeling you offer them crucial support. The staff, however, is confused and feels that little can be gained by your efforts. Even so, they encourage you in deference to the family. However, you now cannot keep up with services to other patients, often staying 1-2 hours late each day.

- *Key issue:* Is your continued involvement a proper use of resources?
- *Conflicts:* The family derives benefits; other patients may be doing without.
- *Ethical views:* Justice and Beneficence are primary in this case.
- *Options:* Continue the services or conclude your involvement.
- *Recommendations*: Priorities must be reassessed. Task neglect and burnout are also of genuine concern. Allocation criteria include: 1) who will realize the greatest benefits; 2) where can quality of life be improved; and 3) where are the needs most urgent. However, a careful assessment must still take place. If benefits can accrue for this patient, it may become necessary to divide interventions among family and staff to properly use your time.

Rights of child

The rights of a child receiving health care services include:
1. To be accompanied by a loved one whenever possible
2. To understand his/her health and treatment situation
3. To receive answers to questions asked
4. To be comforted when in distress
5. To play, even if only in bed
6. To be given honest responses
7. To receive support appropriate to development and needs
8. To be safe
9. To have control of his/her own body
10. To be respected and have rights and feelings honored

11. For well-being to be paramount
12. To be part of a "whanau" (the Maori word for family, used in New Zealand, where this summary was developed).

Adolescent assent

Children should be encouraged to participate in discussions about their health care to the degree it is appropriate for their age and development. Drawing them into discussions together with physicians, parents, and guardians builds trust and strengthens relationships. The degree of involvement varies with the desires of older and/or more mature children holding greater weight. Child buy-in to treatment plans is always important, but final consent or refusal always rests with the parent or guardian. In talking with any given child or adolescent, the following guidelines may help:

- Assist him or her to achieve an understanding appropriate to his or her developmental stage and maturity, major diagnostic and treatment steps, along with expected outcomes
- Evaluate comprehension by encouraging them to relate their understandings back to you
- Inquire after their desires to accept (or reject) the interventions and treatments
- Where reluctance persists and the treatment is burdensome, be direct in the need to impose a plan and do not mislead him or her about this intent. Respect and honesty remain important to the ethical practice of pediatric medicine.

Ideal specialist candidate

Interviewing and selecting potential child life candidates is an important task. The following is a list of personal qualities that lend to positive child life work and outcomes:

- Being particularly warm, comforting, and caring
- Possessing elasticity and adaptability
- At ease in meeting and being with new people
- Able to be directive and assertive when needed
- Possessing the capacity to work well with both children and adults
- Ability to communicate well with all health care providers
- Able to produce a successful working style sufficient to accomplish child life specialist duties
- Emotionally resilient
- Insightful and self-aware, with strong assessment skills
- Able to identify and maintain clear professional boundaries with patients, families, and others

Education and experience

Certification as a child life specialist requires a minimum of a bachelor's degree and a minimum of 10 courses in the following areas: Child Life, Child/Family Development, Family Dynamics, Human Development, Psychology, Sociology, Counseling, Education (if clearly related to the exam content), Expressive Therapies (e.g., play, music, dance, art), and Therapeutic Recreation. Of note, college courses on death & dying, biomedical ethics, cultural diversity, and recreation administration will be accepted regardless of college department. Additionally, preferred candidates will have maintained a 3.0 (B) or higher grade point average in their related courses, will have prior positive experiences working in a variety of settings with children and families, and will have successfully completed a child life internship. Other indicators of an applicant's commitment include child life certification, maintaining membership in relevant professional associations, and evidence of relevant continuing education.

Interviewing strategies

The interview process actually begins with a well-written job description that clearly outlines the expected qualifications and experience, the duties required, and the characteristics preferred. Candidates who respond well to the specific content of the job description would be preferable. Human Resource department staff generally screen out applications missing required background education, skills, and experience. Early interview experiences with human resources staff and program leaders frequently relate to goodness-of-fit with the organization and personal characteristics necessary for child life work. Final interviews involve the strongest candidates and may include: a) actual contacts with children to observe interactive styles; b) meeting other staff members to obtain additional feedback; and c) contact with other relevant professional staff (pediatric nurses, physicians, etc) in seeking broader candidate support. Current interview conventions tend to stress specific prior experiences (contributions in teamwork, problems managed, and goals achieved, etc) more than hypothetical cases, as past conduct tends to better predict future behavior. However, responses to specific scenarios and difficult issues are still commonly used to assess clinical skills and professional knowledge.

Job titles and duties

Certain job titles are common to most child life settings. They include: Child Life Assistant (often uncertified, but experienced in working with children and families); Child Life Specialist (typically a certified person); Senior Child Life Specialist (reflecting considerable experience and/or advanced education); Child Life Manager, Leader, or Administrator (certified and with advanced experience, and often holding a master's degree in Child Life or a closely related field). Primary practice child life clinicians must generally meet the standards put forth by the Child Life Council for clinical excellence. Administrative staff should also be familiar with issues of policy, procedure, professional protocol, quality improvement indicators, budgeting, fund raising, advocacy, and special event management. The Child Life Council's publication, "Official Documents of the Child Life Council" (CLC, 2002) offers further details.

Staffing

Staffing considerations start with an appraisal of a facility's average and maximum admission capacity. Staff in "bed control" is able to speak to the difference between licensed and available beds, typical hospital census, etc. Available program funding is a universal delimiter that must be considered. Facility size and available funds can then be reckoned against the services the program desires to provide – whether limited to inpatient pediatrics only, inpatient and outpatient, and/or to children of adult patients, etc. Coverage issues must also be considered, including whether or not to cover weekends, holidays, and after-hours on call. These are important decisions that will relate to how available the program is for psychological and emotional issues that are often time sensitive. Staff/patient ratios and coverage issues should also reflect the type of services to be provided – whether crisis-oriented or comprehensive, whether all pediatric patients are to be included or primarily those in specific medical departments or those with prioritized concerns. This may be influenced by in-hospital funding sources, as some departments may allocate specific funds for coverage and support so as to lay claim to priority services.

The following variables require specific consideration for staffing: 1) age and developmental issues of the population to be served; 2) special patient needs such as limited mobility, sensory loss, learning disabilities, etc; 3) whether some services can be provided in group settings, or require individual time; 4) the acuity (severity) and stability (changeability) of the target population(s) diagnoses; 5) availability and impact of collateral support professionals (social workers, psychiatry, nurse specialists, etc); 6) special demands of patients in medical isolation, restricted to room, or on bed rest; 7) pediatric patients with terminal illnesses (and long-term vs. short-term prognoses) versus those with chronic conditions (with stability and acuity considerations); 8) parent availability for collateral patient support; 9) whether care is based on geography (unit-based) or diagnoses, and is inpatient, outpatient, or both; 10) other indirect, consulting, and multi-disciplinary team responsibilities; 11) facility-based demands (tours, special events, etc); 12) student and volunteer burdens and assets; 13) idiosyncratic variables (clinic hours, etc); 14) availability of space and resources (rooms, toys, clean-up, etc); and 15) coverage priorities (weekends, evenings, holidays, on-call, etc).

Staffing appropriate to the mission and goals of the program is crucial to success. Only by appropriate staffing and service parameters can patient, family, and facility expectations be met and satisfaction be kept high. Common staffing strategies include:
- Assignment to a specific unit, with age or diagnostic subgroups if needed (for units of 30-40 patients or a busy clinic, 2 staff may be required)
- Assignment to a multidisciplinary "team"
- Assignment to a particular medical service (dialysis, asthma, diabetes, etc)

Coverage can sometimes be enhanced via job sharing, part-time, and "casual" (or "PRN") positions. These positions may also enhance coverage around vacation, sick leave, maternity or family leave, etc. However, service continuity, familiarity, and issues of attachment are important and care must be exercised to keep patient needs primary. Although volunteers, interns, students, and child life fellows can help, they also require supervision and training, and thus cannot be used in lieu of other personnel. Ideally, staffing decisions should be made with input from other personnel, parents, and providers to ensure optimum program benefits and effectiveness.

Patient/staff ratio recommendations
The Child Life Council has not proposed specific staff/patient ratios. However other organizations, such as the American Academy of Pediatrics (AAP) have issued recommendations. They suggest one full-time staff person for every 15-20 pediatric patients. While this may not be possible in many settings, and is perhaps too limiting in others, it is a starting point. In a 1990 survey of 161 inpatient child life programs, staff/patient ratios ranged from 1:5 to 1:180 depending on resources and needs. Adjusted by census, the range was still 1:2.6 up to 1:108. However, 69% of all programs surveyed had ratios ranging from 1:5 to 1:30. Outpatient staffing ratios are harder to determine. While 75,000 annual visits at a pediatric emergency department may warrant 3 child life specialists, a smaller setting may staff 1.5 specialists for only 25,000 visits. One way to learn more about staffing patterns is to participate in benchmark data collection.

Benchmarking is the way hospitals compare levels of service between similar institutions. Many hospitals belong to collection groups.

Development
Child life clinical practice is dynamic and continually changing. New medical advances, medications, machineries, and treatments produce new and varied accommodation challenges. Therapeutic innovations and insights also inexorably expand and demand that practitioners continuously develop their skills and understanding. Hospital settings are particularly sensitive to this process, as continuing education is professionally mandated and culturally ingrained. In like manner, the Child Life Code of Ethics stipulates the need for professionals to maintain competence, enhance services, and regularly update and improve their skills (principles 2, 5, and 6, respectively). Resources by which to accomplish this are readily available in nearly any hospital setting, where a multitude of other disciplines are present and able to share their understandings and skills through in-services, grand rounds, and other presentations of a similar nature. Child life staff should also have access to a medical library, and should maintain an interdepartmental library of specific resource materials as well.

Staff education and development
Quality continuing education is important. Smaller child life programs may wish to join with other outside staff to maximize educational experiences and opportunities. Regardless, potential staff development methods include the following: 1) setting personal skill-based goals; 2) shared staff goal setting; 3) regular child life leader supervision meetings (one-on-one or group); 4) educational staff meetings (may be a part of routine departmental meetings, but focused on training); 5) presenting cases for discussion; 6) creating a "journal club" with rotating staff assignments to present current articles on relevant issues; 7) joining interdepartmental committees relevant to practice; 8) intra-departmental cross-training of staff where work assignments vary; 9) clinical retreats (sometimes called "advances"), with time away focused on training and teamwork; 10) pediatric grand rounds for physician-led sessions to enhance staffs' medical understanding; 11) visitation education, where staff from one facility may share with and learn from another; 12) seminars, webinars (seminars online), conferences, and other training meetings can provide information to attending staff to share upon return; 13) further college studies.

Staff supervision
Ideally, supervision will be provided by a certified child life leader or manager (someone with a master's degree and years of experience), although it sometimes occurs through an outside department such as volunteer services or social work. A few programs use a self-directed model, with leadership rotating among various staff. Key, however, is the use of a person with proper training and experience from which to produce quality supervision experiences. In this way, credible and constructive feedback can be provided, with both parties sharing the responsibility for change. Supervisors must be alert to signs of burnout and compassion fatigue. Burnout is associated with ongoing and predictable work demands. Compassion fatigue arises from the stress and tension of constant exposure to client trauma and suffering. Research indicates burnout to be higher in situations of role stress and ambiguity. Supervisors can aid staff by providing emotional support and release through open sharing and assignment changes as needed. A greater understanding of professional role boundaries may sometimes also be needed to enhance staff coping skills.

Performance evaluations
Continuous staff performance evaluations are essential to professional growth and quality improvement. Recommended practices include staff coaching and relevant and timely feedback. Informal performance reviews should be a regular part of routine supervision; formal reviews with written outcomes should be completed no less than annually. "360 degree" reviews are becoming more common, involving feedback from administrators, peers, clients, and interdisciplinary staff who share roles. Sharing from peers and other non-supervisors should remain anonymous to the staff person for honest feedback to be more forthcoming. This can be facilitated by the use of peer evaluation forms, providing assurance of source confidentiality. If supervision is being properly carried out, the findings presented to staff at their annual review should come as no surprise, having ideally been addressed multiple times at informal meetings in the past. Completion of a self-evaluation can also be helpful for staff as they seek to appraise their own situation and provide recommendations for continued progress and growth.

Promotion programs
Sometimes called "clinical ladders," promotion and advancement programs should be created and encouraged. Where finances and department size allow, the benefits are at least two-fold: 1) these programs provide for open recognition of staff knowledge and skills, which in turn enhances job satisfaction by allowing for greater professional autonomy, broader available avenues of practice, and enhanced feelings of competence and accomplishment; 2) the hospital, patients, and families also benefit from staff with ever greater skills and service capacities. Advancement programs sometimes operate by the concept of levels: a basic child life specialist may receive pay and practice opportunities based at the "CLS I" level, followed by CLS II and CLS III, and culminating with a Child Life Clinical Specialist (CLCS) rating. Advancement is often achieved through a combination of years of experience, additional training, and an application and review process. A level of CLS III or Clinical Specialist will likely require an advanced degree (i.e., a master's) and 5 or more years of experience. Not only will pay increase, but valued opportunities for peer supervision, mentoring, education, and leadership will also accrue.

Tracer methodology
Many aspects of quality improvement are dictated to hospitals by the Joint Commission for the Accreditation of Healthcare Organizations (JCAHO) in the United States, and the Canadian Council on Health Services Accreditation (CCHSA). Historically, much of the accreditation process was driven by records, policy, and procedural reviews. More recently, however, the idea of "tracer methodology" has been introduced. The term refers to tracing patient care experiences across a continuum of services. Primarily, this is carried out via multiple interviews with front line staff, not administrators. Child life staff need to play their part in meeting hospital accreditation requirements.

Quality improvement
Ongoing quality improvement is an essential part of optimum medical care. Whether referred to as quality control, quality improvement, quality assurance, or quality assessment, every department and program in a hospital setting is required to pursue the ongoing processes of improvement. Child life programs may accomplish this in many ways. One approach is to focus on client or customer needs. This is typically accomplished by requesting feedback through questionnaires, satisfaction surveys, or by direct interview. Carefully constructed questions about the helpfulness, timeliness, and effectiveness of interventions and services offered are important elements of such feedback tools. Most

hospital services are interdisciplinary. Thus, the failure of one department to perform well and/or relay crucial information can determine how efficiently and well staff in another department or area may respond. Such problems are sometimes referred to as "cross-functional" problems. Thus, quality improvement efforts sometimes involve assembling interdisciplinary teams or committees with multiple representatives to fully address issues and concerns throughout a continuum of services.

Child life programs and staff must participate in a culture of quality improvement by: 1) knowing the hospital's mission statement and creating a mission statement and program vision statement that is congruent with the hospital's expressed priorities and goals; 2) actively involving themselves in cross-functional evaluation and improvement teams, and providing team input and leadership as needed; 3) developing and utilizing appropriate data collection and statistical evaluation tools and protocols, and adhering to instituted quality improvement strategies; 4) recording quality improvement efforts both within and between involved departments; 5) actively working to improve the way services are rendered and evaluated; 6) soliciting client and family feedback based on experiences and outcomes; and 7) being knowledgeable about changing accreditation standards and incorporating those standards into ongoing service goals and improvement strategies.

Community outreach
Child life staff have many skills and insights of considerable value to their communities. Whether it is in health education, school visits, lectures, etc, child life staff have much to offer. In this process, both the host hospital and the child life staff will benefit. The hospital benefits when: 1) services rendered cast them in a positive and beneficent light; 2) the service is public and charitable; and 3) the service reaches potential customers (parents and others) who may then seek associated medical services. Staff benefit by: 1) increased skills and experiences in varied settings; 2) drawing awareness to a largely unknown profession; 3) having refreshing and energizing contact with well children and families, providing important reminders of the ultimate outcome of most of their services. Costs to child life programs include: 1) participants are absent from the work setting for varying periods of time while outreach is performed; 2) time to meet the needs of clients is reduced; 3) other tasks and priorities may be delayed; 4) energies, supplies, and related resources may be temporarily reduced. Typically, the benefits outweigh the modest costs.

Some ways for child life specialists to become involved in community outreach include: 1) facilitating hospital visits from preschool and elementary school students (which must be carefully planned to prevent patient stress and to maintain confidentiality, etc); 2) outreach visits to preschool and elementary school settings to talk about hospital care and services; 3) joining a speakers bureau as a presenter on issues of child coping, medical experiences, development, rearing, safety, etc; 4) baby sitter safety training, typically for participants aged 11 to 13 (depending upon state laws); 5) health fairs and library reading programs (largely involving hospital and health care stories); 6) career day presentations; 7) Holding "teddy bear clinics" (teddies with treatment paraphernalia in place) or other activities when promoting Child Life Month (March); 8) Children and Health Care activities, such as at shot clinics; 9) committee or board services with childcare and advocacy groups.

Child life care categories

Three categories of child life care are generally recognized. First is "direct care." This involves direct face-to-face contacts between child life specialists, patients, and families. It generally consists of time spent charting, reporting to others involved, and offering consultations. In most settings, direct care typically represents some 75% of all work time and activities. The second care category is referred to as "indirect care." Indirect care usually includes time spent making presentations, attending committees and other non-program meetings, providing in-services as well as student and intern supervision, and time spent in staff meetings. The third category is "non-direct care." It involves administrative activities, such as time spent developing policies, along with environmental design planning, marketing, community event participation and promotion, and responding to media and other educational requests. Time distribution will vary according to child life service goals and the host institution's mission; staff skills (assistants vs. specialists); and the expected benefits from other non-direct and indirect opportunities. Careful collection of activity statistics will help program administrators better understand workload and the need for improvement.

One-person programs
One-person child life programs are not uncommon, comprising as many as 25% of all existing programs. Because of the demands upon single-staff personnel, it is particularly important for services to be planned out carefully in advance. Collaborating with staff from other competing programs in formulating goals and limits can help the planning process. Clear and workable service goals, limits, and priorities must be established. Care must also be taken to address staff isolation. Although single-person programs must only be staffed by specialists with considerable experience and knowledge, these persons still need avenues for professional consultation and collegial sharing. It is also important to understand the demands and limits of reporting relationships. Single-staff programs often report to nurse managers, physician administrators, or family service directors. Any reporting relationship incurs certain advantages and biases. Child life specialists need to be particularly cognizant of all reporting and oversight aspects to ensure optimum program services and time allocation.

Alternative versus non-traditional
Child life services have traditionally been associated with hospital settings. Thus, any non–hospital based programs are referred to as "non-traditional" or "alternative" programs. Among the first attempts to expand child life services beyond the hospital setting were efforts to provide care in outpatient pediatric and dental clinics. These options quickly grew to include ambulatory surgical settings, specialty care clinics (such as those offering dialysis, diabetes, asthma, and other care), and even entirely non-medical areas such as pre-trial court settings where children may be called upon to testify in cases of abuse, divorce, or other similarly traumatic circumstances. These alternative practice programs are expected to continue to grow as child life specialists continue to find new venues for their services.

In considering services in any non-traditional setting, care must be taken to fully assess the needs of the target facility and staff. Particular considerations include: 1) a survey of existing resources and services available to the setting and any overlap with a child life program; 2) basic demographics of the target population and their primary needs; 3) the number of clients to be served and any scheduling demands (i.e., after school programs, etc); 4) the available work environment, and any adaptive space, resources, and options; 5) other caregiver roles to be included along with any further education and training needed; 6) special expertise and skill requirements; 7) tasks and duties shared with other professionals; 8) issues of liability and potentially mitigating factors; 9) funding resources, including any fee structure necessary in order to provide adequate services and staffing; 10) potential referral sources; 11) expected start-up and maintenance costs; 12) administrative personnel for authorization; 13) options for remedy of professional isolation, along with consult and supervision needs; and 14) any anticipated adjustment period and relevant coping skills.

Child life services have long been associated solely with hospital settings. In recent years, however, many child life specialists have begun moving into non-traditional venues. The transition has been made easier by the fact that many child life practice skills are readily applicable to similar tasks in alternative settings. A few such skills and competencies include: 1) reducing the impact of any difficult events and experiences on children, regardless of its source; 2) assessing the burden of specific traumas from a developmental perspective; 3) using play therapy and other interactive and expressive approaches to explore, share, and reduce the trauma of any impending or past events; 4) providing educational experiences that are congruent with development and maturation; 5) highlighting and enhancing the natural strengths of children and families; 6) providing family-centered care; 7) promoting social skills and problem-solving capacity; 8) providing developmentally sound crisis interventions; 9) designing creative solutions to difficult problems; 10) providing developmentally appropriate support groups for children and adolescents.

Child life specialists have entered a number of alternative and non-traditional work settings. Some of these include: 1) pediatric dental clinics; 2) child-oriented ophthalmology and optometry offices; 3) multi-physician pediatric clinics; 4) support programs for children of adults experiencing pregnancy, burdensome chronic diseases, traumatic injuries or acute and severe illnesses, divorce, extended unemployment, imprisonment, court trials, and other legal interventions; 5) organizations and agencies focused on specific diagnoses and/or treatments; 6) recurring camps for medically ill and disabled children; 7) wish-fulfillment programs; 8) hospice and home care programs for both children and adults; 9) grief, loss, and bereavement programs and funeral homes; 10) private practice including contract, consulting, and outreach work; 11) elementary and secondary education and literacy programs; 12) early intervention and remediation programs; 13) legal, law enforcement, and criminal justice settings; 14) child abuse evaluation, treatment, and intervention agencies; 15) community family programs; 16) media and entertainment consulting; 17) architectural and facility layout and design consultation. While the job titles may vary, core skill sets and competencies remain the same.

Volunteers
In most child life settings there is more work to do than available resources can match. In part, this is due to the dynamic and creatively useful nature of child life practice. To better meet expanding needs, it can be important to cultivate a rich and productive volunteer program. The number of needed volunteers will vary according to setting, activities used, and the skills and experiences of the volunteers themselves. Volunteers can provide task-specific assistance such as cleaning toys and playrooms, or administrative support such as organizing and distributing food at busy events. With more training and experience, they may also supervise playroom safety, make bedside visits, read to children, oversee art and craft projects, etc. As most large facilities have specific "volunteer services" departments, specialists must work closely with their staff to offer mutual support and ensure quality outcomes. Volunteers must feel appreciated and productive, and the better the match between programs and persons, the more likely this will be achieved. Further, directors can

also provide invaluable assistance in identifying, training, counseling, and even terminating volunteers if needed.

Establishing a quality volunteer program requires development guidelines and expectations. Some basic criteria include: 1) begin with a needs assessment to reveal key activities and supports that could readily be provided by volunteers; 2) explore the primary volunteer skills and traits necessary to meet the identified needs; 3) produce a recruitment package to summarize common needs and to highlight volunteer contributions; 4) produce need- and skill-specific "job descriptions" so that volunteers can easily locate preferred assignments and better understand expectations; 5) create an interview process that includes background checks, screening, and acceptance criteria; 6) produce relevant interest and skills checklists to ensure good volunteer/assignment matches; 7) assemble a volunteer orientation guide and manual that includes general facility and assignment-specific information, guidelines, and suggestions for involvement; 8) outline a process of ongoing supervision, education, periodic performance review, and termination if required; 9) specifically address any liability issues through formal guidelines; 10) establish formal volunteer recognition activities and traditions, and publicly proclaim the valued roles of the volunteers through newsletters, bulletins, awards, etc.

Interim/event-specific volunteers
Many community businesses and organizations may seek to contribute to the care and support of children. For example, businesses may offer pet visitation, miniature gardening projects, theatrical performances, etc. Sports and entertainment industries may sponsor celebrity visits or memorabilia donations. To ensure safety and success, well-planned guidelines must be in place. Some event guidelines to consider include: 1) provide the guidelines well in advance; 2) offer developmentally appropriate strategies to reduce stress and disruption; 3) acknowledge the ethnic and cultural diversity of all involved; 4) emphasize the need for clear goals and specific benefits; 5) ensure that the event and related activities are congruent with the patient needs and facility limitations; 5) provide protocols for infection control and safety; 6) ensure that a majority of patients be able to participate and enjoy the activity; 7) ensure that adequate staff be available for proper supervision and follow-up evaluations; 8) require that donations be properly secured, safe, legal, and ethically acceptable. Also, special visitor passes and protocols may also be helpful.

Student internships
Child life programs have a professional obligation to try to offer training to individuals formally seeking careers as child life specialists. They may also consider making internships available to students of other closely related disciplines such as pediatric health care (nursing, physicians, allied health providers, etc), psychology and social work, expressive disciplines (i.e., art, drama, music), and elementary, secondary, and special education programs. A key consideration, however, is the twelfth principle in the Child Life Code of Ethics: Practitioners who supervise or train others are personally responsible for providing proper learning opportunities. This refers both to meaningful work experiences and proper supervision and clinical education. When this can be achieved, students from a variety of disciplines can add a great deal to an existing child life program, both in mutual learning and in service contributions.

Accepting student interns requires careful advance planning and preparation. Meaningful guidelines must be formulated and in place well before the arrival of the first intern. Some basic criteria and expectations are outlined here: 1) consensus between all involved entities and staff that both educational and site-specific goals can be met; 2) a formal orientation curricula that adequately provides the student with background and site-specific information essential to success in the placement; 3) an internship "job description" plainly outlining both student and supervisor/clinician goals, duties, and expected outcomes; 4) training materials that explicate key features and understandings of the profession; 5) a supervision contract that provides for ongoing written and oral exchanges; 6) a continuous process of assessment and evaluation that optimizes the potential for mutual success and quality outcomes; and 7) a formal exit evaluation to provide for ongoing internship program improvements.

Budget issues

Child life programs are not revenue generating (i.e., reimbursed by patients or insurance), and they are not mandated for accreditation or essential to medical care. This means that these programs are typically under significant budgetary scrutiny. Although service impact evaluations can sometimes demonstrate indirect savings, child life programs usually remain very budget conscious. Budgets are typically categorized into salaries and benefits, supplies, contracts or purchased services, repairs, and maintenance. Incidental services such as pagers, photocopying, printing, travel, etc, must also be accounted for. Program initiation costs vary according to available donations, but the greatest costs are typically employee salaries and benefits (consuming 86% or more of total costs). Salaries vary regionally and must be researched for any initial budget proposal and then annually reviewed thereafter. Weekend, holiday, and after-hours pay rates are usually higher. Full benefits run 25-30% of base salary. Numbers of employees needed are determined by service goals and patient population. Child life leaders are expected, along with all program managers, to become proficient at the process of budget maintenance and planning.

Program funding

Child life programs are normally financed out of a hospital's operating budget, often referred to as "hard" money. In one survey, more than 75% of the 135 program respondents indicated that 70% or more of their funds came from this source. Other funding sources were philanthropic in nature, including corporate donations, community supporters, grants, and other "soft" monies (so-called because of their uncertain nature). The use of child life "endowment" funding has become more common in recent years, with about 20% of all programs receiving at least some endowment support. Because this source of income is more dependable, many hospital administrators encourage the creation of such endowments. Consequently, it appears, less "hard" funding is being reported in recent years. Regardless of overall funding sources, creative income streams and regular donation efforts remain important to the success of many programs.

Common placements

The organizational position of a child life program within hospital administrative structures delineates chain of command, alliances, and overall hierarchical standing. It will also be influenced by the guiding philosophy of any oversight command structure. Thus, its placement should be thoughtfully appraised. Inclusion under nursing has significant funding and support advantages, but may leave a program somewhat overshadowed by the larger nursing focus. Placement under a physician champion (such as chief of pediatrics)

- 30 -

offers certain political advantages, but fewer resource staff and support services. Surveys of existing programs indicate that larger programs in academic hospital settings tend to report to hospital administrators or patient/family care services. Smaller programs often fall under nursing. Some programs may have dual reporting relationships – referred to as "reciprocal management" or "matrix reporting." Regardless, these relationships are important and meetings normally occur on a biweekly basis in most settings. Ad hoc "as needed" meetings are not recommended as they are difficult to spontaneously schedule. Programs may also benefit from an "advisory committee" which can provide further advice, resources, and direction.

Policy and procedure manual

Any hospital or clinic-based medical program must have written policies and procedures outlining how services are structured, assessed, and rendered. This is a requirement imposed by both the Joint Commission for the Accreditation of Health Care Organizations (JACHO) in the United States and the Canadian Council on Health Services Accreditation (CCHSA). Creating formal policies and procedures has several important benefits. First, these protocols serve as important orientation and educational tools for new staff. Second, they provide valuable guidelines for existing staff who can further consult the manual whenever complex problems arise. Third, they allow for administrative and accreditation reviews to more easily take place. Fourth, a well-constructed policy and procedure manual can provide important benchmarks regarding the scope and nature of existing services that will aid in future program development and expansion.

Many policy and procedural guidelines must be specific to the host facility. However, general content may include the following: 1) child life philosophy and principles of practice as put forth by the Child Life Council and relevant to the specific program; 2) the child life program's mission statement, major service goals, and objectives; 3) administrative and organization charts showing the program placement and reporting relationships; 4) guidelines for basic operations; 5) policies for personnel hiring, promotion, and termination, along with job descriptions, performance standards, assessment tools, and annual review guidelines; 6) clinical practice, ethics, and professional boundary descriptions; 7) coverage, service, and treatment descriptions and protocols; 8) hygiene, infection management, and safety; 9) medical records use and charting policies; 10) data collection tools and guidelines; 11) outcomes-based quality assessment and continuous improvement protocols; 12) common patient intervention and care strategies; 13) mandated reporting guidelines for child abuse; 14) special event guidelines (pet visits, presentations, etc); 15) volunteer, intern, student, and fellows education and supervision policies; 16) interdepartmental and multidisciplinary collaboration guidelines; 17) confidentiality policies; 18) office maintenance strategies; 19) budgeting and reporting guidelines; 20) appendices (forms, etc).

Program development

Child life programs must be developed, maintained, and improved. A common process includes: 1) a review of existing program goals and objectives; 2) collecting/using available data to identify areas needing change or improvement; 3) developing specific goals related to needed improvements; 4) breaking goals down into activities or strategies; 5) creating a timeline with which to coordinate all steps and activities needed; 6) assessing the progress and outcomes of each step taken; and 7) rewriting goals, activities, and timelines to reflect past successes and problems. Goals should reflect the institution's mission and meet upper management's goals, as well as the reported needs of staff and interdepartmental colleagues. Evaluations should involve all relevant participants, including patients and families, staff, administrators, and other departments. Primary resources to assist include the "Official Documents of the Child Life Council" (2002) and the "Child Life Resource Manual" (Brown and Redelheim, eds. Philadelphia, PA: Child Life Education Department of the Children's Hospital of Philadelphia; 2003), which provide information on policies, protocols, clinical enhancement, community outreach, as well as managing internships, volunteers, students, etc.

Annual report

An annual report is a formally written program appraisal and review. It normally includes: 1) a recapitulation of recent goals along with related accomplishments and obstacles; 2) summary performance statistics; 3) prior program revisions; 4) staff changes and development; 5) short-term (coming year) goals, expectations, and plans; and 6) revised long-range goals and planning. The document is typically submitted to the hospital administrator to whom program management routinely reports. Other administrators (i.e., nursing and pediatrics) as well as other closely involved department managers should receive copies so as to better appreciate and evaluate the impact of child life services on their respective programs. Although an annual report is required in most settings, it should still be completed and shared even when not required. It is an invaluable tool for program evaluation and improvement, for improving interdepartmental relations, and for use in orienting new staff and administrators to the program's functions, impact, and goals.

Documentation standards

Appropriate documentation in the medical record is an important component of professional services. Such documentation is a basic medium of communication among the health care team and it serves to bolster patient care and assist in proper discharge planning. It also draws the child life specialist into active recognition by the health care team. Of additional value, well-written chart notes are an important tool for supervisors in evaluating the clinical skills and work habits of their staff. There are no CLC standards as to frequency of charting, content, or issues to be recorded. However, confidentiality and patient privacy remain important. Chart notes should be in keeping with institutional and accreditation standards. Where free form (narrative-style) notes are permitted, care should be used to keep the content concise and focused. Specific formats such as the common medical SOAP construct (subjective, objective, assessment, and plan) may aid some writers. Regardless, child life programs must develop meaningful charting standards that are in keeping with all policies and regulatory mandates and also meet the philosophy and activities of the service being provided.

Program assessments

It is essential that child life leaders be able to plainly demonstrate their program's effectiveness and impact to administrators, fiscal officers, and other relevant reviewers. This requires 3 data management steps: 1) data collection on targeted review indicators; 2) data compilation; and 3) findings summarization and distribution. Meaningful data must categorically capture what kinds of services are being offered and staff hours spent, if any cost/benefit analysis is to be obtained. Data collection examples include: 1) number of patients who received services; 2) number of related family interventions; 3) duration of time spent with intervention type; 4) group activities held, by type and numbers of attendees; 5) special events held, time involved by staff and attendees at each, etc; 6) staff in-services held, by type and number of attendees; 7) community organizations supported and outreach provided; 8) meetings attended, committees supported, reports generated, etc. The data collected should reflect specific goals, objectives, and activities outlined in the annual program goals and report.

Data collection in program assessments
Among the first decisions to be made in establishing a process of program assessment is what activities should be counted. Some programs focus on long-term data collection of specific targeted activities, others on short-term intensive counting of everything a specialist may do in a day. Explicit activity definitions and counting standards must be established if the resultant data are to be of any real value. Productivity data should reveal such things as the usual amount of time spent on each patient, the duration of time required for specific common interventions, etc. Aggregated, this type of data becomes a tool for revealing demand in various service areas, gaps in others (i.e., missed high-risk evaluations or simple needs neglect), revising staffing, reallocating budgets, and planning for new hires and program expansions. Individually tabulated, it becomes a source of feedback for managerial evaluation and counseling of staff members' productivity relative to the productivity of their colleagues.

Individual data points are of little or no value if left uncombined. Only by aggregating data can any trends and relative service weights be identified. Although individual (staff-specific) data tabulation generally occurs by hand and many child life programs continue to use manually generated reports, the use of computerized programs for data analysis is becoming much more common. Nearly any spreadsheet or numerical database system can meet the relatively basic needs of program data compilation analysis, where simple measures of central tendency are used (means, medians, and modes). In general, the simpler the data collection forms and measures, the better. Many hospital systems have departments or specific administrative support staff who can assist in developing record-keeping tools and in selecting computer systems and software fully adequate for data entry, processing, and evaluation. Obtaining early advice and direction can be very helpful.

Once data has been collected and compiled, it must then be assembled into reports for easy review and evaluation. The reports should describe the major findings and meanings of the compiled data. While most of the reports will be narrative in nature, visual depictions will be of particular value in adding meaning and impact to statistical findings. Thus, charts, tables, graphs and other visual depictions can do much to quickly and meaningfully convey the messages obtained through the data analysis process. Interim reports should be carefully written and sufficient to be incorporated into the final annual report of the child life program. Where time and resources allow, aggregate statistics can also be utilized in "benchmarking" projects, comparing services and performance statistics from one program against other programs across a region or even the nation. Benchmarking participation can help identify critical data points for inclusion in future evaluation processes, and ultimately in further program optimization and effectiveness.

Role of research

There are many areas in child life practice that need continued study and investigation. Even some of the most commonly held professional assumptions may lack empirical evidence. For example, it has long been presumed that medical procedures should not be administered in a formally established play area, lest negative play-setting experiences produce lingering negative feelings in a setting that should evoke feelings of respite and safety. Child life specialists have an obligation to try to advance significant clinical understandings and evidence where possible. Quality research should utilize well-established research designs and approaches such as: 1) descriptive studies, also called observational research; 2) survey research, frequently utilizing a questionnaire format; and 3) experimental designs, comparing intervention and control group outcomes. Ethical standards involving proper prior institutional review and informed consent must always be honored.

Valid findings emerge only where an appropriate process of inquiry has been followed. An expanded version of the scientific method includes the following steps: 1) form a research question into a statement of presumption, reasoned from theory or experience, and referred to as a research hypothesis; 2) review existing literature that may more fully inform the process of inquiry; 3) create a research proposal, including desired study design, subject selection, and data collection and evaluation methods; 4) submit the proposal in an application to the proper institutional authorities; 5) gather the data by approved methods; 6) analyze the data, seeking assistance from hospital research analysts (bio-statisticians, computer specialists, etc) where needed; 7) compare findings to your original hypothesis, and prepare a written summary of the outcome(s); 8) share the findings with others by publication, presentation, and other avenues of communication and information dissemination.

Merging into existing facility

There are many skills necessary to carry out a child life practice, some of which are particularly essential to integrating the program into existing health care settings and services. This skill subset includes the following: 1) a strong knowledge of child development, allowing for unique and essential perspectives on how developmental stages and processes may relate to externally imposed events and situations; 2) strategies and approaches necessary to operationalize and adapt developmental understandings to specific health care experiences and interventions; 3) manifold communication skills, including patterns appropriate to professional and interdisciplinary interaction and exchange as well as those appropriate for use with very young children and adolescents; 4) the capacity to carry out a professional needs assessment coupled with program-specific problem solving; 5) acceptable methods of advocacy in the hierarchically constrained health care environment (i.e., many layers of power and authority both above and below the nexus of the child life program); and 6) skills in multidisciplinary interaction.

Applying development understandings

Health care settings are already personnel laden and highly constrained by finances, regulations, and other delimiters. Consequently, child life staff must be able to quickly and meaningfully demonstrate their capacity to add value and effectiveness to the health care team. One way this is accomplished is by utilizing a broad definition of "client" or

- 34 -

"customer." Because the child life definition includes health care departments, organizations, and agencies, along with individual physicians, nurses, patients, and families, child life specialists are able to design interventions and strategies that account for the needs and concerns of all participants. Second, child life practice specializes in using knowledge of child development to design techniques and approaches which will mitigate age-specific fears, anxieties, and misapprehensions arising from health care interventions, treatments, tools, and/or personnel. Only through the skilled use of these specialized understandings and approaches can essential program value and efficacy be adequately demonstrated.

Communication skills

Child life specialists must possess not one single facility in communication, but a manifold capacity. Not only must a child life specialist be able to communicate and interact well with other professionals, but with medically uninformed adults (i.e., laypersons) who may easily become overwhelmed with technical jargon, and with a broad array of children and adolescents at varying developmental stages. In working with children in particular, communication skills must also incorporate a considerable range of expressive media, including verbal, non-verbal, symbolic, written emotive, behavioral, and activity- and play-based. Further still, the child life specialist must be able to translate the communications, understandings, and insights obtained from one population into terms and expressions useful to each of the others. The capacity to communicate in terms of program marketing and advocacy is also essential if others are to recognize the unique, sometimes initially obscure, but ever essential contributions arising from a child life program. Lacking these skills, a child life program could not long survive in the highly dynamic and demanding environment of modern health care.

There are many ways to develop better communication skills. These include the following: 1) reading relevant professional publications such as "Children's Health Care", "Journal of Pediatric Psychology", "Developmental and Behavioral Pediatrics", "Journal of Pediatric Nursing", and "Child Development"; 2) increase mutual interdisciplinary understanding by sharing particularly pertinent articles with other professionals; 3) providing relevant presentations in the community; 4) engaging in shared discussions about patients with health professionals and therapists; 5) clarifying ways that child life interventions made difficult situations better for patients, providers, and family members; 6) read the medical record and make meaningful entries; 7) provide in-services and case presentations for colleagues and other staff; 8) attend presentations provided by other disciplines; 9) complete occasional environmental review to ensure that play spaces, offices, and other departmental areas project uplifting messages; 10) become a "reflective practitioner" by consistently reviewing past efforts and regularly looking for avenues of improvement.

Problem-solving approaches

Needs assessments are accomplished, first, via an open commitment to personal, institutional, provider, and program success, coupled with an active engagement in continuous quality improvement (sometimes referred to as "total quality management"). Considerable literature is available to assist practitioners in pursuing quality improvement and in identifying gaps in practices and environments needing further address. Beginning with personal and program examination and improvement is always an ideal way to begin. Proposing changes in broader environments and approaches requires carefully garnered input from all vested participants and the building of a joint commitment to any suggested changes. With their unique perspectives on children, development, and environmental issues child life staff are in a position to make valuable contributions in many areas.

Multidisciplinary collaboration
It is essential for child life specialists to recognize that they cannot function in isolation. Without insights into a child's diagnosis, the tests, treatments, and procedures that are being utilized, or advance referrals with adequate preparatory time for a high quality intervention, child life services are dramatically muted. It is necessary for child life staff to become part of a collaborative team if a child life program is to be effective. Close team collaboration is also a standard measure for program accreditation by the Joint Commission for the Accreditation of Healthcare Organizations (JCAHO) as well as the Canadian Council on Health Care Services Accreditation (CCHSA). Collaboration is particularly important where other departments' services may overlap with child life involvement, such as pediatric social work, etc. Thus, understanding a team role, building relationships, sharing workload, and providing useful feedback and support are functions integral to program success. To optimize efforts, child life staff should regularly review the mission and vision statements of the institution, and look for ways to collaboratively support congruent interventions and activities.

Role of advocacy
Advocacy involves identifying neglected areas of concern, bringing relevant participants into discussion, influencing opinions, and reaching agreements on change. Advocacy efforts are most effective when high quality, trusting relationships have been nurtured, where intervention burdens are shared, and where all major stakeholders have been able to contribute to any proposed solution. Effective advocates have quality people skills, use a team approach, possess good problem-solving skills, are able to sustain the energy necessary to pursue change, and are familiar with relevant regulations, institutional constraints, and community guidelines and resources.

The child life profession is relatively new and often unrecognized. The goal is to provide quality services and sustain a program so that other health professionals may recognize and appreciate the value of its contributions. Staff will not derive these insights unless child life staff participate in team activities and model interventions, provide positive experiences, and offer other valuable contributions. Team visibility is important and may be improved by: 1) participation in new employee orientations; 2) providing unit-based orientations to new pediatric staff; 3) role-playing interventions with interns and residents; 4) videotaping children sharing their views about health care experiences and experiences with child life staff; 5) posting notices and hosting activities relevant to Child Life Month (March) and Children and Health Care Week (also during March) which also identify the role of child life services; 6) providing and/or sponsoring CEU-qualified presentations; 7) participating in conferences, perhaps co-presenting with medical staff; 8) design patient satisfaction and service surveys and share the results; 9) establish a "family and children advisory council"; 10) participate in a facility speakers bureau, offering to speak about child life.

Overcoming challenges
When child life services receive resistance, typically the root issues are misunderstanding, or low trust, or both. One way to negotiate staff-specific resistance is to develop alternate partnerships until the resistant staff person becomes more accommodating. Another approach is to place the highest skilled child life staff in areas of resistance in order to

optimize positive experiences and understandings until resistance diminishes. A comprehensive or multi-tiered approach to overcoming resistance targets virtually all levels of staff in a given department or area until better understanding and acceptance has been realized. Child life staff must maintain a commitment to children and families sufficient to diligently pursue ways to overcome resistance and establish a well-functioning program.

Planning for the future

Child life professionals must anticipate changes that will influence the profession as far in advance as possible. In this way, optimum strategic planning can take place in ways that minimize service disruption to children, families, and other staff. Further, by staying well-informed child life staff may be able to influence the path of change. Ways to remain abreast of impending changes include: 1) staying familiar with strategic plans and the annual report of the organization; 2) reading information releases and updates found on the website of the Joint Commission for Accreditation of Healthcare Organizations (JCAHO) or, in Canada, the Canadian Council on Health Services Accreditation (CCHSA); 3) accessing other resources such as the National Association of Children's Hospitals and Related Institutions (NACHRI), the Canadian Association of Pediatric Health Centers (CAPHC), and the Child Life Council (CLC); and 4) reading materials and bulletins from other health care organizations, journals, and management magazines.

Child Life Council

Mission statement
According to the Child Life Council Mission Statement, child life professionals are to serve infants, children, and adolescents with an emphasis on nurturing and sustaining important family relationships. Primary goals include the reduction of distress and trauma arising from difficult life events that may otherwise hinder or prevent normal "development, health and well-being." The use of play strategies is seen as "a healing modality," with well-being and development further pursued through "assessment, intervention, prevention, advocacy, and education."

Major themes
According to the Child Life Council Values Statement, child life professionals are to: 1) acknowledge and support individual and family diversity, support systems, and resources through the use of family-centered care; 2) view play as natural and essential to childhood, as a tool to promote healing, coping, expression, and learning and to buffer children and adolescents from ongoing challenges and traumas; 3) build therapeutic relationships of trust through mutual respect and professional service that fosters family strengths and problem-solving skills; 4) recognize that children and youth communicate not only through words but through behavior and play activities as well; 5) build upon appropriate theoretical foundations including family systems theory, child development, crisis and coping, and therapeutic play theory; 6) collaborate effectively with other professionals, organizations, and agencies, and to mentor and support child life students; 7) hold professional practice standards of excellence, including a commitment to life-long learning and ethics; 8) acknowledge research as essential to professional growth, whether by direct participation or through reading and education.

Vision statement

The Child Life Council Vision Statement describes the profession's commitment to meet children and family needs in times of trauma and distress, as well as a recognition that child life philosophy and skills can be adapted to any non-traditional work situation or setting, that services should be "holistic" (emphasizing the whole person and individual interdependence within a broader social and relational construct) and theory grounded, with objectives to maximize individual growth, development, and relationships, and to minimize the impact of negative life events.

Rationale, goals, and standards

Since 1986, child life staff has been granted certification via the Child Life Certifying Committee (CLCC) when appropriate criteria have been met. The rationale for certification includes: 1) consistency in practice standards and ethical conduct, and increased professional credibility; 2) protection of clients; 3) validation of essential skill levels; and 4) requiring continuing education to maintain certification. The goals of certification include establishing a standard for entry-level competency and holding certified specialists accountable where needed. Requisite standards for certification include appropriate education and internship, and continuing education requirements for recertification. Certifying body administration includes: 1) a standing certification committee; 2) a triumvirate (3-member) chairpersonship with each serving 3-year elected terms; 3) an executive board; and 4) subcommittees for role delineation, exam development, and exam assembly.

Environment issues

Pediatric waiting spaces

Modern medical care has become an increasingly ambulatory, outpatient experience, with patients hospitalized less often and for shorter periods than in the past. As more complex procedures and treatments are compressed into shorter contact periods, pediatric waiting areas have taken on greater importance. Not only are they needed to occupy children and to distract them from the stress accompanying impending events, they have also taken on important educational and acclimation roles. Properly planned, pediatric waiting areas will engage and engross children and assist them in becoming more familiar with the staff, machinery, and processes they will experience. For example, a radiology waiting area may host a "medical play" corner containing illuminated x-ray viewing panels, mock films, and pictures of the exam rooms and equipment. Staff photos will display images of people smiling, relaxed, and dressed in typical medical garb. When properly situated in a secluded corner, these play areas may also be used for private consultations and important education. Given this importance and their unique understanding of children's needs, child life specialists should be involved in planning the layout of these areas.

Entryways, lobbies, and hallways

Donor plaques have often been the decor of choice for the entrances to many hospitals. However, children and families are in need of information and resources more pertinent and user-friendly than these traditional displays of philanthropy. Colors and decor in the entrance area should be family- and child-friendly, selected to engage but not overwhelm. Entrance architecture should be carefully chosen to enable easy access by those with adaptive equipment, including no-seam floors, ramps, and hallway grab rails low enough to be reached by children. Signs should be clearly posted and use simple language that children can understand. Information booths should be centrally placed in a lobby area and should offer information pamphlets and other resource materials useful to attending families. Well-placed larger artwork items such as paintings, statuary, etc, are particularly useful as landmarks in sizable facilities where it may otherwise be difficult to find one's way. If properly planned, entryways, lobbies, and hallways can be attractive and very user friendly. Comforting families and children allows them to feel at ease and welcomed by their environment.

Staff area needs

Child life staff spend the majority of their time interacting with children and families. However, adequate office space and resources remain essential for productive work. Ideally, an office area will be located near pediatric patients and available play areas. If carefully planned, the office space may also double as a conference area for private patient and family discussions and meetings. In larger facilities, multiple staff may utilize shared office space. This can facilitate mutual professional support and consultations. Given the emotionally demanding nature of child life work, however, the office should also serve as a quiet respite setting where thoughts and energies can be quietly reorganized. Desk and filing cabinet space, telephones, computers, printers, fax machines, etc, will complete the basic office setting. Space for office supplies as well as resource information will also be important, and access to digital cameras, scanners, and document laminating equipment can be important and cost-effective additions. A well-planned office area can contribute greatly to an efficient and effective child life program.

Children's libraries

Reading and being read to are common activities for children. As such, they induce feelings of normalcy and security when repeated in unfamiliar settings. Further, bonding between parent and child and between child and staff are enhanced by activities such as shared reading and play. Because of the importance of familiar stories, reading, and being read to, child life programs need to maintain reasonably well-stocked libraries of books suited to the various ages and interests of the patients they most frequently see. An extension of simple reading is the concept of "bibliotherapy" – wherein specialized stories help children cope with particularly difficult experiences. For example, The Kissing Hand by Audrey Penn (1993) is a story addressing the issue of parent-child separation. Older patients may appreciate more direct narratives, such as Young People and Chronic Illness: True Stories, Help, and Hope (Huegel, 1998). By drawing upon important literature, child life specialists can help children and adolescents better cope with their own unique situations.

Family Resource Center

One important tenet of family-centered care is the full and unprejudiced sharing of medical information in a supportive manner. Laypersons often have difficulty grasping the intricacies and details of technical medical information and may frequently benefit from less jargon-laden narratives. One way to assist families is to maintain a Family Resource Center containing lay literature on those childhood conditions most frequently seen in any given setting. Other relevant materials include resources for finding additional help (telephone hotlines, disease-specific associations and support groups, etc). These materials may be integrated into a larger medical library setting, or maintained by child life staff for use as needed. In some larger settings, where funding permits, a children's librarian or Family Resource Center librarian may be engaged to assist with more extensive collections. Regardless, providing families with well-suited information, as well as access to computers for literature searches, etc, can go a long way toward meeting the important goal of family-centered care.

As other multidisciplinary participants have become more involved in pediatric and adolescent care issues, the limits of a simple playroom and family lounge area have been more acutely felt. Where resources permit, some health care facilities have creatively expanded child life and family-centered care services into a variety of additional resources. Some of these include computer rooms, closed-circuit television studios, sibling play areas, stage and performance settings (for puppet shows, plays, etc), teen lounges, gardening areas, pet support programs, parent volunteer share-and-care programs, and support groups. The growing influence of technology in interpersonal relationships (social websites, e-mail, text-messaging, etc) has influenced teen services in particular, as ongoing efforts are being made to meet the special needs of this dynamic population. Although considerable planning is required to initiate and maintain such additional services, commensurate benefits may also be realized.

Intervention

Negative event/positive outcome

Research, observation, and the professional literature confirm that health care experiences often initially negative in nature can be shaped to promote positive growth and development. For example, teaching a child how to cope well with surgery can be empowering and can aid the child in developing skills that may be useful in later medical events and even throughout life. Utilizing unique communication strategies, such as play-based engagement, and placing interventions in a family-centered context while applying understandings of normative growth and development, child life specialists are able to enhance each child's coping abilities and minimize the stressors accompanying a health care experience. While all medical care team members share an interest in optimum psychosocial care, no other service offers the unique skills and developmentally informed perspectives applied by the child life specialist.

Children's universal needs

It has been noted that there are certain needs children have, independent of any given physical setting or experience. These include the need to feel competent and empowered, the need to understand their situation, and the need to express and receive love. Child life specialists work to meet these needs by optimizing the family context, maintaining normalcy through established routines, and by providing avenues for expression within the developmental capacity of each child. A sense of self-competency and situational mastery is fostered through play activities, personal expression, peer interaction, and family involvement. Stressors and medical intrusions are engaged and mitigated by age-appropriate education, rehearsal-induced familiarization, coping skill development, and threat reduction. In this way, psychological trauma is minimized and the potential for positive outcomes is greatly increased.

Additional support for children

The Joint Commission for the Accreditation of Healthcare Organizations (JCAHO) requires environments and programs that provide age-appropriate activities, information, and orientation for all pediatric patients. The Accreditation Council for Graduate Medical Education (ACGME), which approves and accredits medical residency teaching programs, strongly supports teaching by varied health care providers such as child life specialists where hospitals have pediatric residency programs. Finally, child life programs have been shown to produce enhanced work environments for physicians, nurses, and other allied health care professionals who work with pediatric patients. Thus, child life programs not only meet unique and specialized patient needs, but they also aid in processes of accreditation, education, and in measures of staff satisfaction.

Historical pediatric hospitalization

Overwhelmingly, in the past, children were routinely kept unaware of their health conditions, and were told little or nothing about diagnoses and treatments that were to be given them –being left to experience each intervention as it actually unfolded. Children and parents were nearly always separated from each other upon entry to the hospital, with children left to cope with unfamiliar environments and persons in the near total absence of any familiar figure of support. Family visiting hours were often limited to just a few hours each week. The resulting responses of children to chronic emotional deprivation, isolation, environmental and stimuli losses, and loneliness led one researcher to coin the term "hospitalism" in reference the ultimate outcome (see Bakwin, 1949). The specific neglect of pediatric issues in hospital environments continued well into the post–World War II period.

Following World War II there was a burgeoning interest in psychiatry. During this time, a number of researchers took a special interest in the deleterious and often lingering effects of child-maternal bonding, separation, and loss. In the light of this growing understanding, and with the advent of antibiotics to successfully stave off visitor-borne infections, a new willingness was seen to allow greater parental presence and interaction with their children. Finally, the needs of children in hospital settings began to be explored more fully. This led to substantial increases in visiting hours, the establishment of live-in facilities for parents, and efforts to sustain and support maternal-child bonding. Early "play programs" began to appear, from which modern child life programs ultimately emerged.

Professionalization

Some child life programs had been established in forward-thinking settings between the 1920s and 1940s. However, substantial growth did not occur until the 1970s and 1980s. Early programs were often staffed by nursery school educators, referred to as "play teachers." Use of the term "child life" did not emerge until 1961, with many prior programs referred to simply as "recreation" or "play" programs. The establishment of the title "child life" was an important step, as it more fully encompassed the many tasks and goals emerging as important to children's well-being in medical settings. The first professional organization was called the Association for the Well-Being of Hospitalized Children and Their Families, founded by 6 child life specialists in 1965. It became the Association for the Care of Children in Hospitals (ACCH) in 1967. In 1982, the name was changed to the Child Life Council (CLC). By the mid 1980s, membership exceeded 4,000 and included not only child life specialists, but administrators, social workers, physicians and nurses, and many others involved in pediatric health care. Eventually membership was expanded to include parents.

Child life service model

Intervention
Interventions are the direct services provided by the child life specialist. They may consist of conversations, environmental adjustments, play sessions, relationship building, etc. Most interventions begin by establishing rapport and trust, and many should also involve joint parent-child activities to further nurture bonding and feelings of normalcy and security. Interventions are based upon plans that arise out of a quality assessment. For example, an assessment identifying issues with appetite and acceptable food might lead to a cooking activity. Anxiety over an upcoming procedure (assessment) might result in a time set aside (plan) for an educational session to familiarize the patient/family about the planned procedure and how best to cope (intervention). Interventions should be consistent, timed and sequenced, and adapted to the availability of the specialist and the child's needs. Some interventions may require support from an entire care team for adequate reinforcement,

and are best presented and discussed in a team conference before being shared with the patient and family.

Evaluation

The final component of the child life service model is "Evaluation." Follow-up evaluations are sometimes overlooked. However, they are an essential element if optimum services are to be provided. An evaluation is conducted by using objective criteria to measure intervention success. Appropriate measures may include a patient describing their understanding of their diagnosis or a child finally talking about previously repressed feelings and thoughts. Often, behavioral indicators are measures that are more objective and more in keeping with the capabilities of children. Behavioral measures include:

- Showing compliance with a given procedure
- Modeling coping with a catheter
- Using symbolic play to show their understanding of an impending separation and later reunion with parents
- Demonstrating the self-selected play activities they will use during their recovery at home.

Finally, it is essential to evaluate whether patient, family, and team members feel their own needs were met. Doing so shows respect for their views, and allows for an even greater refinement of future services.

Programming and practice

A well-run child life program should leave the appearance that all participants are relaxed and comfortably engaged in activities. This can only be fully accomplished, however, when there is an underlying basis for all activities taking place. Child life programming involves preemptive planning to address anticipated concerns (i.e., upcoming shots at the outset of flu season or immediate pre-surgical distractions). Decisions must be made in advance about whether to match specific children up with like issues or personalities (i.e., will that adolescent awaiting a gastric PEG placement benefit by spending properly structured time with another adolescent who is post-PEG placement and doing well?). Practitioners must also carefully prompt their activities and then remain on the alert for insights and understandings that may reveal hidden concerns and questions (e.g., what activity would both fit – and perhaps reveal something about – the first-grade child recovering from reconstructive leg surgery who has been undergoing negative emotional changes?). Even parent involvement must be carefully planned and followed. The process of making and monitoring these decisions is referred to as "programming and practice."

Stress point care

When services are being directed toward one individual, group, or population, another person, group, or population must make do without services. In close corollary, if one staff person is assigned to a great many service areas and groups – or to one that is heavily utilized (i.e., a pediatric presurgical waiting area in the early morning) – either most children are receiving only token care or just a few are receiving quality care. One way to accommodate limitations is to focus on "stress point care." This involves identifying the most crucial or highest stress points in a care experience and focusing services there. However, it is important to properly identify the key stressors. For example, while the idea of surgery may stressfully preoccupy adults, many children experience their greatest

- 43 -

stresses during presurgical lab work, IV placement, and other events involving needles. Finding and mitigating these key stress points is crucial, for if ignored or identified belatedly the child may develop treatment-specific distress patterns which can become very entrenched, obstructive, and difficult to remedy.

Child preparation

Steps commonly taken to help children cope during medical procedures include: 1) EXPLAIN: using simple, plain terms describe (or review) what will be done, why, and how it will feel – a needle prick that may sting, a stethoscope that may feel cold if it wasn't warmed first, the smell of anything used such as alcohol wipes, that taste of anything that must be swallowed, etc; 2) GIVE HELPFUL DIRECTIONS: tell the child what they need to do for things to go quickly and well – i.e., remaining still when an x-ray is taken; 3) PREVENT FEAR: rehearse the upcoming event with a medical play doll and allow the child to do so after you; have the child practice sitting still during most of a rehearsal of the procedure, and praise every success.

Managing a child's fear during medical procedure
To help a child cope: 1) set a good example by remaining calm and speaking in a relaxed matter-of-fact manner; 2) use honesty to avoid surprises (if something will hurt even briefly, say so); 3) give positive, simple directions ("hold your arm very still") rather than vague and negative statements ("don't cause any trouble"); 4) offer choices when reasonable, such as what to hold or who to have beside them – but don't delay the procedure; 5) offer simple coping suggestions; 6) give praise for any success no matter how small – a small treat (like a sticker) may help; 7) provide positive limits and follow through with what you say (no idle or extreme threats); 8) if the child becomes upset, offer brief sympathy but focus on positive coping by noting they can do better next time and praising the successes you noticed. Plan for the next event by: 1) talking with the child and the family about how they felt things went; 2) what was most helpful; 3) what was least helpful; and 4) what they might like to try next time.

Common coping strategies
Coping strategies that can be taught to a child include: 1) holding a stuffed toy, doll, or a loved one's hand (decisions such as holding tightly, loosely, to one's chest, face, or side may also provide a sense of control and further distraction for some children); 2) deciding whether or not to watch the procedure (some may prefer, others want to be distracted); 3) engaging in an enjoyable activity such as singing a song, hearing a story, sharing a story, describing a favorite toy, or telling about a favorite activity or memory or plans for the summer; 4) using deep-breathing to relax – taking in a very deep breath and letting air out slowly "like a leaky tire"; 5) going limp and relaxing totally "like spaghetti"; or 6) counting to 3 to launch the procedure. All these are simple approaches to helping a procedure unfold more easily and less painfully.

Play

Health care play

Health care play is focused on activities involving actual health care experiences. Specific health care play forms include: 1) "expressive" play – helping young patients to express

- 44 -

feelings where limited vocabulary or burdens of stress have restricted their capacity to vent (examples include syringe target shooting, messy play [finger painting, making slime, etc], throwing activities, art, even cooking); 2) "familiarization" play – allowing children to play with anxiety-producing medical objects in a fun rather than threatening way (i.e., making figures with tongue depressors, collages with swabs, painting using syringes, water play with IV tubing, etc); 3) "drama" play or "medical" play – focused on health care processes using dolls, puppets, teddy bears, etc, where equipment (such as stethoscopes, blood pressure cuffs, tape, and surgical scrubs) is used to reenact experiences to empower children who have been through threatening and painful medical events; and 4) "guided" play – not true play in that it is not freely chosen, is conducted by a facilitator, and incorporates information about impending procedures, events, and sensations, along with coping strategy rehearsal to prepare children for fearful and unfamiliar events.

History of play

It remains unclear whether play is an outgrowth of child development or if it directs processes of development. Many researchers suggest it does both. Regardless, play seems to be related to development across its full continuum, providing many direct, indirect, and delayed contributions. Essential amounts of play for normal development are not known. In the complete absence of play, however, children quickly develop severe emotional and even physical problems. Qualitative studies reveal the following characteristics: 1) play permeates children's activities in every culture and historical era; 2) play amounts and types differ significantly according to culture; 3) children in more impoverished and less developed countries and areas tend to neglect drama play (imaginary play) and use less elaborate play approaches; 4) play varies considerably by gender; 5) play differs according to age and maturation; 6) play affects the development of key physical, emotional, social, and mental measures; 7) play remains individually unique, even when otherwise regimented and rule-bound; 8) children must feel safe, both physically and emotionally, before they will fully engage in play.

During the 1970s and 1980s play held a prominent place in the holistic treatment of hospitalized children. Both spontaneous (child-initiated) and directed play were seen as complementary and important aspects of play that both comforted children (via the familiar) and helped them to assimilate and overcome the stressors that hospitalization and medical interventions induced. Soon the role of play in exploring, diagnosing, and remedying children's issues also emerged and was affirmed through research. However, increasing health care costs, shorter medical stays, and other constraints of the 1990s resulted in diminished support for play in health care settings. Directed medical play became the primary focus, gaining greater acceptance from its greater semblance to a process of diagnosis and treatment as divergent from simple recreation. A return to understanding the core value of play as a strategy for coping and for subsequent recovery enhancement is now in order.

Equipment

Child life play/activity equipment
Child life specialists require considerable equipment by which to facilitate treatment and therapy approaches. Some of the following are common general items: 1) for art: paints, crayons, markers, paper (in various sizes and colors), brushes, scissors, paste, glue, beads, yarn, balloons, string, pipe cleaners, Play-Doh; 2) for family play: dolls and a doll house,

- 45 -

miniature furniture, people, pets, food, household appliances, kitchen utensils; 3) for outdoor play: balls, chalk, bicycles and tricycles (with attachments to hold an IV), basketball hoop, Nerf balls and rockets, bean bags; and 4) for water play: squirting and pouring items, sponges, targets, aprons, shower caps, and treasure chests.

Equipment for coping with emotions
Child life specialists use specific equipment to aid children in coping with emotions. Some examples include: 1) for anger/aggression: hand and finger puppets, puppets with faces that can be drawn, pounding and throwing toys (soft target and Koosh balls), punching ball and bag toys, animals (for making sounds), and graffiti boards; 2) for separation: "parent" and "child" animals, telephones, separation songs/games/books, bubbles (go away), and any toy with parts that the child can control; 3) for issues of loss: journals, memory books, photographs, amputation dolls, stories of loss and coping, videotapes, and wigs/scarves/hats (for chemotherapy hair loss).

Extended-stay/isolation patients and for treatment room/distraction
Child life specialists use specially planned play to help children cope well with long stays or medically imposed isolation, as well as to distract children's thinking away from unpleasant experiences. Some of the following are examples for each: 1) for extended stay patients: miniature gardening, window painting, room decorating, remote control toys, long-term projects (such as paper mache crafts), video and audio taping, visits from mascot puppets, and school work; and 2) for treatment rooms and treatment distraction: blowing toys, squeezing toys, pop-up and I-Spy books, flashlights, magic wands, and toys that make sounds.

Equipment used for developmental promotion
When infants and young children require extended medical stay, it is important for their normal physiological and mental development to continue. Some of the materials used by child life specialists to this end include: hand-eye coordination toys, tracking toys, blocks and building toys, duplicate toys for parallel play, mirrors, puzzles, push and pull toys, toys that use large muscle groups, color and shape sorting toys, board games, musical instruments, microphones and keyboards, tape recorders, books, textural items for tactile development, comfort toys, bells and sound-making items, name-that sound toys (barnyard sounds, etc), pick-up sticks and Jenga-style coordination games.

Medical play toys and equipment
Child life specialists spend considerable time endeavoring to minimize the trauma that accompanies painful, burdensome, and anxiety-producing medical treatments and diagnostic interventions. Special medical toys and medical equipment significantly aid this process. Medical play toys include x-ray viewing boxes, stethoscopes, medical staff and patient dolls (with varying hues in skin tones), the Fisher-Price medical kit, emergency vehicles (ambulance, police car, fire truck, life-flight helicopter, etc), play wheelchairs and medical furnishings, and mobile hospital sets. Medical equipment for play includes: band-aids, butterfly needles (plastic tab only, with the needle cut off), syringes (without the needle), alcohol wipes, gauze pads, tape, tourniquets, oxygen masks and nasal cannula, blood pressure cuff, operating room attire, an anesthesia mask, mirrors, videotapes, and dolls.

Welcoming environments
Any environment in which a child spends significant amounts of time needs to be welcoming, clean, and safe. This includes rest and recovery areas (such as a patient's bed and immediately surrounding area) as well as any play and recreational areas. Familiar, colorful, and valued items help to make rest and recovery areas inviting (such as family pictures, treasured dolls or teddy bears, posters, cards, and other similar items and decor). Play areas need to be stocked with toys and activity items that are kept clean and safe for use even in situations when the child life specialist cannot be present to provide professional supervision. These include: magnetic mazes attached to tables or walls; "busy boxes"; secured block, bead, and wire mazes; "cube" play units with revolving, spinning, switching, and turning items mounted on all sides; electronic games; books, audio and video media; etc. By contrast, art and paint supplies and toys containing removable and interchangeable parts, etc, will require supervision lest they become lost or pose some danger (sharp pencils, small parts that can be swallowed, etc). When personal areas and play areas are welcoming and safe, optimum efficacy can be realized.

Normalizing structured play activities
No matter how unfamiliar and frightening surrounding events and circumstances may be, and no matter the culture, personality, or disposition of a given individual, play is the universal constant for all children. Play makes children feel normal and enhances a sense of well-being. Consequently, it also normalizes related environments and participants. Well-prepared and structured play activities and games can produce a powerful sense of safety even under the most trying of circumstances. Play is also therapeutic, development enhancing, and stress reducing. It facilitates relaxation, bolsters coping reserves, and becomes a medium through which communication can occur and relationships can be strengthened. Otherwise tedious information can become recreational when incorporated into structured activities and games. Children's play is also frequently revelatory, illuminating fears, disputes, confusion, and misunderstandings – all particularly important features given the limited expressive and language capacities of childhood. Little wonder that games and play are of inestimable value when coupled with the skills of a child life specialist.

Psychological and medical preparatory play
Structured "health care play" or "medical play" involves activities designed to familiarize children with unexpected and potentially fear-inducing experiences and/or facilitate communication, target emotional issues, and help them develop needed coping skills. All activities must be adjusted to relevant medical, psychological, social, situational, and developmental factors to produce optimum benefits. Medical play is designed around specific medical items such as simulated or real medical equipment, facility settings (i.e., the doll "house"), miniature furniture, various dolls or other figures, etc. Health care play varies greatly, and may include:
- Role play (especially health related)
- Guided play, often to address specific medical issues
- Symbolic play (such as peek-a-boo or games rehearsing "leaving and coming" events
- Story play, allowing illustrative expressions
- Drama play, where stories are developed and enacted

Communication is particularly enhanced when a specialist can speak "through" a doll or "around" games and activities, reducing the direct-focus pressures that so often inhibit children.

Sibling playroom
Criteria for the management and use of a sibling playroom include the following:
- Siblings must be screened for potential infections or illness before using the room.
- An armband may identify those already screened.
- Sign-in and sign-out should be by the same person.
- Overflow children should be put on a waiting list and families told when to check back.
- The number of children allowed in may vary according to age, disabilities, etc, with play periods capped at 1-1½ hours.
- A pager may be given to families so they can be reached promptly.
- Security information must be used to ensure children leave with a proper adult.
- Family members must remain in the hospital during a sibling's play time.
- Ages may range from 18 months to 14 years.
- No food/drink is permitted; families must provide any diapers/changing supplies.
- Supervision may be by staff or trained volunteers.
- Siblings cannot enter if they have visited an ill child under isolation precautions.

Play spaces
Regardless of their health situation, all children desire to play. In many ways, play is the medium through which children conceive of and engage their world. Properly structured, play can become the means of introducing new skills, ideas, and coping strategies to children, thereby fostering and enhancing each child's growth and development. However, effective play therapy requires a conducive environment and necessary accoutrements. In order to "play through" (and thereby normalize) crucial hospital experiences, the child life specialist will ideally have access to representative and symbolic items with which to draw the child into the interpretive play process. The ideal setting will allot 30-35 square feet per child indoors, and 75 square feet outdoors. A "natural playscape" may feature trees, shrubbery, grass, water sounds, wind chimes, and variable light, along with various play toys themselves. Outdoor play spaces may be situated on rooftops, adjacent parks, or a nearby playground. Optimally, every child will have access to play experiences in a conducive setting. Planning and managing play space is primarily the duty of the child life specialist.

Planning a play space
Considerable literature is available to assist child life specialists in planning appropriate play settings. Some necessary considerations include:
- Determining key population characteristics, such as age range, expected primary diagnoses, likely disabilities, numbers using the setting, etc
- Appraise anticipated limitations including funds, available space (existing or remodeled/expanded), and access to utilities (plumbing, electricity, ventilation, etc)
- Expected medical equipment demands, such as portable ventilators, IV poles, oxygen tanks, wheelchairs, roll-in beds, etc
- Desired activities (individual, group, age-based) as related to available space
- Necessary supervising and attending parent space
- Essential storage area space and equipment
- Space for expected sibling participants
- Issues of safety (ease of monitoring entrances and exits), cleanliness, and infection control

- 48 -

- Space supervision plans
- Hours of operation
- Adequate proximity to medical staff and care and treatment areas

Goals and assessment

Common goals sought through use of medical play equipment include: 1) preparing the child to better cope in a hospital setting; 2) reductions in fear, stress, and anxiety; 3) a better understanding on the part of the child about the medical equipment to be encountered and how it is used; and 4) sufficiently preparing the child so that some control can be gained over accompanying emotions during any medical intervention. Initially, the contents of a medical play box may induce some measure of fear in a very young child. Consequently, it is important to begin with an assessment. This may take place by: 1) putting the child and parent(s) at ease by establishing a rapport; 2) determining the child's developmental level; 3) asking gently probing questions to ascertain the child's understanding of the purpose and use of medical equipment pertinent to the child's diagnosis and treatment; 4) learn of any relevant past medical experiences that may have bearing on this one; and 5) introducing the medical play box stocked with items relevant to the child's situation.

Spontaneous play

Child development researchers increasingly see play as that medium which integrates and maintains the manifold elements of a child's being, from physiological, to emotional, to cognitive and intrapsychic aspects. For example, children at play have heart rates that are lower and more variable – thus on a healthier continuum – than during episodes of exploration or other learning activities. Play appears to enhance cognitive development, as measured in overall learning capacity and degrees of interhemispheric integration. Indeed, studies suggest that in the absence of play children may even develop smaller brains (Brown et al, 2002). Play in early childhood education also appears to bestow greater long-term benefits in self-esteem, social skills, and academic achievement indices than other non-play approaches.

Medical play box intervention

Preparation phase
In order to bring to bear the full value of the medical play box and its stocked equipment, there must be a preparatory period consisting of some seven steps: 1) introduce the box by telling the child that it contains some of the things that may be seen when in the hospital; 2) allow the child to explore the box while supervised; 3) tell the child about the purpose and uses of various medical equipment as represented in the box; 4) take time to point out the sensations associated with each item (the "cold" stethoscope, the smell of alcohol wipes, and the squeeze and sounds associated with inflation of a blood pressure cuff); 5) role- play the use of some of the items, taking care to let the child be in control of this process; 6) remain vigilant for signs of fear and respond in a relaxed, understanding, and calm way to any item that causes anxiety and then model its use on yourself; and 7) begin use of the medical play box under your supervision and then, once the child appears relaxed, allow him or her to continue to explore without your guidance.

- 49 -

<u>Equipment selection phase</u>
It is necessary to stock the medical play box with equipment that will be relevant to the child's upcoming hospital experience. Use the following steps to guide your selection of items: 1) learn of the child's underlying condition or diagnosis; 2) inquire/read about commonly related diagnostic processes and/or medical interventions likely to be used; 3) inquire of involved medical staff if there are to be any special procedures, treatments, and/or interventions that should be familiarized prior to the hospital stay; 4) consider the child's age, developmental level, personality, and maturity; 5) select equipment that is to be used and consider potential explanations for each that are within the child's capacity to understand; 6) carefully place the items in the box with the simplest and least threatening items on top, so that you may introduce only a few uncomplicated items initially and then add more as the child's comfort level increases.

<u>Activity phase</u>
When presenting the medical play box, the following steps may contribute to a more positive experience: 1) allow the child to explore items from the box under your supervision as you pass them out; 2) defer to the child and await his/her attempts to role-play the use of each item; 3) place yourself in the role of "patient" so that the child can experience early measures of control; 4) be realistic during the role playing, reacting with appropriate responses to item – acknowledging "that's cold" to the stethoscope or alcohol wipe, and "ouch" to needle sticks; 5) liberally praise every successful interaction; and 6) openly discuss any fears that surface, and allow the child to back away from any item or the activity altogether if it causes too much anxiety or fear, returning when he or she chooses.

<u>Evaluation and follow-up phase</u>
After completing a period of interaction with the medical play box, move into an evaluation phase. This should be conducted with the parent(s) or an accompanying adult who observed the experience. Address the following specifically: 1) what interactions, behaviors, explanations, and experiences helped; 2) what seemed to inhibit, complicate, or detract from the child's experience; 3) how the experience might have been improved; 4) what content and interactive changes might be helpful; 5) review vocabulary used, descriptions provided, role-playing accuracy, pace of the interaction, reassurances and comforting efforts that worked, etc, to seek optimum changes where needed and to capitalize on what worked well.

Treasure chest distraction

Many methods may be used to distract and engage children during an examination and/or medical procedure, including fantasy, imagery, and breathing exercises. Yet another one is referred to as the "treasure chest protocol." The basic premise is to create a very intriguing and interesting source of distraction, both by the use of engaging symbolism (treasures) and by the introduction of one or more items that has considerable capacity to absorb a specific child's interest. This intervention works well on short notice, when other accommodation and familiarization options were not available, and/or to enhance immediate responses. The primary goals of a treasure chest intervention are: 1) to aid in coping and distraction from any distressing or burdensome experience; 2) to decrease anxiety and fear, and to increase the tolerance threshold for pain and discomfort; 3) to refocus attention away from difficult medical procedures and interventions; and 4) to establish and enhance measures of emotional control during procedures and interventions.

- 50 -

Basic assessment steps

Any intervention must be preceded by an assessment if it is to be optimally effective. Basic assessment steps include: 1) putting the child and parent(s) at ease by establishing rapport; 2) determining the child's developmental level (normal development, special needs, etc); 3) explore whether or not a distraction object would help, or if some other support approach would be better; 4) inquire of the parents their willingness to be involved in offering support, and determine their level of tolerance for the medical event(s); and 5) decide who would be the best to implement the technique (parent, nurse, or child life staff).

Preparation and object selection phases

Prior to introducing the treasure chest activity certain preparations should be completed: 1) using simple, plain terms explain (or review) the pending treatment or procedure; 2) describe what will be done, why, and how it will feel – a needle prick that may sting, a stethoscope that may feel cold if it wasn't warmed first, the smell of anything used such as alcohol wipes, that taste of anything that must be swallowed, etc; 3) tell the child what they should do – i.e., remaining still when an x-ray is taken; 4) address any fears directly, calmly, and empathetically. After the child has been prepared and calmed, the following steps should be used in selecting a distraction/engagement object from the treasure chest: 1) consider personality, age, and developmental level; 2) keep the number of distraction objects to 2 or 3 to avoid confusion; 3) choose an object consistent with the child's interests and energy level; and 4) select for a child under the age of 6, allowing those who are older to choose for themselves.

Procedure and evaluation phases

Recommended procedures for the intervention include: 1) provide time for the child to play with the object immediately prior to the procedure (but not so long as to become bored); 2) allow the child to continue playing with the object throughout the procedure, or use it in the child's behalf in plain view to maintain engagement (i.e., blow bubbles, etc); 3) praise every success and endurance, even when only small (10-15 seconds of sitting still, not pulling back, etc); 4) if it seems an object is ineffective select an alternate or allow an older child to choose, if possible; 5) return object(s) unobtrusively to the chest immediately following the event. After the procedure is complete, evaluate and review. Common steps include: 1) talking with the child and the family about how they felt things went, what was most helpful and least helpful, and what they might like to try next time; 2) reevaluate the treasure chest regularly (use a list of items to rank at each event), moving out objects that are often ineffective and replacing them with new or other more reliable objects.

Playing hospital

Among the many ways there are to help children adjust to an impending hospital stay, one of the primary methods is the use of the "play hospital." Assembled as a scale-sized hospital setting complete with staff, rooms, and medical paraphernalia, the play hospital is an ideal tool for desensitizing children to the concept of hospitalization. Through it, multiple medical care goals can be met, including: 1) preparing children to cope more easily in the hospital environment; 2) mitigating the potential for excessive fear and anxiety; 3) helping children understand the various medical equipment likely to be encountered, along with their specific applications; and, 4) rehearsing specific impending medical treatments and procedures in advance to reduce the potential for unwanted surprises.

Assessment steps and the preparation phase

Prior to any intervention attempt, an assessment must first be completed to optimize the potential for success. Basic assessment steps include: 1) putting the child and parent(s) at ease by establishing trust and rapport; 2) determining the child's developmental level (normal development, special needs, etc); 3) exploring whether or not the play hospital protocol would be effective, or if some other support approach would be better. If this approach is deemed appropriate, the following preparatory steps should be taken: 1) review the role of medical equipment in helping doctors to help their patients; 2) display some of the medical equipment (actual or miniaturized models) that the child may expect to see during the upcoming medical stay; 3) use medical dress-up and role-play to explore the upcoming experience.

Process and procedure phase

The following procedures should take place in engaging preadmission children with the play hospital: 1) produce the play hospital model, equipment, and staff and allow the children to engage the items in a natural and unforced way; 2) as the children's comfort level increases, gradually prompt them into playing and exchanging various roles (patient, nurse, doctor, allied health support staff, parents, etc); 3) join in the role play process at any time that it might help or if interest in the intervention lags. After an appropriate and productive period of play, follow up with a short evaluation: 1) consider the quality, quantity, and accuracy of the information elicited and shared through the play intervention; 2) clarify any misconceptions; 3) elaborate where more information may be needed; 4) upgrade the play hospital model and equipment if it seems inadequate in any way. In this way, optimum use of the hospital model should be enhanced in an ongoing fashion.

Body outline doll

The "body outline doll" is one among many ways there are to help children adjust to an impending hospital stay. The body outline doll consists of a doll with no features or identifying marks. It is made of a material that can be drawn on, allowing a child to customize the doll to his or her liking. Hair, features, and expressions can be added as preferred by the child. Importantly, too, additions such as IV sites, surgical wound stitches, and other medical interventions can also be drawn on the doll. In this way, a child can have a comfort doll that reflects their personal experiences. Primary goals involving use of the body outline doll include: 1) to enhance preparation and improve coping for a hospital stay; 2) to bring something to a hospital environment that typically takes things away; and 3) to promote a child's more complete comprehension of the hospital experience.

Assessment steps and the preparation phase

Prior to any intervention an assessment must be completed. Basic assessment steps include: 1) putting the child and parent(s) at ease by establishing trust and rapport; 2) determining the child's developmental level (normal development, special needs, etc); 3) exploring whether or not the "body outline doll" would be effective, or if some other approach should be considered; and 4) discussing a parental role (the child may want to use the doll only with the parents) and parental comfort with participation. In preparation for a body outline doll intervention the following steps may be helpful: 1) bring up the body outline doll around the time of admission; 2) open discussion with a statement such as, "I have a 'hospital friend' for you!" and add further comments such as, "It is your very own, and can stay with you the whole time you are here and can even go home with you." 3)

- 52 -

After explaining how to personalize the doll, the child life specialist can stay and help or leave the child and his or her parents to finish it together.

Process and procedure phase
To engage the intervention, the following steps are recommended: 1) give the child a few minutes to play with the doll; 2) provide colored markers and explain how the child can personalize the doll to be his or her "special hospital friend"; 3) help the child with the personalization process by suggesting finishing touches – hair, face, IV site, etc – potentially prompting other additions throughout the stay (surgical stitches, etc); 4) invite the parents to join in; 5) regularly make use of the doll in explaining how procedures and treatments will be given, and that the child and his or her "special friend" will be experiencing together.

Current research
The proper "dosage" of play and how to derive its benefits in health settings has generated considerable debate over the years. Most agree, however, that play is a primary medium through which children interact with their environment and a crucial experience necessary for learning, growth, and development. In recent years, the focus on children's play in health settings has waned and little new research on play has been generated since the late 1980s. With over 60 prior years of undergirding research, it is important for the role of children's play in health care to be reestablished. Childhood is an extremely brief, important, and vulnerable period. Neurological research suggests limited years during which neocortical connections can be made, and strongly suggests that stress and constant threats in these years can produce aberrant cognitive and emotional pathways. High levels of prolonged threat (i.e., serial hospitalizations and/or traumatic procedures) may interfere with language development, socialization skills, and other developmental tasks. Play, even in the last moments of a child's life, remains a key mode of communication and comfort (Kossoff (1996). It must not be neglected.

Theoretical orientations to play

Classical theory holds that children's play renews energies, revitalizes, and is a means of rehearsing for adulthood. Competence Motivation Theory suggests that acting upon their environment through play enables children to develop competency, to enhance feelings of efficacy and control, and thereby enables them to derive personal satisfaction regardless of other rewards. Arousal-Seeking Theory posits that children are innately driven toward information seeking, environmental stimulation, and arousal, and play is the mechanism by which levels of stimulation can be mediated and moderated to an optimum level. Thus, children's play is seen as a source of progress, adaptation, power, imagination growth, and physical, emotional, and social development, as well as a way of integrating and optimizing personal learning and capacity.

Principal development of play

Bolig (2005) specifies that play is the means by which children: 1) demonstrate and derive developmental concepts and feelings; 2) manage and organize emotions; 3) ameliorate conflicts and discord; 4) enhance imagination, and develop higher thinking through fantasy; 5) find ways to demonstrate and derive what is unacceptable or unavailable to them in reality; 6) integrate, rehearse, refine, and enhance experiences; 7) seek sources of internal empowerment and confidence; 8) expand actual and perceived competence; 9) encourage and challenge the world and others around them; 10) regulate internal and external

- 53 -

stimulation; 11) promote post-play relaxation and calm; 12) communicate, both between themselves and adults; 13) develop resilience and adaptability; and 14) symbolically integrate and communicate values, beliefs, and culture.

Principal elements of play

Reuben, Fein, and Vandenberg (1983) identify 6 recurring criteria in the literature, suggesting that play must be: 1) motivated from within; 2) focused on means rather than structured ends; 3) internally controlled rather than externally imposed; 4) comprised of non-instrumental actions (as opposed to goal-oriented or instrumental actions); 5) free from imposed regulation or rules; and 6) actively engaging. Bolig (2005) suggests that play must be: 1) voluntary; 2) self-motivated; 3) enjoyable and relaxing; 4) in the present; 5) self-dominated (as opposed to object-dominated); 6) unpredictable and novel; and 7) physically and mentally activating. However, for children, it is often the context that is primarily important, with the single most compelling factor being its voluntary nature.

Theoretical categories

Developmental researchers Piaget (1962) and Smilansky (1968) have provided the more influential classifications of play. Piaget began by defining the categories of "practice play," "symbolic play," and rule-based games. Smilansky revised the nomenclature by referring to practice play as "functional play," symbolic play as "dramatic play," and adding the category of "constructive play." Because constructive play involves the pursuit of goals, debates continue as to whether or not it is true "play." Specifically defined, play types include: 1) constructive play – modeling life activities, including the activities of adults; 2) functional play – involving physical movements that may or may not include the use of objects; 3) dramatic play – focused upon use of the imagination; and 4) rule-based games – recreational activities carried out within the parameters of special rules. Play descriptors frequently incorporate Parten's (1932) classification of social participation (unoccupied, solitary, parallel, associative, cooperative), leading to terms such as "dramatic-solitary." Recent findings preclude the idea of a developmental play hierarchy, and "language play" and "rough-and-tumble" play were not addressed by early theorists – only being more fully examined in recent years.

Categorization of play by types, forms, context, and content
The specific activities and concepts involved in play may be referred to as its "content." Much of this arises out of the agreements and exchanges arranged between participants (ages, social relationships, gender, etc) and the environment (space, objects, available participants, etc). Play context and content options tend to result in certain play forms and types – whether the play is unstructured or structured, free play or nested in the context of work – all of which can either migrate along a continuum (beginning as unstructured and evolving into structure) or produce activity polarities. Regardless, play may be categorized by many criteria including intended goals, object selection, or degree of participation by adults.

Most prominent theories
Historically, psychoanalytic theory was used as the primary explicator for the function and value of play as related to medical and hospitalization events. Theorists posited that there is a "cathartic" aspect to play (i.e., expression and stressor release) by which to manage experiences that cannot otherwise be reduced through logical cogitation alone, and a

"mastery" component by which external threats (pain, etc) are mitigated and ultimately overcome. Later, Piaget (1962) saw play as a way for children to assimilate and internalize difficult experiences into an age-appropriate understanding and resolution.

Review Matthew's views
Matthews (1991) has described "therapeutic play" as a method to limit or prevent psychological damage, with primary goals to: 1) accommodate normal developmental requirements; 2) produce a sense of familiarity in an unfamiliar setting composed of strangers and foreign instruments and demands; 3) enhance children's understanding of medical experiences and the treatment process; 4) produce and expand feelings of self-efficacy, control, and situational mastery; 5) improve opportunities for shared communication and individual expression; and 6) to aid children in coping with health and setting restrictions, including isolation and familial separation.

APT and NAHPS
The (National Association for Hospital Play Staff) NAHPS describes the goals of health care play as follows: 1) to produce circumstances that are naturally conducive to the reduction of anxiety and distress; 2) to enhance feelings of security and confidence; 3) to effectively channel feelings of hostility and frustration into positive activities; 4) to develop a child's understanding of disease and related interventions, and to prepare them for procedural and treatment processes; 5) to serve as an adjunctive avenue for evaluation, diagnosis, and treatment of emotional and psychological issues; and 6) to enhance the rate of recovery. The (Association for Play Therapy) APT concurs with the above, adding that manipulation of toys provides "a way of talking" and "playing out" fears and concerns, resulting in emotional release and renewed energies to move forward.

Research

Key deficits and gaps in children's health care play research
Bolig (2005) notes that considerable gaps and deficits exist in research on children's health care play and its benefits and effects. These include: 1) a substantive drop in the numbers of students and professionals conducting health care play research; 2) the lack of any consistent nomenclature, including definitions, types, and subtypes focused on the field of child play itself and its relevant processes, roles, and activities (limiting research design and finding comparisons); 3) the predisposition to use play as a mediating variable instead of as a dependent or independent variable in research designs; 4) the virtual dearth of studies exploring whether play interventions correlate with post-treatment and/or post- discharge adjustment; 5) the predisposition to study outpatient populations due to inpatient curricula, resource, and staffing variations; 6) the total lack of studies on children's play in long-term care and home care settings; and 7) the lack of studies (only 2 field studies found) on parental presence as related to children's play patterns. Additional research-complicating factors include: age variation, illness disparity, and equipment and resource diversity – all of which have been found to be significant predictors of specific positive outcomes.

Significant research findings
Gilmore (1966) found that frightened and anxious children were least likely to engage in free play; and Bolig (1992) found that this reluctance could be reduced by the presence of an encouraging and supportive adult. Lockwood (1970) found that medical doll play did not reduce children's pre-procedural stress, but did significantly reduce children's anxiety-defense scores (suggesting a greater likelihood of cooperation, etc). Clatworthy (1981)

found that children receiving hospital play did not maintain lower anxiety scores throughout their full hospitalization, but, by contrast, the anxiety scores of children in the control (non-intervention) group increased markedly during the course of their stay.

Schwartz et al (1983) found that children playing under supportive adult supervision remained less upset and more cooperative than children not supportively supervised. Thompson (1985) found that any play session, whether or not with hospitalization-related materials, might improve behavioral stress and anxiety during a medical stay. Phillips (1988) found that short, 30-minute play interventions were capable of reducing children's anxiety substantially, and multiple additional researchers have since confirmed this finding. Wolfner et al (1988) found that preparation play, more than a freeplay focus, improved adjustment, coping, and recovery. Rae et al (1989) found that short therapeutic play sessions decreased reported fears far more than diversionary play, talking, or no intervention.

Variables on child's responses

Play environment and psychosocial and behavioral responses
Past researchers have shown that environmental circumstances are greater predictors of human behavior than either demographics or past behavioral predispositions (Barker, 1968). Kritchevsky et al (1977) studied day care settings and determined that quality of space predicted teacher warmth and children's interest and degree of participation in activities. Nash (1981) found that well-planned environments enhanced children's language development, cognition, and creative tendencies. Smith & Connolly (1981) found that positive behaviors in children increased in environments with higher quality planning as compared to environments of lower quality. Tiza et al (1970) found that children needed an average of 3 days to begin active play. Harvey & Hales-Tooke (1970) found that a "play leader" helped children move more quickly into "settled play." Williams & Powell (1980) found less anxiety and more engaged play when a play "facilitator" was involved. Eisert et al (1988) found that engaging play toys, setting, and space increased the time spent in play; Bolig (1992) found that longer supervised play periods resulted in more play (as did the presence of medical play equipment).

Parental contact influences adjustment and play responses
Brian & Maclay (1968) found that children with parents "rooming in" adjusted far more favorably to hospitalization than those without parents consistently present. Lehman (1975) found that children of rooming in mothers were better able to express themselves. Cormier (1979) found significant indicators of depression in children who had little parent contact. Hall (1977) found increased play between parents and children with the establishment of a playroom. Bolig (1992) noted increased play by children when a parent was present (with similar, but less complex play when substituted by a child life specialist).

Child's age
Most research suggests that children between the ages of 6 months and 4 years are most vulnerable to the disruptions and stressors inherent in hospitalization and related medical events. Demonstrations of distress and upset in this group continue both during and following hospitalization. Older children tend to fare better, but adolescents have not been adequately studied. Most studies have focused on preschool-aged children. These studies reveal that preschoolers measurably benefit from any play, but normative play activities appear to provide the greatest preventative, balance-maintaining, and recovery-oriented

benefits. More studies are needed on the benefits of play on older children and adolescents, especially those focused on play alternatives such as bibliotherapy, art, humor, and drama.

Illness type and gender
There is a lack of research regarding the influence of illness type on children's distress and adjustment. Shade-Zeldow (1976) discovered that emergency admissions increase distress and predispose coping problems. Pass and Bolig (1993) revealed that children requiring surgery were less likely to become involved in play than children with other needs for admission. It makes sense that illnesses of a more acute nature would inhibit play, as might restrictions such as medical isolation. Rutter (1981) found differences in coping patterns based on gender in stress-specific studies. Other studies directly related to hospitalization adjustment have produced conflicting results, largely due to confounding variables and/or group and age differences that prevent accurate gender comparisons. Pass & Bolig (1987) found boys involved in more constructive play, with girls exhibiting more observational behaviors. Johnson et al (1999) studied play in nonmedical settings, and found boys engaged in more aggressive play and girls using more varied toys and play activities. Thus, it is likely that gender will be a significant variable in health care setting play, as well.

Challenges of facilitating play

Unplanned play encounters between children and adults can potentially extinguish play in progress or fail to produce play experiences where no play is occurring. This most typically results when adults are not sensitive to children's cues and responses. Adults prefer play related to cognitive functioning, and frequently use strategies of demonstration and interrogation that predispose takeover of play and play planning by the adult. Skilled play facilitation reflects children's cues and interests back to them as encouragement, and allows for subtle migration of play activities toward optimizing play strategies. Rae et al (1989) noted that certain play strategies under specific circumstances may predispose enhanced in-hospital coping and post-hospital adaptation. Thus, thoughtful care should be taken in activity facilitation and promotion.

Theoretical orientation

Psychoanalytic theory focuses on children's play as expression of feelings and mastery of circumstances in order to prevent situational repression or stress-inducing fixation. Psychoanalytic perspectives predispose unstructured and non-directive play options with a maximum potential for self-expression. Its voluntary, open-ended, untimed, child-controlled nature predisposes the optimum use of fantasy and imagination and all the social and emotional benefits that such play produces. However, psychoanalytic processes also require substantial time for the establishment of familiarity and trust in order to facilitate exploration and ultimate play. This may be difficult to accomplish in time-constrained settings. By contrast, cognitive theories posit play as a path to knowledge and understanding. This predisposes guided or even outright structured play experiences, directed toward specific goals and outcomes. The more active the adult role required the greater the likelihood that true "play" may be transformed into "work" and "non-play" experiences that leave children feeling burdened. However, carefully calibrated approaches can produce an adult-child reciprocity that facilitates trust and attachment. Theoretical perspectives, therefore, may be utilized for guidance based on time, environment, child attitude, and desired goals and outcomes.

<u>Roles that adults assume</u>
In studying classroom and childcare settings, Johnson (1999) defined 6 active adult teaching and interactive roles, with the 3 most productive roles found in the mid-range between total control and total disengagement. The 3 roles have been described as: 1) "stage manager" – by which an adult remains on the sidelines, responding to children's requests for help only; 2) "co-player" – wherein the adult partners with the children and assumes the role of follower and assistant as needed; and 3) "play leader" – by which the adult more actively extends play experiences by suggesting ideas and options. Wolfgang and Bolig (1979) have also described an adult involvement continuum stretching from "structured" to "open," with involvement ranging from physical direction and modeling, to verbal direction, to simple questioning, to non-binding statements, ending in observation. To be fully effective, health care professionals may need to assume approaches oriented more toward the structured end of the continuum, given resource and time limitations. Even so, reducing directive demands can enhance children's feelings of self-efficacy and control, thereby further supporting coping capacities.

Organizations providing resources

Organizations focused on promoting play and educational play for children include the following: 1) the Association for Play Therapy (APT); 2) the Child Life Council (CLC); 3) The Association for the Study of Play (TASP) with its regularly issued journal, "Play and Culture Studies"; 4) the National Association for Hospital Play Staff (NAHPS) in the United Kingdom; 5) the International Council for Children's Play (ICCP); and 6) the International Play Advocacy (IPA) organization. The importance of play in children's development is sufficient for many countries to have issued governmental policy statements in support of play, along with similar statements generated by educational oversight bodies, governmental health advisory services, and other organizations dedicated to children.

Child Life Programs and Issues

Continuum of life programs

There are 5 types of child life programs. First, there are "comprehensive" programs. They operate using psychoanalytic, cognitive, psychosocial, crisis, stress, and other relevant theories. These programs focus on environmental normalization, socialization, communication, family relationships, and coping. Second are the "therapeutic" programs, using psychoanalytic theory as a foundation. These programs aid children in expressing feelings, fears, and fantasies regarding upcoming events and changing circumstances. Third, some programs focus on "child development" by way of psychosocial and cognitive theory. Such programs target the specific developmental stages of child maturation and include specific experiences, group activities, and settings appropriate to the age and development of participants. Fourth, other programs are "activity/recreational" in nature and draw primarily upon relaxation-recreation and arousal-stimulation theories. They are intended primarily to induce child involvement, stress reduction, and relaxation. Finally, fifth, there are "diversionary" programs, based upon theories of surplus energies, attention management, and relaxation. Their goal is to engage children and direct their attention to or away from specific events and circumstances. Each program offers unique benefits, and will be more or less adaptable to specific situations and needs.

Medical preparation kit

A basic medical preparation kit should include:
- Cloth dolls with washable blank "faces" for children
- Readily fastened medical ID bands
- A working stethoscope
- Infant-sized blood pressure cuffs (to model on dolls)
- Latex gloves (for familiarization)
- Syringes, with and without needles (familiarization goal)
- Band-aid, tape, cotton balls, gauze, and tongue depressors
- An adult- and a child-sized hospital gown
- Butterfly needles and arm-restraining board
- Lancets, antiseptic swabs, and rubber ligature bands
- "Magic wand", compressed air "spray," and "pixie dust" (powdered chalk) to simulate healing, pain relief, and becoming well
- Reward stickers (stars, smile faces, popular images, etc)
- IV tubing, catheters, and an IV bag
- A 30 ml bottle of water or saline solution with ½ strength red food coloring, which can be "injected" into tubing, etc, to illustrate blood flow and the like

Common activities

Services rendered by child life specialists are extremely varied. However, the following are commonly identified responsibilities and activities: 1) prepare children to cope with medical procedures and treatments often producing fear and anxiety; 2) provide child and parental support during difficult procedures; 3) provide diversion, stress release, and normalizing experiences; 4) use play to enhance newly emerging developmental capabilities; 5) rehearse and desensitize health care events through play; 6) screen for developmental markers and provide other assessments; 7) supply substitute support in the absence of parents; 8) enhance parent/family-child bonding through attachment activities; 9) provide adaptive activities and toys for children with disabilities; 10) serve as a liaison for school/tutoring services; 11) build memories (or create new ones for brain-injured children) and legacies for children facing serious illnesses; 12) arrange holiday, birthday, and other celebrations; 13) manage special programs, such as "pet therapy"; 14) maintain libraries of books, audio tapes, videos, etc; 15) run patient, parent, and sibling activity and support groups; 16) organize specialty camps, cookouts, and other outdoor activities; 17) educate staff, attend team meetings and case conferences.

Team communication

Child life specialists must maintain close and active involvement with all members of an interdisciplinary care team. Appropriate and effective professional practice requires that they be well advised about each patient on a daily basis in order to respond to the many unique needs and stressors of changing medical circumstances, and to anticipate and plan for upcoming medical events in a timely way. Similarly, child life specialists must also actively respond to team members. Child life specialists have many unique skills and resources with which to enhance and facilitate optimum communication with children. They also have specialized developmental perspectives and understandings necessary for the recognition and interpretation of various emotional and behavioral problems – along with insights into the many idiosyncrasies of childhood behavior that might otherwise be inaccurately assessed. It is therefore essential that child life specialists maintain a commitment to sharing information both verbally and by reading and recording observations in the medical record. A timely summary of every contact should be provided, including relevant observations, insights, expectations, goals, and recommendations.

Children of adult patients

Over many years numerous understandings have been gleaned from research into children's illness-related needs and coping patterns. More recently these findings have been applied to the issues that arise for children when their parents and other significant adults become ill. As child life services have grown, health care staff has naturally gravitated toward these programs whenever they encounter children coping with distress over the illness of an important adult figure. Skills already present in child life practice can readily be applied to this new perspective, as practitioners work to interpret complex medical information into developmentally appropriate expressions, utilize play strategies to release stress, normalize unfamiliar environments, engage sharing and communication, etc. Where children face the death of a loved one, developmentally appropriate bereavement counseling skills and proper referrals for further support can be provided during the course of short-term intervention. Child life services are not intended to replace more formal counseling and psychotherapeutic services. Even so, they provide useful emotional decompression strategies that can substantially help otherwise normal and healthy children to cope during a brief crisis period.

Changing views

20th century
The prevailing social view of the era was that children were to be "seen but not heard." When parents visited their hospitalized children and left, the children often cried and required considerable consoling. The result was to curtail parent visits. In further keeping with the "seen but not heard" perspective, parents were also coached not to tell children when they were sick, nor even that they were to be hospitalized. In this way, involved adults (parents and medical staff) could avoid difficult questions from the children and new arrivals would be calm and unaware of their impending admission. Most certainly, however, children did not remain calm when they became aware that they were not returning home with their parents, but were instead being put into strange hospital clothes, rooms, and beds, and subjected to painful tests and procedures entirely without family support. It was not until Beverly's work (1936) that researchers began to explore children's responses to medical and hospital events, whereby it was learned that unnecessary emotional trauma often had lasting adverse effects.

21st century
Progress in medical technology and care now means that a great many children are undergoing surgeries and other medical treatments and procedures on an "outpatient" basis. Follow-up care is also ever more likely to occur in the home, rather than having the child return to the medical setting. Nurses, physical therapists, respiratory therapists, and other staff can now be sent out to children's homes. In addition, sophisticated in-home monitoring equipment can now be used to further diminish the need for facility-based care. Even when children are hospitalized, a pediatric stay today averages only about 3½ days — very different from the weeks or even months of yesteryear. Thus, child life specialists

today are required to provide meaningful interventions, teaching, and support during much shorter and fewer contacts with children, and with more attention devoted to transitional needs as the children move through various medical services.

Continuum of care

Olson's "continuum of care" refers to 10 specific progressions in the rendering of medical care, from discovery of an illness or injury through an eventual complete recovery or into maintenance care for those with chronic conditions. An individual's specific care experience need not encounter all 10 progressions, depending upon: 1) the events that draw one into the care continuum (identification of an illness in a doctor's office versus an emergency room setting, etc); 2) the kind of care needed (outpatient vs. inpatient, etc); 3) the duration of the condition (transient vs. chronic); and 4) the kinds of treatment needed (intensive care, home care, rehabilitative care, etc). Although each care progression generally moves one "forward" through the care continuum, subsequent medical events, relapses, or treatment transitions, may cause an individual to repeat or encounter new parts of the continuum.

First 2 phases

Olson has noted that each progression in the continuum of care is associated with specific stressors and burdens for both children and their families. The first phase is the diagnostic phase ("identification" of a disease or injury.) This phase may be precipitous and prompt or more protracted, depending upon whether the discovery occurs during a routine doctor visit or after an extensive diagnostic work-up. Other considerations relevant to the diagnostic phase are whether medical attention must be rendered urgently or gradually over time. The second phase refers to an escalation from simple medical discovery into immediate care need (i.e., "urgent care"). Primary stressor differentiation for this phase of care devolves upon whether or not required treatment is rendered in a familiar setting versus a strange and foreign environment.

Third and fourth phases

Olson's third progression focuses on emergency medical treatment, as differentiated from urgent care. Because of the trauma frequently accompanying emergency interventions, it warrants a category of its own. Significant child and family burdens affect the anxiety accompanying emergency events, as well as issues of familiarity versus unfamiliarity, depending upon whether travel for treatment involves family members and vehicles or an ambulance and strangers, and whether subsequent facility transfers are needed. The fourth progression or phase arises from the care setting, specifically, treatment in a hospital environment as opposed to a doctor's office or clinic. Primary burdens include: 1) whether the admission was planned or not; 2) whether admitted by age to a pediatric unit or grouped by diagnosis in a mixed-age environment; and 3) whether important figures (typically parents) are able to remain nearby.

Fifth and sixth phases

Olson's fifth progression focuses on the level of hospital care – specifically, the need for intensive care. Primary stressors include: 1) transferring from the emergency department into the ICU; 2) whether the transfer was planned or unplanned (generally unplanned, due to the nature of acute treatment demands and related health changes); 3) whether a child's familiar pediatrician continues the care or if it must be entirely relinquished to intensive care staff; and 4) the degree to which family is able to remain involved and present. The sixth progression addresses intermediate or, as it is sometimes called, "step down" care. The major burdens and stressors are: 1) less medical staff support and monitoring (when arriving from an ICU) versus increased intrusion if arriving from a lower level of care (outpatient or hospital "floor care"); and 2) whether or not family was given time to accommodate and prepare for the change in level of care and transfer setting.

Seventh and eighth phases
Olson's seventh progression addresses processes of rehabilitation. Because medical rehabilitation usually requires transfer to another facility, changes in setting and staff are significant stressors for a child and involved family. Whether or not there is a source of payment is yet another stressor, primarily for parents, as rehabilitation services may not be covered by many policies. The eighth phase in the continuum of care refers to specialty outpatient services. These services may be encountered during a diagnostic exploration and evaluation, or as part of a recovery plan. Principal stressors include: 1) whether or not the services involve invasive or noninvasive diagnostic or treatment interventions; 2) whether or not there has been time or opportunity for child coping skill preparation and family orientation; and 3) whether or not there are follow-up home care demands placed on the family or not.

Ninth and tenth phases
Olson's ninth continuum of care phase deals with issues of home care. The major stressors and burdens identified include: 1) whether or not home care demands were arranged during a hospital stay or were initiated precipitously in the home setting; 2) whether the home care plan devolves solely upon family members or is shared by medical professionals; and 3) whether or not the care is provided by a limited number of familiar people or by multiple providers who may be strangers. The tenth phase addresses issues related to the movement from acute illness and/or transient disability to chronic conditions. The primary stressor features include: 1) whether the resultant chronicity was expected (emerging over time and through multiple events or as a sudden extension of a disease or injury); 2) the nature of the response of the child and family to the diagnosis of chronicity; and 3) whether treatment demands and processes are similar or very different from those incurred during the acute phase of the illness or injury.

Nehring's levels of care

Nehring conceived of 3 levels of care when considering a continuum of care. The first level is termed the "primary" level, and includes: 1) all routine and preventative health services; 2) the treatment of simple injuries and illnesses; 3) health monitoring and management of stable conditions; 4) education and counseling services; 5) support resources, referrals, and case management; and 6) any direction provided via physician contacts in an office or clinic. The next level is a "secondary" tier of care. It includes specialty care as provided by consultants, specialists, and interdisciplinary teams. It involves: 1) caregiver training; 2) patient and family counseling; and 3) the establishment of care plans. This second level is typically required to manage irregular and complicated medical conditions. The third care level is termed "tertiary" care. It refers to highly specialized services provided in hospitals, medical centers, and university-affiliated facilities. These services include: 1) multidisciplinary group involvement; 2) specialized patient and family education and counseling; 3) collaborative discharge and community care plans; and 4) research.

Managed versus academic care

It has been noted that 85% of all employer-based health insurance plans utilize a "managed care" approach. Managed care is different from the traditional academic model in many ways. The academic model treats problems as they arise; managed care uses "population-based medicine" based on a prevention model. Academic medicine demands that "everything" be done even if continuing treatment is futile; managed care utilizes an "evidence-based" approach that rejects futile or unproven treatments. The academic model calls for independent physician practice (sometimes resulting in wide practice variations); managed care requires physicians to adhere to treatment protocols and "best practice" treatment guidelines. Given these differences, it is expected that managed care will continue to dominate the medical arena for the near future.

Rights of children

Bioethicists and others now advocate strongly for children to be integrally involved in their own health care. The United Nations "Convention on the Rights of the Child" (CRC) also supports eliciting children's views on health care needs and decisions. While adults may still make most final decisions, their choices should take into account a child's personal view, concerns, and wishes. In recognition of children's "evolving capacities," their views should carry greater and greater weight as they mature and develop increasing insight and appreciation for varying situations. This requires that children of all ages be encouraged to communicate their views in ways that are appropriate to their developmental capacity – whether through medical play, drawing, storytelling, or by some other means.

Erikson's (1963) theory

Erik Erikson's theory of personality development is the most widely accepted and used. He proposed that there are 8 stages in the process of personality development, with a core conflict inherent in each stage, which must be resolved before further development is possible. The age-related stages are as follows: 1) birth to 1 year is characterized by the conflict of trust versus mistrust; 2) ages 1 to 3 years covers the stage of autonomy versus shame and doubt; 3) 3to 6 years poses the conflict of initiative versus guilt; 4) 6 to 12 years focuses on the conflict of industry versus inferiority; 5) 12 to 18 years addresses identity versus role confusion; 6) the early 20s involves intimacy and solidarity versus isolation; 7) the late 20s to 50s encompasses generativity vs. self-absorption; and 8) the 50s and beyond addresses integrity versus despair. While no stage-related conflict is ever fully mastered, each must be reasonably resolved for growth to continue.

Hospitalized children

Unsupported hospitalization experiences
By 1965, more than 200 articles had been written about the effects of hospitalization on children. Between 1963 and 1983, research on the impact of hospitalization on children had already documented numerous post-discharge problems, including sleep disturbances, behavioral problems, persistent separation anxiety, and undue problems with authority. Other studies revealed that teenagers who were hospitalized when young had greater adjustment difficulties than those who were not. This was particularly true for children with hospital stays exceeding 7 days or who were repeatedly hospitalized even for shorter periods before the age of 5. However, research by Chess and Thomas (1984) found that

- 63 -

with adequate support and direction, emotional stability could be retained and even some psychological benefits could be realized.

Characteristics of hospitalized children today
Almost 13% of all hospitalizations are for children under 1 year of age, even though they comprise only 1% of the population. 5% of all hospitalizations involve children between the ages of 1 and 17. Hospitalization periods for children are shorter than those for adults by an average of 29%. The most common diagnoses for extended neonatal and pediatric hospital stays are: 1) intrauterine growth retardation, premature birth, and below average weight at birth; 2) infant respiratory distress or any similar respiratory failure; 3) leukemia; 4) psychological disorders prior to adulthood; 5) birth defects of the heart or circulatory system; 6) pneumonia due to aspiration of meconium (newborn fecal matter drawn into the lungs during birth) or any other such aspiration due to an infant's poorly protected airway; 7) other psychological disturbances such as anxiety or personality disorders; 8) depression (or other "affect" disorders); and 9) graft, implant, or medical device infections or complications.

Intensive care versus general "ward" care
The responses of children to various medical and health-related stressors vary not only by developmental stage, but also by: 1) past health care experiences (including associated pain, forced parent-child separations, length of stay, etc); 2) available coping skills; 3) family and other supports; and 4) the severity of an illness or injury. It was long assumed that children hospitalized in a pediatric intensive care unit (PICU) might fare more poorly than children receiving care in a general pediatric ward. However, studies have found that children hospitalized today are all markedly ill and thus they receive roughly equal numbers of invasive tests and procedures whether or not they are in the PICU or in general pediatric care (although children in the PICU were given more sedatives and pain medications). However, the younger the child, the greater the illness or injury severity, and the higher the number of invasive procedures and tests, the more prone children are to post-traumatic stress symptoms for at least 6 months after hospital discharge.

NIDCAP guidelines
The Newborn Individualized Developmental Care and Assessment Program (NIDCAP) was designed to support developmentally appropriate care in hospital neonatal intensive care units. Key guidelines include: 1) caregiving that is uniform and consistent (where a primary team and the family jointly design infant-specific care plans); 2) structuring the full 24 hours in a newborn's day (including particular attention to promoting growth by supporting the infant's sleep-wake cycles); 3) transitional support (between care activities and sleep-wake intervals); 4) proper positioning (enhancing infant comfort using optimum positioning); 5) nutritional support (selecting bottle or breast as ideal to circumstance, and optimizing the feeding schedule); 6) shared care (all medical interventions planned by both the family and care staff); 7) environment enhancement (home-like settings, quiet music, gentle lighting in concert with day/night cycles, bedside seating for family interaction, etc); 8) developmental attending (care that includes specialists in developmental and psychosocial care, including child life staff).

Needs of older infants (ages 6 months to 1 year)
The greatest threat to older infants is separation from their parents, typically referred to as "separation anxiety." Therefore, the greatest protection that can be provided a hospitalized infant is maximal parental presence and participation in care. Resolution of Erikson's first

- 64 -

developmental phase (trust vs. mistrust) is optimized by parental presence. Infants seek control and confidence (i.e., trust) in their surroundings through cues of movement and expression (smiling, crying, kicking, etc). When these cues are noted and met, confidence and trust increase. Minimizing movement restriction and changes in routine also promotes successful development. Providing opportunities to explore beyond the crib further ensures essential developmental learning and growth.

Separation anxiety

The 3 stages of separation anxiety and the end-phase consequences were provided by Robertson (1958) and Bowlby in 1960. The first stage is referred to as the "protest" phase. In this stage, the child aggressively and physically reacts to the separation by crying, kicking, and screaming – all the while remaining alert to any sign of parental return. The second stage is described as the "despair" phase. As hopelessness grows in the child, crying and other protests become intermittent and eventually cease altogether. Depression ensues. Historically, staff interpreted this as successful adjustment, and because protests were renewed at parental return and re-exits, it was used to justify major limits on parental visitation. The third stage is that of "detachment." It emerges after extended parental absence, following which the child attempts to produce new attachments and to re-engage in the environment and activities. However, alternate attachments tend to be superficial, and the child becomes self-centered and focused on material items over relationships. Little more than apathetic responses meet parental return, and the ability to form normal attachments may never be regained.

Needs of hospitalized toddlers (aged 1 to 3 years)

Need for parental presence remains paramount. However, toddlers are also facing the next Erikson developmental phase: autonomy versus shame and doubt. Toddlers develop autonomy by play, movement, socializing, and exploring. Environmental engagement is maximized by promoting security (parental presence) and through predictable routines and rituals. Major challenges arising through hospitalization include: 1) parental absences; 2) environmental restrictions; 3) routine disruption; 4) unrescued experiences of pain; and 5) body image and boundary perceptual limits. Successful coping is promoted by: 1) keeping the hospital environment as homelike as possible; 2) limiting environmental and movement restrictions; 3) retaining homelike routines (bathing, eating, play and nap times, etc); 4) using coping and distraction to minimize pain; and 5) using medical play approaches to aid in body understanding. Toddlers are likely to perceive the hospital and painful experiences as "punishment." Understanding exceeds communication skills; thus, preparation for procedures using medical play and alternative approaches is valuable. Parental preparation is also essential, as a calm parent results in a calmer child.

Challenges of hospitalization to preschool children (aged 4 to 5 years)

Stanford and Thompson (1981) note that children aged 9 months to 4 years are impacted the most by hospitalization. Preschoolers are egocentric, have a high need for independence, and cope poorly with environmental and physical restrictions. They view negative experiences as punishment, and operate with "magical thinking" (wishes and thoughts make things happen). Self-blame is common when bad things happen. Consequently, they are particularly vulnerable to pain and bodily injury. Play is the primary coping approach. Concrete thinking leaves them vulnerable to fears about physical mutilation and requires simple explanations (surgery to fix something, etc). The use of medical models and equipment is particularly helpful. "Safe" places are important. Bedside tests should be limited or negotiated to reduce the fear of invasive events disturbing sleep

- 65 -

(using care to let the child define what is invasive); play spaces should also be pain- and test-free zones. Parents and important people should be present for all distressing events, carried out in settings that minimize impersonal, clinical, and sterile feelings.

Challenges of hospitalized school-age children (6 to 12 years of age)
School-aged children are capable of cognitive reasoning, can build alternate trusting relationships, and socialize more skillfully. They understand events more easily, cope with staff and changes better, and can remain apart from parents for longer periods. Possessing "concrete operational" thinking, they follow "cause and effect" explanations. Even so, school-age children rate "being away from family" as the greatest stressor of hospitalization, followed by anxiety about shots and hearing "something is wrong" from staff. Erikson's industry versus inferiority stage helps explain anxiety about missing normal activities and friends. Family visits, augmented by telephone calls, e-mail, cards, etc, remain vital. Complete medical explanations to include current and future implications are needed, as they will seek to fill in any gaps. "Industry" activities such as socializing, crafts, writing, and computers will aid in coping. Child life programming focuses on normalizing events and providing appropriate structure and routines. Procedure preparation remains important for fear reduction. Body image awareness is high, and role and response rehearsal build confidence where image changes are faced.

Most stressful events of hospitalization cited by school-age children
The 6 most stressful events school-age children themselves cited as having happened during hospitalization were studied by Bossert in 1994. The 6 most stressful events cited by children ages 6 to 12 were: 1) intrusive events (body entry through the skin or an orifice); 2) physical symptoms (illness sensations, as well as pain, medication side-effects, nausea, blurred eyesight, etc); 3) therapeutic interventions (being examined by a physician, probing of the abdomen, awakening following surgery, having others awaken them at night, bandage changes, stitches being taken out); 4) restricted activity (keeping still for radiographic imaging, restricted to one hospital area, being confined to bed); 5) separation (from family, friends, and pets); 6) environmental stressors (upset or impatient medical providers, difficult roommates, machines and wires that look scary in the dark at night).

Primary challenges for hospitalized adolescents (puberty to adulthood – generally, ages 13 to 21 years in males)
Adolescents have entered Erikson's developmental phase of "identity versus role confusion." Already inclined toward separation from family, adolescents are particularly stressed when medical events keep them away from friends and group activities, and impact future plans. Strict medical isolation is particularly challenging (i.e., following transplant or with certain cancers). Other stressors include loss of control and overexposure to rules, regulations, and adult supervision. Major medical fears are related to changes in appearance, physical prowess, and sexual functioning. Common responses include anger, rebellion, and frustration. Mid-adolescence (from 14 to 18 years of age) is the period during which hospitalization is most stressful for adolescents. Primary coping strategies should be directed toward developing and maintaining peer supports. Access to computers, telephones, e-mail, video games, music, and movies is also important. Relaxed visiting policies for friends will be helpful. Issues of privacy, bodily modesty, and confidentiality are significant. Quality medical explanations, preparatory procedural reviews, and meaningful involvement in decision-making will round out primary adolescent coping interventions.

Particularly vulnerable children

Children seen as particularly vulnerable and in need of special attention include: 1) young children hospitalized in the past who have developed overwhelming fears and/or misunderstandings; 2) children with preexisting emotional disturbances; 3) children of parents who cope poorly with hospital experiences, tend to overreact, and are hyper-anxious, or those who are inattentive, neglectful, or harsh; 4) children with a history of significant abuse; 5) children who are developmentally delayed, sensory disabled (i.e., hearing, sight, etc), as well as those with neurological damage or defects.

Particularly resilient children

Resilient children are defined as those able to return to a stable physiological and/or psychological state very quickly after disruption. Resilient children tend to be able to involve themselves in their treatment, to respond at their own pace, and to appropriately express needs and give useful directions to others. Resiliency is supported by: 1) clearly connecting events to outcomes (i.e., "straighten your arm so your IV doesn't get blocked"); 2) giving praise when something is done right, and not before; 3) acknowledging partial successes (initial efforts, first steps, and meaningful trying); 4) motivating extra efforts and task completion even if stressed; 5) demonstrating "feelings" sharing and positive "self-talk"; 6) teaching new skills and reinforcing existing positive actions. Resilience is increased by useful and constructive perceptions, by maintaining quality family support and contact, and by giving voice to feelings to decrease anxiety and fears.

Family stress and priorities

There are many sources of stress for a family when one of the children is hospitalized. These include: 1) the health status of the ill child (diagnosis, prognosis, involved pain, treatment decisions, etc); 2) facility issues (coping with strangers, uncertainties, and unexpected demands); 3) system entry (emergency vs. planned admission, with some, little, or no preparation time); 4) duration of hospitalization (exacting increasing demands on time, energy, and resources); 5) child's coping (developmental regression, emotional compromise, transient vs. permanent impairments and disfigurements); 6) loss of routine (sleep, work, household upkeep). In order to cope, most families default to the following hierarchy of priorities: 1) meeting the needs of the ill child (particularly for mothers); 2) attending to siblings (extended family and friends' support may be accepted); 3) work demands (less of a priority for mothers, greater for fathers); and 4) household demands (meals, laundry, etc, with many non-essential tasks deferred or transiently ignored).

Assisting families to cope

The stability of parents and the extended family has direct bearing on the status and recovery path of an ill or injured child. Thus, substantive attention to the family's needs is warranted. Assisting parents with personal care needs and comforts by providing access to telephones, showers, laundry, meals, and quiet can provide profound support. Parent pagers are a relatively new innovation, but one that can give parents significant peace of mind when they must be away from the bedside or out of the facility. Ensuring parents receive regular and meaningful medical updates is especially important. As parents accommodate and adjust to the new situation, they move through predictable stages: 1) acquiescence to staff; 2) information seeking; and 3) advocacy. Where distress continues, much of it will be due to: 1) feeling out of control; 2) the use of a confrontational style of coping; and/or 3) an avoidance or escapist coping style. Reduced stress is most closely associated with becoming involved in caregiving, participating in decision making, and accepting other responsibilities.

Needs identified by parents when recalling the hospital experience
The top 10 needs reported by parents are: 1) to be told about everything that is being done for their child in a timely way; 2) to see staff comfort their child; 3) to become medically well informed and educated; 4) to receive honest and complete responses to questions; 5) to have open visiting hours; 6) to be confident (by explicit assurances) that top quality care is being provided; 7) to be informed about the expected short-term and long-term prognosis for the illness or condition; 8) to feel that medical staff genuinely care; 9) to be sure the child is being treated gently by health care staff whether or not the parents are present. When staff is made aware of these needs and works to meet them, parental stress is substantially reduced.

Needs identified as least important to parents
When asked, parents tended to identify the following needs as being among the least important to them during a child's hospital stay: 1) for others to be concerned about the parent's health; 2) ready access to a restroom; 3) availability of pastoral staff or clergy; 4) transportation issues; 5) visitation by the child's siblings; 6) help from others in coping with other sibling's reactions; 7) to be accompanied by others during visitation; 8) comfortable furniture in the waiting area; 9) talking with other parents in a similar situation; and 10) access to a family support group. When more important priorities are met, however, these needs may subsequently grow in significance to the family.

Age-related variables and common reactions of siblings
Numerous concerns come to bear on siblings with the hospitalization of a child. Siblings quickly become aware that serious events are occurring, and often must cope with this awareness in the absence (whether physically or emotionally) of parents. Their capacity to cope depends upon: 1) age and developmental maturity; 2) how much they know about the medical problems (ignorance may also give way to fearful fantasies); 3) perceptions of parent anxiety and their altered interactions; 4) deviations from routine and the presence of surrogate caregivers; 5) the social and economic status and resources of the family; and 6) their own prior experiences. Common reactions include: 1) disruption in sleep; 2) changes in eating; 3) academic and concentration problems; 4) feeling anxious, angry, or withdrawn; 5) behavioral problems; and 6) increased dependency on parents.

Children under the age of 7 have distinctive cognitive and developmental deficits that leave them particularly susceptible to stress at the hospitalization of a sibling. One study suggested that the greatest coping difficulties are experienced by children between the ages of 4 and 11. Younger siblings will most acutely feel the absence of parents who remain at a hospital bedside. Many children may also draw upon their propensity to self-blame when "bad" things happen, leading to unwarranted internalized guilt. All children may well worry about contracting the same affliction or sustaining a similar injury at some future time. Older children in particular may feel angry at the increased attention given the ill child and the increased responsibilities shifted to them during their parents' absences. The pattern of onset of the affliction also influences children's coping. The more acute the condition and the more sudden the onset the more difficult it is for children to cope well.

Siblings with the closest relationship to the hospitalized child typically experience the greatest levels of stress. Those closer in age and/or those who share room space and activities often find closer attachments. Other bonding factors include an older (now ill) child who routinely babysits, supports, or otherwise cares for a younger sibling. When this

- 68 -

child is absent, the sibling may feel abandoned, along with feeling unloved, unimportant, or punished. Much younger children may respond with separation anxiety, as with the absence of a parent. While changes in routine are always difficult, sometimes a child's illness results in displacement of siblings from the home and into care by other relatives. When this occurs, all stressors are further amplified, particularly where different home and parenting styles are involved. Higher socioeconomic status makes such displacement less likely, and a mother's higher educational and occupational status has also been shown to decrease sibling anxiety – perhaps due to greater awareness of situational stressors engendering greater compensating efforts.

General efforts to include siblings in the hospital experience will usually lessen the distress that they feel. Being given age-appropriate explanations about the illness, disease, or injury is very important, as is time at the sick child's bedside. Being prevented from seeing the ill child may engender fears and flights of fancy and fantasy that could well be worse than seeing the actual circumstances even if they are difficult. However, adequate preparation is essential if young children are to avoid being unduly impacted by seeing an acutely ill loved one. Where distance prevents sibling visitation, exchanges of cards, letters, phone calls, and photographs can help draw the ill child and the siblings closer and reduce some of the distress they may otherwise be feeling. Being given opportunities to talk, share fears, and receive reassurances most certainly aids sibling coping. At such time, misconceptions may be corrected and unfounded fears and self-blame put to rest. Child life specialists are particularly well suited to meeting these unique needs.

Safety checks

Staff supervising any children's art activity should adhere to the following checklist of concerns before beginning: 1) find and check the labels found on all supplies – note: the term "nontoxic" includes only short-term health effects and does not rule out long-term issues that may arise from the ingestion of or exposure to larger quantities; 2) use common sense – discard old, damaged, smelly, and/or moldy items that may have become unhealthy or unsafe; 3) olfactory senses are not definitive – even things that smell normal, sweet, or odorless may still be bad, so follow labels and expiration dates carefully; 4) plan every step in an activity in advance – including techniques, equipment, etc; 5) reevaluate each child's condition – some may be immunosuppressed, allergic, contagious, have food restrictions, be overly susceptible to odors and nausea, or have medical devices that need special protection; 6) evaluate the setting – look for environmental safety issues, including elopement risks or potential problems with noise; 7) assess supervision needs – especially when working with higher risk items (sharps, etc) or in larger groups.

Medical staff in general and child life specialists in particular have an ongoing responsibility to ensure the safety of all children involved in program activities. This responsibility requires careful event planning, proper supervision and monitoring, and appropriate post-event clean up and organization. Primary safety concerns requiring ongoing attention include: 1) art materials (sharp pencils, ingestible paints, etc); 2) activities and methods (when they may predispose falls or other injuries); 3) children of very young ages and/or developmental thresholds (especially when they are interacting with other children or involved in more risky events); and 4) children with disabilities or markedly poor conditioning (i.e., at greater risk of falls, disturbance to medical devices, etc).

Emergency Room

Unique stressors
The emergency room is perhaps the most daunting and stressful area in a hospital for both children and adults. The activities inherent to that setting are generally urgent and hurried. Great numbers of people – patients and medical staff alike – move through the area, causing substantive congestion, noise, and chaos. Law enforcement, firefighters, and other first responders hasten to ancillary duties. Sounds of the injured and ill may be heard, and considerable medical machinery and other paraphernalia are encountered in and though that setting. All during this time patients and families are usually coping with questions, uncertainties, as well as the pressing symptoms of their personal medical malady. Therefore, it is not difficult to comprehend that the emergency room is among the most stressful aspect of hospitalization.

Issues and strategies for managing emergency admissions and unplanned procedures
When emergencies and unplanned medical events arise, the following suggestions and approaches may be useful: 1) focus on coping distractions, parent involvement, positioning for comfort (seated in a parent's lap with an arm out for an IV is much better than on a gurney), and treatment area/atmosphere (noise, privacy, etc); 2) setting limits – protective limits are also important ("the restraints help when you forget and pull at the tubes, and we can take them off whenever someone is with you"), not just choices; 3) negotiation – sometimes options can be helpful, but undue delays usually make things worse; 4) professional support – use child life staff or others similarly trained to assist during the procedure (bring them in proactively, rather than when all are already upset); 5) honesty – never damage trust with untruths or betrayals about what, when, with whom, or how events are expected to unfold.

Infancy, toddler, and preschooler
Processes of examination, evaluation, and testing in the emergency room tend to separate patients from families and involve numerous strangers. Key insults relate to separation anxiety, impairments to the secure base, and reduced trust. Interventions to reduce these issues include: 1) enabling the parents to remain with or at least near the infant, holding the baby whenever feasible; 2) not conscripting parents to aid in distressing procedures (i.e., holding the child down, etc), but instead have them focus on comforting and soothing interactions; 3) keeping the numbers of personnel involved to a minimum and deferring nonessential intrusive tests or procedures until the infant is admitted into the more ordered hospital environment. Toddlers benefit from the above as well. However, their growing need for autonomy should be engaged through choices, medical play activities and preparations, and distractions, while minimizing restraints and limitations. Where preschoolers are involved, magical thinking, fears of mutilation, and desires for competence are paramount. Thus, greater preparatory detail is needed prior to procedures, more candid conversation is important with questions answered honestly, and specific coping strategy teaching is beneficial.

School-aged children and adolescents
School-aged children are particularly distressed over loss of control over the body, feeling overly dependent, and feeling less than competent. Consequently, interventions such as procedure preparation, coping strategy teaching, providing choices and options, and specifically involving them in activities of medical care where possible must be given increased age-appropriate emphasis. Adolescents are sensitive to issues of trust,

- 70 -

restrictions, forced dependence, loss of bodily capacities, threats to future plans, and perceived issues of competence. To compensate, interventions should foster fully candid discussions, direct address of emerging physical and psychological changes and problems, honest appraisals about the long-term consequences of an illness or injury, along with ways to ameliorate and compensate for any residual deficits. Greater involvement in carrying out treatments is helpful, as is offering ongoing communication opportunities combined with useful responses, direction, and guidance.

Improving family capacity to cope with emergency department experiences
Brunnquell and Kohen (1991) studied family issues as related to emergency care and then developed the following recommendations: 1) Never escalate your emotions and agitation to compete with family anxiety. Focus on empathic responses, soothing speech, and offering answers to calm their fears and produce greater family stability. 2) Ensure that a specific person is assigned to attend to the family's emotional needs, and make sure that all involved (patient, family, medical staff) know who has been assigned. 3) Patients and families have heightened information needs during an emergency room stay. Empower them with complete and timely information. 4) Prepare both patients and families prior to undergoing any procedure, intrusive treatment, or test. Be candid about any distress expected, and offer recommendations to support both themselves and the child. 5) Be particularly vigilant about uncontrolled pain. Ensure adequate time passes after administration of any anesthetic for it to be fully effective. Because anxiety increases pain, use alternative coping resources such as relaxation therapy and imagery to reduce pain and other stressors.

Pediatrics

Improving pediatric ambulatory care experiences
Ambulatory (outpatient) medical care is increasing in prevalence. With the shorter periods for interaction and preparation that this form of care affords, careful attention must be given to numerous details in order to adequately compensate. Ambulatory care facilities should be designed with pediatric patients in mind. Engaging and positive entryways, waiting areas, and pediatric furniture should be included. Play areas equipped with toys, age-appropriate literature, and educational materials should be included. Accouterments such as decor, music, magazines, aquariums, and other sensory enhancements are also important. As health care systems encounter increasing time constraints, staff turnover, and program consolidations, these extra measures become ever more important. Children who feel relaxed and comfortable upon entering the health care facility will be easier to work with, more tolerant of unfamiliar staff, less anxious over treatments, and generally more effective and cooperative patients to serve.

Improving pediatric home health care experiences
Care that used to be rendered only in an acute care medical setting is now routinely provided through visiting nurses in the home setting. Reduced environmental accommodation and stranger intrusion are significant benefits for children who are able to return home more quickly. However, there are certain drawbacks to the home health care approach. First, patient monitoring and complex medical equipment must be managed without readily available professional support. This produces stress for both parents and the ill child. Siblings may feel more marginalized and ignored when these care demands further draw parental attention toward the ill child. Interrupted peer visits, household chore shifting, and other challenges may create further family stress. Consequently, the

transition into home care must be carefully planned. Child life staff and other providers can reduce children's stress through open sharing and creative activities such as art, crafts, music, and journal writing. Building in care opportunities for siblings is also important, as it more fully facilitates coping. Ongoing family monitoring is essential, as needs and circumstances will evolve and change.

<u>Outpatient pediatric medical daycare centers</u>
When home health care of a child is expected to be protracted or even indefinite in nature, staff and families will want to look for outside resources to assist the family with unremitting health care tasks and demands. A resource of particular significance is that of "pediatric medical daycare." These child health care centers are staffed by multidisciplinary teams of professionals, including nurses, physical and occupational therapists, speech therapists, developmental educators, and child life specialists. These daycare centers can manage very complex medical patients and can provide parents and others with much needed respite from the demands of long-term care. Of considerable additional value, daycare centers such as these can also provide important socialization and developmental assistance so that children can maintain normal patterns of growth and progress. Group activities, field trips, guest presentations, outdoor play, and a host of similar events help a child who is otherwise unable to return to normal community involvement. As most such centers are located in or very near hospitals, medical concerns are kept to a minimum.

Theoretical concepts of stress

Sources of stress may be physical, psychological, social, or any combination of these. Berk (1997) refers to children's stress as either "normative" (arising from usual life events and typical developmental processes) or "nonnormative" (e.g., trauma, abuse, severe illness, etc). The stress model most frequently applied to children is the "transactional stress model" developed by Lazarus and Folkman (1984). This model has 3 key stages: 1) stressor identification; 2) appraisal of resolution options; and 3) stressor mitigation (behavioral or cognitive changes and efforts). Resources, developmental capacities, and circumstances will constrain available options. Coping efforts may be categorized as either "problem" or "emotion" focused, or some combination of these. Coping outcomes are seen as either "adaptive" or "maladaptive." Child life staff must use caution not to prematurely judge a child's coping efforts to be maladaptive. A state of "denial," for example, may actually be transitionally adaptive and only maladaptive if it persists for an extended time.

Child preparation programs

By the mid-1970s, research detailing the positive benefits of preparing children for medical procedures and treatments had begun to be recognized by medical providers. By the early 1980s it had been determined that optimum preparation programs included: 1) essential information shared in age- and developmentally-appropriate ways; 2) opportunities for children to share their feelings about the information and upcoming medical plans; 3) parent (or other significant adult) participation and joint preparation; 4) the creation of a trusting bond with key medical staff. Studies also found that child-specific preparation programs were demonstrably effective (i.e., reduced emotional stress by self-report and follow-up behavioral observation, and improved physiologic stress indicators such as pain tolerance, blood pressure, etc) for children ages 4 to 6 and older. Primary benefits to younger children were realized through preparation efforts directed toward parents (principally mothers). Common preparation activities included medical play, role rehearsal, "stress point" care, and therapeutic play such as interactive medical puppet shows.

Coping

Coping has been referred to as a process by which one engages stressors. It implies only effort, not necessarily success. Many different thinking processes, strategies, and behaviors may be utilized in the effort to cope with any given stressor. The overall trend and predisposition of one's efforts and option selections may be referred to as one's "coping style." Children rarely rely on only one coping strategy, with their own individual coping styles still very much in development. Further, children are quite malleable and impressionable, and thus readily able to adopt new and different coping strategies that are presented to them. Child life staff may capitalize upon this and teach children additional or replacement coping strategies in order to maximize their potential for coping success.

Intrusive medical events

It has been noted that 40-60% of the 3 million children who undergo surgical procedures annually in the United States will experience significant stress prior to surgery. Much of it is manifested behaviorally, with common reactions including tearfulness, nightmares, fear of doctors and hospitals, or tantrums. Other internalized and repressed emotional and psychological stress reactions may be less apparent but are no less traumatic and burdensome to those children who suffer with perioperative fears and anxieties. The prevalence and degree of such stress underscores the need for age-appropriate and effective interventions.

Common preparatory efforts

There are a great many preparatory programs and approaches used. Some of the more common specific approaches that are also supported by research findings include: 1) pre-anesthetic sedation (sedatives given to relax the child before actual anesthesia), which reduced preoperative stress and postoperative negative behaviors; 2) cognitive-behavioral preparation using written, verbal, and practical advance instructions (procedure descriptions with practical prompts, etc), which allowed for reduced stress and anesthesia-free transurethral catheterizations and better pain management; 3) distraction as coping, which produced benefits enduring beyond the immediate procedure for two-thirds of children studied; and 4) hypnosis, which may be more effective for some children than certain cognitive approaches.

Programs using approaches to meet children and family needs

Most preparation programs will draw upon a diversity of interventions and approaches in an effort to most fully meet patient and family needs. For example, one published study relied upon an art therapy approach that utilized the following interactive modes: 1) a pre-procedural medical review and discussion; 2) the use of outcome visualization and positive imagery by which to manage discomfort, divert attention, and soothe concerns; 3) medical play to enhance feelings of understanding, control, and confidence; 4) structured drawing by which to ground reality, identify misconceptions, and mitigate fantasy fears; 5) free drawing through which to allow children to identify, describe, and otherwise externalize their anxieties; and 6) drama play to aid children in accommodating and resolving issues related to appearance, function, and/or other body changes. By use of these multiple modalities, the researchers were able to document significant decreases in pre- and post-hospital problems and distress, as well as measurably improved collaborative behaviors.

<u>When families are unable to attend onsite preparation meetings</u>
In situations where the child and family members live at great distance from the admitting medical facility, they may not be able to attend a face-to-face preparation experience. In such circumstances, it becomes necessary for staff to look for alternative approaches to preparation and teaching. Some literature documents measurable success on preparation indices using illustrated pamphlets, videos, and other booklets and handouts as substitute teaching materials. Where the family has access to technology and computers they may also access information online and take virtual tours of a medical facility, see pictures of key personnel, and access additional preparation or program information and resources. The benefits of advance preparation and familiarization are significant enough that every available opportunity should be made available to the family and child involved. In this and all preparation processes, special language, culture, and background issues should also be met to the degree possible.

<u>Development and maturation</u>
In order to be successful, preparation programs must be tailored to the age and developmental level of the child. Indices of success must also be selected with developmental perspectives in mind (i.e., measures of anxiety for those younger, as opposed to information-seeking skills, etc). This may be one reason why the literature largely fails to document preparatory success with preschool and younger-aged children (also considered to be those at most risk for negative emotional outcomes). Indeed, some studies specifically recommend that preparation programs should not be employed with children preschool age or younger. However, other more recent studies suggest that the approach and coping strategies selected may well be determinative. For example, one study noted that the use of role-play was effective in reducing anxiety in all studied children, with the greatest effect seen in children under the age of 5. Other research emphasizes that older children (age 6 and beyond) benefit from preparation earlier (5 to 7 days pre-event) as opposed to only 1 day or less in advance.

<u>Coping strategies and practical interventions</u>
Weisz, McCabe, and Dennig (1994) observed that most natural coping behaviors were self-protective, with others identified as reaching out, situation controlling, and information seeking. From these observations they classified 3 categories of coping strategies employed by children: 1) primary control (consisting of behaviors to revise ensuing circumstances); 2) secondary control (efforts to adjust self to circumstances); and 3) relinquished control (deferring to others). They found that secondary control strategies resulted in the most successful and beneficial outcomes. Thus, these should be taught, modeled, and promoted. In keeping with the natural tendency toward primary control, another researcher found that children of all ages benefit from program components allowing children greater control and choice, such as letting the child select the arm for the IV, negotiating timing and other options in the procedure, or postponing if necessary. When options were offered and control shared, cooperation was substantially enhanced for all ages. Because not all elements of any given procedure can be negotiated, it is essential to seek out those that can and capitalize upon them at every appropriate opportunity.

<u>Role of language development</u>
Child preparation programs are typically offered starting at 2½ to 3 years of age. The focus for children younger than this is on the parents, who will benefit from learning specific supporting strategies and becoming familiar with what will occur in advance. Younger children rely more on enactment, object manipulation, and play strategies to learn, with

verbal skills much less predominant. Preparation programs must recognize this and create interventions and approaches that more fully accommodate these basic skills and needs. Particular care should also be taken with medical terminology. Technical terms should be carefully explained to minimize anxiety and fearful fantasies upon hearing them. However, explanations should be interactive to ensure a full understanding. Some terms might be avoided altogether, where possible, due to the distress they may provoke in certain children. For example, getting a "shot" might be persistently seen by some children as a threat of gunshot ("injection" is an alternative). Thus, staff should remain alert to unique language issues and emphasize those words and phrases that best meet the child's needs where possible.

The first "language" of newborns is crying. The next stage is "cooing" at about 4-6 weeks. This is followed at about age 5 months by single syllable sounds ("da," "ga," etc). From about 6-8 months onward a child can recognize its own name and "babbling" begins. First words ("mama," "dada," etc) appear about age 10 months – an understanding of "no" is acquired very quickly. From about 12-18 months, vocabulary increases on average one new word per week; basic commands begin to be understood. Between 18-20 months, an infant uses some 20 words properly. At or near 24 months vocabulary is up to about 50 words, with one or more new words gained daily; two-word sentences begin ("give me"); and, attending to two-step requests starts ("don't touch!"). From 24 to 30 months "telegraphic speech" starts, including subject, object, and verb sentences ("me want up"). By about 36 months, a toddler can understand some 800 words, and very basic prepositions ("put it in that box"). From the age of 4 onward, children usually speak so others understand them most of the time.

Communication

<u>Strategies for infants, toddlers, and young school-aged children</u>
Infant/toddler communication: 1) requires a careful focus on the intensity, inflection, level, and rise and fall of infant sounds; 2) relies heavily on body language, such as positioning and motion; they are usually most attentive and comfortable when in an upwardly-inclined or fully upright position; 3) is most effective when they are nearer their parents, as stranger fear emerges at about 6 months; and 4) should be engaged using a quiet voice, along with comforting gestures such as patting, cuddling, and stroking to induce calm.
Preschool/young school-aged children: 1) allow them to approach you first whenever possible; approaching or moving too quickly easily startles children this age; 2) avoid overly broad smiles or lengthy direct eye contact when first meeting; 3) keep parents close by, and move to the child's eye level to limit the threatening sense of disproportionate size; 4) talk plainly to avoid confusing the child, staying away from phrases such as "got a frog in your throat" or "a hitch in your giddy-up," which children of this age interpret literally, if at all.

<u>Strategies for older school-age children and adolescents</u>
Older school-age children: 1) employ plain and direct methods of communication; 2) lead with explicit explanations and basic reasons for anything discussed or demonstrated, as these children are coming to place greater emphasis on knowledge and understanding than on seeing and showing alone; 3) keep in mind that knowledge is also an increasingly meaningful way of coping; 4) explanations about how the body functions become especially important in helping older school-age children cope with hospital experiences.
Adolescents: 1) keep in mind that teens are more moody and emotional than their younger selves; 2) focus on specific concerns to retain necessary engagement; 3) when teens use

words or phrases you don't understand, make a point of asking, rather than assuming a meaning that may not be correct; 4) avoid asking questions in ways that seem demanding or intrusive; 5) emphasize non-threatening topics early on, until greater trust has been built; 6) start with broad, open questions first ("What's up at home?") before being more specific ("Are you and your Dad getting along?"), to minimize the potential for perceived intrusion.

Techniques that improve the "preparation" process for children

The following techniques are helpful: 1) try to appear unhurried and relaxed in voice, movements, and questioning; 2) use few words, in word sequences equal to the child's years of age plus 1; 3) begin with play to engage a child (i.e., addressing their teddy bear first), and then move to questions; 4) recognize play as communication – watch and listen to children play to learn things they may not express; 5) provide options and choices when possible ("We need your shoes off – do you want help?"); 6) be truthful if something will hurt, but describe feelings ("stings for a minute") rather than just pain; 7) use clear explanations ("check how warm you are" instead of "take your temperature" – which might leave a child wondering what is being taken away); 8) stay away from words with double meanings (see "take" above); 9) choose words that are not emotionally laden ("slip this in" instead of "stick you", etc); 10) use positive directions ("Can you stay real still?" instead of "don't move"); and 11) keep away from private topics, awkward feelings, embarrassing questions, and lecturing.

General procedure preparation principles

When preparing for an impending surgery or other medical procedure, small children generally need to meet key participants in advance and in a non-threatening situation (where they can sit, talk, and/or play in a non-threatening way), to explore involved medical equipment (either as represented by models or as real items), and to explore involved settings (visiting the surgical area, waiting areas, play rooms, etc) Preschoolers and young children benefit from the above, but can gain further benefits from event and coping strategy rehearsal as well as being provided with available choices to enhance feelings of control. Older children and adolescents have the greatest desire to talk, to ask questions and receive meaningful answers, and to otherwise learn more about an impending medical experience.

Benefits and timing of procedural preparation for infants and toddlers (from birth to 2½ years)

Offering procedural or medical event preparation to children under the age of 2 lacks specific research validation measures of efficacy. However, many practitioners and researchers have noted that infants as young as 9 months of age are able to manipulate medical utensils in meaningful ways, and may well benefit from a process of familiarization prior to the medical event itself. It is postulated that because sensory exploration is the primary mode of environmental engagement for infants and toddlers, being allowed to explore medical equipment may lead them to some internal sense of mastery and/or accommodation that could lessen their distress during subsequent procedures. Modeling the use of the equipment may enhance these benefits. As infant and toddler perceptions of time remain limited, preparatory experiences taking place just prior to the procedure should still be optimally effective. Children aged 4 and above have the capacity to track time and events, and will thus benefit from more advance preparatory experiences.

<u>Concepts and steps essential to preparing infants and toddlers (aged 9 months to 2½ years)</u>
Infants and very young children benefit most from the presence of a parent. Thus, many researchers suggest that the greatest preparation efforts should be directed toward familiarizing the parents with an impending procedure, teaching ways to keep calm and emotionally available, and to optimally comfort and support their child. Thus, recommended steps include: 1) introductions – greet the parents, and use a game or toy to engage the infant/child; 2) exploration – give safe medical equipment planned for use to the infant/child while talking further with the parents; 3) demonstration – a) show the usual use of masks, tubes, tape, etc; b) allow the child the use of each; c) give the child/parents a doll prepared with these items; d) the doll should come back for the procedure, and the parents should rehearse with the child and doll in the interim; 4) mastery – take parents and child to see relevant areas and staff; prompt the child to use things like light switches, remote controls, and scales, so that he or she can feel a sense of mastery over the environmental setting.

<u>Concepts and steps essential to preparing preschool children (ages from 2½ to 5 years)</u>
Providing preparatory experiences some 5-7 days in advance, coupled with social supports and assurances from staff reduces stress for both parents and children. Useful preparatory techniques include: 1) introductions – greet parents and the child by name, and clearly explain that this is a visit only, with the procedure to happen later (to eliminate any fear); 2) explore – walk them through all relevant areas, pointing out useful details, and let the child thoroughly enjoy the play area; 3) explanations – from admissions, to pre-op, to postoperative recovery in the "wake up" room, explain the entire process and people involved – use proper equipment and dolls for a detailed review of the procedure and related events (reminding the child that his/her parents will be there throughout); 4) choices – offer realistic choices, from flavor of anesthesia to which parent is with him or waiting where, to toys and movies, but never offer a choice that is not truly available.

Four concluding preparatory steps for preschool-aged children include: 5) role – tell the child his/her "jobs" (drink fluids, eat popsicles, watch movies, avoid touching the IV site, etc) to gain buy-in and cooperation; 6) coping – teach appropriate coping strategies (with parents as supportive coaches to give them a positive role and help them reduce their own anxiety); 7) cues – give the child ways to know when each step in the experience is complete (i.e., "the IV comes out just before you go home", etc); 8) questions – field questions and answers until the child and parents are both clear about what is to happen (leave contact information for missed questions); 9) positive ending – give praise, rewards (stickers, candy, etc), or their own medical doll to take and bring back, and then let the child lead the way out, pushing any elevator buttons and opening all automatic doors themselves (something much enjoyed and empowering for all children, and something they can then do when they return).

<u>Concepts and steps essential to preparing school-age children for medical procedures (ages from 6 to 11 years)</u>
In addition to many of the preparatory suggestions for younger children, school-age children also benefit from: 1) increased information – curiosity increases and they are more interested in the workings of the body, particularly if models, pictures, and non-medical terms are used to explain; 2) more sophisticated coping strategies – they use imagination and visualization well and thus can benefit from engaging music, images of a favorite place, or favorite activity (encourage choices to further empower them); 3) greater participation – these children can often help by holding bandages, tape, tubes, a thermometer (again,

- 77 -

choices help); 4) timing – school-age children should be told a week or more in advance of the procedure, given a schedule if further treatments are required, allowed opportunities to plan life events around their treatments, and be given routine reviews of long-term goals and expected outcomes to minimize the stress of short-term treatment burdens.

<u>Concepts and steps essential to preparing adolescents for medical procedures (ages 12-18+)</u>

Teens must cope with body changes, a need for independence, peer attachments, emotional changes, etc. This can result in periods of dependency followed by "tough" indifference, making it difficult to offer support. Approaches for younger children still work, with adaptations: 1) question lists – teens can readily write down questions to ensure they receive answers; 2) realistic teaching tools – substitute dolls and rudimentary drawings with photographs and diagrams; 3) coping – engage coping approaches at any stressful step (ask what they think might help – watching, looking away, humming, counting, deep breathing, etc, then do it together); 4) modesty – bodies are changing and they need greater privacy via careful placement of gowns, closed doors, and pulled curtains; 5) menstruation – stress can bring on unexpected menstruation and girls may bring preferred supplies for comfort; 6) participation – teens can monitor vital signs, help in treatments, and manage meal menus, and will be more resilient if encouraged to do so; 7) peers – find ways to help teens stay in touch with peers through visits, notes, or e-mail – no adult support can entirely replace peer needs.

Postvention

Post-intervention

There are occasions when a child is admitted and experiences various medical interventions without the benefit of any preparation, coaching, or preplanned support. The remedial process for calming a child and establishing post-trauma trust and equilibrium is referred by Mahan (2005) to as "postvention." One approach to postvention is to introduce medical play as early as possible. This can involve supplying a medical doll and basic medical paraphernalia and encouraging the child to provide care for it. By use of open-ended questions and clarification requests many fears, questions, and misconceptions can be identified, addressed, and corrected. In this way, the child is also able to establish some measure of mastery and control over the things and events that recently caused them distress.

Role of art

The use of the arts in health care has been recorded since ancient Greece, where music was used in healing centers. While the arts are unable to produce "cures" for illness, they nevertheless promote emotional and physical healing. Because the arts can be so deeply therapeutic and tension relieving, they are of particular value for use with children who are vulnerable to the traumas of hospitalization and medical interventions. The arts are used in ways similar to the use of play in health care settings. Artistic activities promote self-expression and situational mastery, and reduce stress. They may also symbolically represent fearful thoughts and feelings otherwise unwelcome or too complicated to put into words. While exploring well-being by way of art, professionals must use care not to encroach on the domain of "expressive therapy." These therapists are licensed professionals with special training to prescribe specific artistic activities and interpret the results. While others may do great good with art, they must not practice as expressive or art therapists.

The "arts" include a great variety of activities and creative endeavors, including: 1) visual arts (painting, sculpture, photography, needlepoint, flower arranging, etc); 2) performing arts (dance, drama, storytelling, etc); and 3) literary arts (writing, symbolism, poetry, etc). All can be used with children, and mixed and matched as optimally beneficial. Creative activities evoke and enable emotions, and allow for expression of feelings and thoughts in ways not otherwise readily available. Artistic activities can also be used to soothe, calm, reduce pain, or circumvent conflicts. Further, they provide children with opportunities to be actively in control, empowered, and directive in settings where deprivation, pain, and loss of control are unavoidably common. Finally, the arts bring a sense of the familiar, produce enjoyment, and relieve the stress associated with illness and intrusive medical experiences.

Managing pain and other medical and health-induced discomforts
Pain and physical distress and discomfort are endemic in situations of illness and injury. It is well known that children use art and expressive activities to distract themselves from pain, nausea, and other health stressors. Gate Control Theory (Wall, 1973) helps explain how this works. The theory postulates that unmediated emotions (fear, excitement, anxiety, etc) heighten sensations of pain and discomfort by opening a "central control" in the nervous system (i.e., the "gate"). Creative endeavors, by contrast, tend to close the gate of pain pathways by means of neurological and cognitive diversion, including relaxation, positive imagery, distraction, and suggestion. Finally, the use of artistic modeling and drawing can also be an invaluable tool for health care professionals who need children to show them where they have pain or other discomfort, and to illustrate its intensity and radiance into surrounding tissues.

Restrictive nature of health care environments and regimens
Medical settings are fraught with restrictions and losses of control. Doctors' orders, medication regimens, dietary guidelines, positional demands, and a plethora of similar limitations round out the total surrender of self in an era of technology-driven medical care. These issues are only heightened and expanded for children, who typically have very few choices or options, and who are even more confused than their adult counterparts by the environs, tests, and interventions involved. Further, patients must also remain passive and cooperative during experiences involving the infliction of pain, such as blood draws, surgical interventions, or dressing changes. While adults can resort to verbal exchange and discussion, children typically have no such voice available to them. Consequently, the arts provide an important outlet for children's frustrations, distress, and communication needs. Choices almost endlessly abound – selecting activities, colors, media, etc – all of which the child can control. Physical outlets are also available, where children can build, stack, pound, squash, and form shapes and structures to meet their desires. Little wonder that the role of the arts in health care is of such importance.

Assisting children to manage difficult emotions
Painful experiences, varied limitations, restrictions, and confusion all combine to produce considerable distress, fear, and frustration in children undergoing medical interventions and hospitalization. Unaddressed, these emotions can transform into feelings of depression, anger, and despair, and may manifest as withdrawal, misbehavior, and refusals to

cooperate. This can in turn lead to poorer health or immunity suppression. Opportunities for expression and emotional release are primary tools for coping. One medical center uses the novel intervention of a "wet room." Children dress in bathing suits and "paint" their distressing feelings onto the walls. Later they "wash away" the feelings down the drain, literally and symbolically ridding themselves of their distress. Artistic endeavors are marvelous tools for capturing and conquering difficult emotions and experiences in all their dimensions, and guiding them into safe and positive modes of expression and resolution. Joys and moments of contentment, too, can be artistically illustrated and thereby heightened.

Children with disabilities and the arts
Hospitalized children may be physically unable to participate in all available activities. Sometimes physical problems are transient (e.g., temporary immobilization of an arm due to an IV) while others may be permanent. Some children may be undergoing treatments or suffering from illnesses that leave them too fatigued to fully participate. Even so, virtually every child should be able to participate in one way or another. Certain children can "dance" only by moving limited parts of their bodies (or even using just their eyes, moved in time to the music); other children cannot wield a paintbrush unless it has been specially fitted with a holding device; still other children will need someone to actually carry out an artistic task for them, but under their specific direction. Children in medical isolation can participate in group activities by having their artwork joined into a collective show with the work of others. Another example is the "Life Necklace," where every child helps by making his or her own bead for the necklace's ultimate colorful composition. By being creative, every child can receive the benefits of the arts in medical settings.

Activities and experiences that produce positive health and well-being
Certain artistic endeavors are particularly engaging. These include music, visual arts, storytelling (including humor), dance, creative writing, and drama. Properly engaged, these arts can profoundly lift mood, enhance healing, improve immune and endocrine system functioning, reduce stress, and moderate pain. Of the 15 major stress management categories Ryan-Wenger (1992) found most commonly used by children, 5 could be significantly enhanced through the arts: 1) behavioral distraction; 2) cognitive distraction; 3) emotional expression; 4) self-controlling activities; and 5) social support. The relationship between efforts such as these, the senses, the environment, and the well-being of the mind and body (particularly as related to stress and optimum functioning) is currently being studied in the relatively new field of psycho-neuro-immunology (PNI). PNI studies have clearly demonstrated both positive and negative outcomes based upon physical and expressive activities and environmental influences. The arts in health care, therefore, continue to grow in importance and meaning.

Medical art therapy
Medical art therapy involves directed art strategies used with individuals who are ill or injured. Specialized techniques such as "projective artwork" are best left to certified therapists. However, other useful techniques include: 1) "Illuminative" artwork – where the child is prompted to think of art as a way to communicate, and then asked to explain meanings in their art themselves. Two specific benefits have been noted: a) the quality and meaning of expressions are increased; and b) the art becomes a focus around which conversations are easily expanded (referred to as "the campfire effect"). 2) The "draw-write" method – where children draw pictures and then write out what is occurring in the artwork. Helpful information is often elicited, even when young children must seek help in

recording their descriptions. 3) The "ipsative method" – which assesses children's adjustment and coping over time by looking for changes in sequences of artwork. 4) Past-present self-portraits – asking a child to draw a self-portrait of how they looked before becoming ill, during treatment, and after treatment, and then discussing the differences. Many significant insights may be gained through these methods.

Providing activities or art support in a child's home

Advances in technology and medical support have provided opportunities for many children to return home with significantly debilitating chronic conditions or for protracted recovery periods. Child life staff may be called upon to offer support, ongoing evaluations, and art and activity resources. These opportunities are very valuable, as it is so much easier to assess overall patient and family functioning, and to develop much closer bonds and trust. However, it is also important to recognize the following important limitations: 1) never assume simple supplies will be available, or when present that they may be used (i.e., bring along a toaster oven to cure clay beads, rather than depending on the oven in the home which may be unavailable); 2) obtain permission before using anything and use care to not burden families with too many requests; 3) additional protection against accidents and spills may be necessary (damage to expensive items, heirlooms, etc, may be very problematic); 4) be prepared with alternative activities and options should circumstances change.

Planning needed before initiating a pediatric art program

There are many considerations and planning steps that should be taken prior to starting a pediatric art program. Some may include: 1) surveying existing programs in the community and/or other health care settings and consulting with their staff; 2) considering whether to pay involved artists or to recruit volunteers (funding sources, community size, and other factors may substantially influence this decision); 3) considering where to base the program (in a hospital, clinic, school, or other community setting, and surveying possible sites in advance); 4) seeking advice from organizations such as the Society for the Arts in Healthcare Consulting Service (SAHCS) or the Society for the Arts in Healthcare (SAH) to minimize the possibility of unforeseen complications.

Artists who would work well with pediatric populations

In engaging artist-professionals to work with children, the following characteristics are recommended: 1) a desire to work with children, and a caring nature and openness to diverse groups; 2) professional level of skill in their art; 3) open to nurturing unique artistic differences in children; 4) an understanding of the true power of the arts and personal limitations; 5) adaptability to circumstances; 6) a humorous, fun side; 7) works well with others; and 8) free of health problems or background problems harmful to children. Note: A genuine desire to work with children (and their parents) is more important than having specific prior experience.

Important elements of an activities/visiting celebrity checklist

To make sure activities/celebrity visits go well, review the following checklist: 1) ensure an activity/celebrity visitation policy is in place; 2) activities/celebrity visits must be monitored by trained staff and parents; 3) copy policies to all celebrities/media representatives; 4) entertainment must: a) be age appropriate; b) not cause disruption or misunderstandings; c) not generate images or fears of harm; d) not use cultural or religious themes that could alienate; e) avoid allusion to violence or dying; f) not use frightening masks or attire; and g) avoid competition; 5) instruct visiting celebrities, media, and groups on how to approach and talk with children; 6) escort all visitors at all times, adding an additional monitor when the media is present; 7) allow children and families to decline contacts; 8) maintain confidentiality and privacy; 9) include otherwise confined children; 10) obtain signed permission from parents for photos, interviews, or videotaping; 11) plan for patients and families who are sleeping, grieving, or in pain; 12) ensure that gifts are screened for safety and appropriate for all present; 13) time for a relaxed pace; and 14) ensure the event is not being inappropriately used for publicity.

Continuing growth and learning

Health care facilities and processes are foreign to normal activities and environments. Sterility, machines, and strangers make the experience further stressful. Through the arts, children can re-engage familiar and normalizing activities, and escape by way of imagination into an atmosphere that is much more appealing and supportive. Learning and growth, too, can be fostered through the arts. Drawing pictures of the body, the procedures involved, and expected outcomes, children can come to better understand themselves and their bodies, and can feel more fully empowered. These same drawings can be used to correct misconceptions and misunderstandings, as well as serve as a medium by which to illustrate and then talk about specific fears and concerns. In these, and many other ways, the arts can further children's growth and learning even in medical settings.

Role of music

Research into the use of music as a coping and life-enhancing strategy in health care situations has identified numerous benefits. Music: 1) reduces stress; 2) produces relaxation during medical procedures; 3) decreases anxiety during the preoperative period; 4) reduces nausea; 5) boosts immune function; and 6) reduces depression symptoms while increasing a sense of enjoyment and expressive feelings. Music has also been identified as one of the 4 most effective strategies used by children with asthma, and among the top 5 for pediatric oncology patients. In part, these benefits accrue when music induces a relaxation response – including decreased anxiety, blood pressure, stress hormone release, and heart rate. Music also aids in managing both situational and chronic pain, and makes distressing medical procedures tolerable. Optimum benefits are realized by matching music to personal taste and culture, with "designer music" (created especially to induce certain effects) being the most efficacious. Even newborns and premature infants benefit, with "heartbeat music therapy" inducing sleep and reducing stress and crying time.

Role of visual arts

Visual arts (painting, photography, drawing, etc) are primary aids to communication and may be used to uncover and illustrate complex feelings and fears. Creating visual art also provides an avenue for catharsis, and is an ideal tool for monitoring children's emotional states. Stressed children, in particular, are more likely to include emotional indicators in their drawings than non-stressed children. However, care should be exercised not to over-interpret children's drawings, which may simply contain images for distraction, escape, or enjoyment. Other times drawings include references unrelated to health concerns – such as family issues – that sometimes produce greater stress than an illness or disease process.

Capacity for visual arts to assist in pain control

Drawing and painting have been reported by children coping with cancer as effective ways to distract themselves from pain. One explanation for this effect arises from neurological interhemispheric theories. Artistic activities such as drawing and painting derive from cognitive skills situated in the right side of the brain. By contrast, verbal descriptions and conceptual recognition of pain reside in the left side of the brain. Thus, while engaged in intense right-brain activities, it is possible that left-brain awareness is diminished or even turned off altogether. This may, then, account for reported pain decrease or transient management through visual art activities. Of additional interest and benefit, it has been noted that the right brain tracks time poorly. Thus, art sessions can often be carried on for extended periods without a sense of tiring or over-attending to the activity.

Benefits of humor

The benefits of laughter and humor on healing and coping have been of particular interest since Norman Cousins first proposed its importance in his work with those who are ill. Many studies have documented related benefits, including improvements in immune function and serum antigen levels. Humor has also been identified as a very effective way to cope with stress and anxiety, providing catharsis, comic relief, and diminishment of the otherwise difficult threats that may arise with profound health changes. These same benefits have since also been recorded in school-age children and adolescents. The use of humor has been found to be a particularly important asset in working with adolescents. Consequently, many health care centers have produced "humor programs" to maximize the beneficial effects.

Benefits of storytelling

Storytelling provides children with many substantial benefits. Well-chosen stories provide indirect ways to look at overwhelming fears. Highly engaging stories often provide greater distraction from pain and treatments than can behavioral distraction approaches. Stories offer important catharsis, as emotions and feelings can be more readily channeled through story characters than through oneself. Stories generated by children provide measures of assessment, as stressed and anxious children tell stories that are more negative than children who are coping well. Stories may be used as tools to teach relaxation, and as sources for a relaxation response. This technique has been used to reduce medical visits and hospitalizations in children coping with asthma. Familiar stories create feelings of safety, comfort, and confidence, and reasons for extended human contact and sharing. A carefully selected story allows children to open up if they wish, or simply to enjoy a short fantasy. In short, children may take from a story only what they need and want, and the rest is simply irreplaceable fun.

Benefits of dance

Dance is an important therapeutic tool for children in health care settings, in part because it is another meaningful way to address the whole child and not just a disease, illness, or injury. Further, the earliest way children build a view of themselves and the world, and find communication, is through movement. This makes it particularly important for children's well-being. Dance and other significant movements are differentiated from simple mechanical motion by the infusion of emotion (via expression, posture, gestures, etc), and by the way specific movements can change and improve emotional states.

Among the many benefits derived through dance and movement are those identified by Warren & Coaten (1993): 1) to develop better control over musculature; 2) to achieve an enhanced body awareness and image; 3) to serve as an outlet for modulated emotional transfer and release; and 4) to enhance individual social skills (when shared with others in a group setting). Hanna (1995) indicates that dance assists the body and mind in healing by: 1) eliciting spiritual strength; 2) nurturing physical mastery; 3) reducing stress and pain through elevated emotion, distraction, and improved physical strength; and 4) attacking stress and its effects by using movement as a coping skill.

Koshland & Curry (1996) identified 4 specific benefits and outcomes of movement and dance that can be received by children in any hospital setting and situation: 1) facilitation of trust – dance and other gentle and artistic movements incorporate gestures and posture, and readily integrate voice sounds and tone, imparting a physical sense of sharing and empathy that facilitates trust (a simple example is the shared experience of a game of peek-a-boo with a young child); 2) improved body comprehension – via shared therapist/child experiences, often incorporating gentle props such as colorful movement streamers, wands, feathers, or stretch bands; 3) better sensory appreciation and control – includes enhancements in range of motion, breathing, circulation, etc; and 4) enhanced expression of burdensome feelings and emotions – where therapeutic and rhythmic movement, sensations, body awareness, and vocalization leads to release of fear, anxiety, anger, and fatigue.

Creative writing

Once children have attained the capacity to write, many find great stress relief and enhanced coping by way of writing. Those with particularly acute diseases and difficult experiences may be specifically encouraged to keep a journal of their experiences. Selecting a journal with unlined pages makes it easier for children to add artwork and/or paste in pictures to aid them in better capturing their feelings and experiences. It has been suggested that the link between reading and writing is storytelling. Thus, recording personal stories and feelings is an important link between learning by reading and wholesome emotional releases via the sharing of personal stories and the creation of poetry or music lyrics. Using props such as bubble blowing as inspiration for images, stories, and sharing can be helpful. Displaying poems as "sky writing" (i.e., on the ceiling above their bed), or as "poem posts" (on racks in postcard form), helps to further nurture the process. Surprising insights and growth often occur through creative writing.

Value of drama

Drama has long been used in health education, learning, and recovery programs for children. Opportunities for role-playing and Life Theater (particularly for adolescents) may be especially fruitful. Such approaches significantly increase the likelihood of discussion and insightful thought. For younger children, puppets are a particularly useful drama approach. Puppets provide natural outlets for both verbal and behavioral expression and the sharing of feelings. Conflicts are lower and a sense of safety is high because puppets do not innately produce personality threats or other intrinsic barriers. Speaking through a puppet is often easier, as there is a greater tendency toward honesty and toward message acceptance. Puppets are also an ideal tool for preparing children for upcoming health procedures and other similar events.

Drama, in its most basic form, refers to "doing things" in some active and engaging way (typically, acting out stories or events, using puppets, and/or engaging in hypothetical role-play). McKenna and Haste (1999) found drama therapy is helpful for individuals coping with chronic illness or disability in 4 key ways: 1) it enhances feelings of personal space in otherwise impersonal and often formal care environments; 2) it provides an enriched medium of entertainment and diversion from the constant stress of health care issues, treatments, and procedures; 3) it produces feelings of efficacy, involvement, and creativity in environments that intrinsically suppress these much needed feelings; and 4) it also offers up a multitude of metaphors and imagery through which to engage and resolve internal fears and challenges.

Concept of "clowning"

Sick or seriously injured children are often easily disturbed by strangers. It has been found that clowns in particular may inspire anxiety and fear in little children unless they are particularly careful about their interaction patterns, gestures, and modes of entertainment. Where they are specially trained, however, great benefits may result. Therefore, a number of training programs have been established for training "doctor clowns" in the unique skills required for medical clowning. The New York Big Apple Circus Clown Care Unit (CCU), for example, has been preparing clowns to work in medical settings for more than 20 years. Medical clowns are professionals, not volunteers, rotating through hospitals every 3-5 days. They work closely with medical staff and are briefed on special children's issues or concerns in order to minimize the potential for a poor response. Qualified clowns should have completed specialized training and should have subscribed to a code of ethics such as that provided by the CCU group noted above.

Relationship-centered care

Simply having programmatic supplies, resources, and opportunities available to children is insufficient to realize maximal benefits. The greatest benefits accrue through activities that engage children with each other and/or with other adults. In particular, having a concerned and caring adult involved and participating directly with a child is far more likely to produce a beneficial therapeutic result. For example, creating artwork can aid children to cope better and relieve more stress and anxiety than in the absence of artistic opportunity. However, when the artwork can be used as a tool for sharing and communication, its efficacy increases many-fold. Only through such sharing can trust, empathy, understanding, reassurance, and strengthening fully take place. Consequently, live music is preferred to recorded music, and live storytellers are preferred to video-recorded images.

Professional artwork and artists

The famed nurse, Florence Nightingale (1860), was once noted to have said that things of beauty were not simply aesthetically appreciable, but that they have meaningful influence on the physical being, as well. For example, researchers have found that individuals recovering from surgery who were provided with views of an attractive park containing trees and flowers took less medication, were seen as better patients by their nurses, and were discharged more quickly than patients with views limited to a back brick wall. Similar effects have been measured when patients were afforded views of paintings or photographic images of natural scenes as opposed to abstract art images. Researchers have also noted that children are more sensitive to their surroundings than are adults. Consequently, the beneficial or harmful effects of an environment are likely to be more pronounced with children.

Encouraging creativity

Essential guidelines for enhancing creativity in children include: 1) making a variety of creative options available; 2) combining creative modalities when necessary to optimize the results (i.e., painting and music, etc); 3) prompting children to include details (i.e., questions such as "Should he have a coat and shoes on out there?" or "Does someone else live in that house?'" will help children expand their thinking and increase their enjoyment); 4) supplying ideas and suggestions (recommend activities until the child hits upon something he or she feels they will particularly enjoy); 5) respecting emotions and individual concerns (e.g., art may well bring out many emotions and reactions – accommodating these will enhance ultimate outcomes); 6) working through irregular, regressive, and/or messy expressions, fantasies, feelings, and behaviors (provided no harm is being done); 7) becoming the hands, arms, legs, ears, and/or eyes for a disabled child, allowing him or her to participate more fully; 8) encouraging and praising special talents and interests; 9) celebrating and encouraging children's art through displays, performances, or awards; and 10) helping, but not taking over, for a child who is struggling.

Special needs children

Demographic characteristics
Variation in past definitions of special needs created many obstacles to research and understanding. In 1998, the Maternal and Child Health Bureau, Division of Services for Children with Special Health Care Needs produced this definition:
"Children with special health care needs are those who have or who are at an increased risk for a chronic physical, developmental, behavioral, or emotional condition and who also require health and related services of a type or amount beyond that required by children generally." (McPherson et al, 1998, p. 138). 12.8% to 20% of all children in the United States may meet these criteria through various conditions such as asthma, attention deficit disorder, cerebral palsy, depression, and sickle cell disease. The incidence of special needs in boys is 33% higher than in girls, and African American incident rates are the highest of all racial groups. Single parents and others of low income are also represented disproportionally. Children with special health care needs require more advanced medical technology, undergo more medical procedures, and are more likely to be transferred between care facilities.

Guiding principles in caring
Vesey and Maguire (1999) note 2 overarching principles that should guide the care of special needs children: 1) that there is more that special needs children have in common with other children than not; and 2) an awareness of these similarities should be the focus of most care, rather than the condition driving an interactive focus (often referred to as the "noncategorical approach"). Important commonalities between children include: meeting developmental markers, nurturing self-esteem, and maintaining important family and community relationships and involvement. Utilizing a child's developmental age (instead of chronological age) in planning interactions and interventions, and focusing on strengths rather than weaknesses, may prove particularly helpful.

Family-centered care

Family-centered care recognizes that families understand their own children best, and are their best source of support. Thus, their role is central to the health and well-being of children, and they should have an equally central role in evaluating, arranging, and providing care. Further, the needs of the child should be balanced with those of the family, to ensure that both can properly thrive. Balance is best achieved by openly and completely sharing information. Families may be supported by: 1) mobilizing internal resources; 2) providing referrals to community resources; and 3) encouraging family-to-family support (i.e., self-help for families). Indeed, research suggests that families of special needs children, in particular, are especially well qualified to offer assistance and support to each other.

Role of culture and ethnicity

Special needs children are more vulnerable than other children, and thus issues that influence children's care and well-being are felt more acutely in this unique population. It has been noted that culture and ethnicity may well influence: 1) the meaning of disease and illness; 2) approaches to providing care; 3) patterns of communication; and 4) the use of available services. Families from different backgrounds report that health care providers seemed to believe things about their culture or ethnicity that were not true as much as one-third of the time. Further, as many as 25% of these families perceived health care providers as insensitive to their unique needs, and felt providers did not properly inform them about their child's diagnosis. To improve these issues, health care providers need to focus on cultural and ethnic diversity and traditions as strengths rather than weaknesses, and to find ways to use their traditions to advantage. Part of this requires providers to secure adequate interpreters for non-English speakers, to ensure adequate communication and understanding.

Concept of "normalization"

Normalization is a process by which difficult experiences or situations are made more familiar and acceptable. Special needs children are in greater need of normalizing influences than other children, in part to aid them in coping with their more chronic conditions. Knafl and Deatrick (1986) provided 4 key steps to take in pursuit of normalization: 1) accepting that an illness or condition exists; 2) interpreting new family patterns as normal; 3) conceiving of the social consequences as minor; and 4) establishing new family routines consistent with normal life. Special needs (SN) children also benefit from: 1) having similar rules and expectations as other children; 2) being included in conversations and decision making; 3) self-control and choices; 4) a focus on abilities instead of deficits; 5) self-care; 6) adaptive resources to foster independence; and 7) special care needs being incorporated into usual family routines.

Stress and coping theory

A widely used stress and coping framework has been provided by Lazarus and Folkman (1984). They note that potential stressors for families of special needs children include: 1) changes in the disease over time; 2) resultant role strain and role confusion (terms as established by T. Parsons); 3) finance, time, and energy demands; 4) social, emotional, and psychological stressors; and 5) long-term uncertainty about the path and endpoint of the disease. Gartstein et al (1999) cite 3 specific theoretical orientations to psychosocial adjustment: 1) the "discrete disease" model focuses on learning about: a) adaptation of the family; b) unique condition-related stressors; and c) the specific familial, social, and emotional consequences involved; 2) the "non-categorical" model focuses on common issues for families, including: a) stressors specific to the child's condition; b) disturbances arising from family caregiving; c) relevant condition commonalities; and d) the potential for developmental disruption; 3) the "mixed" model is focused on: a) blending other models; b) identifying similarities between clustered conditions; c) recognizing and guarding against the potential for developmental disruption.

Application of systems theories
Sociological and human behavior researchers have long used "systems theory" to help explain the complex interactions found within social groups, organizations, and families. These theories generally hold that: 1) human systems are comprised of many parts that are dependent upon and interact with each other; 2) there is usually a steady-state balance existing between each part and the surrounding environment; and 3) family systems accommodate and adjust depending upon degrees of cohesion and their capacity for adaptation. Through systems theories, researchers are better able to understand the influence and impact of special needs children in their families, and to recognize dynamic relationships between the child and family members, health care systems, community organizations, and society as a whole. These insights enable more comprehensive and effective assessments and interventions.

Comprehensive, multidisciplinary, and coordinated
Special needs children, by definition, have one or more highly complex problems. Systems theory highlights the fact that chronic changes in a child's health will translate into significantly increased needs and demands upon all others involved. Further, these demands and needs typically require multiple service modalities and interventions to produce effective care and maintenance strategies. Common domains affected include social, emotional, financial, developmental, educational, emotional, and those of the family and involved healthcare and community organizations. No one service or professional perspective is adequate to address these many domains and needs independently. Thus, to be effective, the care of special needs children must be: 1) comprehensive – addressing all major facets of well-being; 2) multidisciplinary – drawing upon numerous specialists and providers to properly identify, evaluate, and address all involved concerns; and 3) coordinated – in order to produce cost-effective and appropriately efficient services and interventions. Goals should target both short-term needs and long-term management plans. Care coordination should be vested in a single care professional when possible, to enhance communication, produce overall clarity, and reduce both service redundancies and fragmentation.

Children's chronic disease categories
Children's chronic conditions can be classified as follows: 1) chronic medical illnesses as well as disabilities arising from post-natal injury (includes conditions developed following birth such as thyroid dysfunction, diabetes, traumatic blindness or paralysis, etc); 2) developmental disabilities – includes conditions originating during fertilization or gestation such as genetic disorders (i.e., sickle cell disease), intellectual disability (microcephaly, etc), congenital deafness, and phocomelia (truncated or entirely absent limbs); and 3) mental health problems, including attention-deficit disorders, cyclothymia (fluctuating endogenous depression), etc. While prominent developmental disorders have an obvious impact on the normal progression of childhood development, all complex chronic conditions will influence developmental processes. Whether arising from an inability to participate in normal activities, fatigue, recurring illnesses and serial hospitalizations, or unremitting medication side effects, such persistently disruptive problems can ultimately influence developmental

processes and accomplishments. Deficits may include emotional, social, academic, and/or physical developmental delay or dysfunction.

Optimizing planning
Regardless of the severity of medical problems or the degree of dependence on medical technology, careful planning can assist every infant and child to more successfully develop and achieve their optimum capacities. Three principles have been identified to enhance the developmental planning process: 1) Obtain and apply a comprehensive grasp of a child's medical problems to enhance effective developmental planning, considering issues of strength, endurance, stress signals, and coping styles to design a plan of care that optimizes the child's capacities; 2) design care plans and interventions that are specific to the child's personal interests and needs; and 3) become sufficiently acquainted with any required medical technology and equipment to successfully and innovatively meet essential developmental goals and progress. Proper developmental goals also require that children become integrally involved in their own care planning and innovation processes. This includes ensuring that they also understand their specific conditions, medical equipment, and progress expectations, sufficient to participate and provide meaningful input.

Care leadership
Care leadership refers to the locus of care activities – whether vested in the parent, the child, or both. Kieckhefer and Trahms (2000) designed a care leadership model that emphasizes a developmental perspective. Their model is structured in the following 5 stages: 1) identifies the parent of an infant or very young child as the "CEO" of care, with the child solely operating as a care recipient; 2) the parent moves into the role of "care manager," with the young child providing at least some of their own simpler care, in accordance with their growing capacity; 3) as the child's abilities allow him or her to begin serving as "care manager," the parent becomes a "care supervisor"; 4) the parent then becomes a "consultant" to the older child, who has now become their own "care supervisor"; and 5) ultimately the child becomes his or her own "CEO" of care operations.

Pediatric to adult care transition
There will come a time when pediatric care is too restrictive and developmental progress indicates a transition into adult care. Thoughtful planning is essential to ensure a smooth transition. Preparatory considerations include: 1) an adolescent's understanding of his or her medical condition, including all medications, treatments, and related dangers and precautions; 2) the capacity to communicate needs and wishes to others; 3) the degree of compliance with care requirements; and 4) the level of interest in making the transition. Other concerns include insurance coverage (which may change with age), the level of care needed (in-home support, residential care, independent living, etc), and the capacity to progress into vocational activities and eventual employment. Finally, long-term planning should include preparations for any time in which parents and/or other extended family may no longer be available to provide support, with particular focus on financial planning and other adjunctive support options.

Adaptive tasks common to successful parents
Clawson (1996) has identified 8 key adaptive tasks common to successful parent and family coping with a special needs child. They are, successively: 1) coming to accept the medical condition; 2) assuming daily treatment and care tasks; 3) tracking and meeting key developmental markers for their child; 4) successfully meeting the needs of others in the family; 5) coping adequately with the emotional and developmental needs of other family

members; 6) handling crises and continuing stressors successfully; 7) teaching other transiently involved individuals about the condition and management requirements; and 8) developing needed resources and supports.

Coming to accept a medical condition: To fully transition into the role of a long-term caregiver of a special needs child, parents need to come to terms with their child's condition. They need less to "accept" the condition (implying that it is somehow suddenly "okay" for their child to be disabled) as much as to fully acknowledge the situation and its reality. Medical staff can assist in their adaptive transition by: 1) telling parents of the diagnosis in a caring manner, in private and when together rather than separately; 2) emphasizing their child's strengths along with limitations; 3) using language free of medical jargon; and 4) attending to cultural variations and meaning of a disease or disability. With ongoing support as needed, parents can more readily avoid the syndrome of "parent straddling" – living in the past and the present, and focused on the need to see their child as "normal" when disability is obvious. Assisting parents with "grief work" as they mourn the loss of the expected future of their child will also help to facilitate this process.

Assuming daily treatment and care tasks: The burdensomeness of daily management tasks varies greatly according to the condition. Some conditions do not appreciably progress and require only vigilant monitoring to prevent further problems (i.e., cerebral palsy); others require active managing (i.e., cystic fibrosis), and still others require management coupled with "controlling activities" (i.e., diabetes injections coupled with diet and blood sugar level monitoring). In this process, Knafl et al (1996) identified 5 family management styles in a continuum from most successful to least: 1) thriving (focused on normalcy and feeling confident), 2) accommodating (some uncertainty and discord), 3) enduring (feelings of burdensomeness although they are capable), 4) struggling (meeting bare minimum standards and very negative), and 5) floundering (in the process of failing as caregivers). It is essential that coping skills be learned and new caregiving techniques applied where success is not in evidence.

Tracking and meeting key developmental markers: Parents who have the greatest degree of caregiving success and confidence are typically those who have a thorough understanding of their child's condition and all relevant needs. When they are also educated about an appropriate and expected developmental course, they are better at highlighting a child's strengths over weaknesses, incorporating necessary developmental activities, and presenting the child with proper guidance and discipline. Comprehensive family education should also include ways to merge caregiving and treatment needs into a normal family schedule – medication dosages timed to let the parents sleep at night, coordinating diet requirements with family food preferences, physical therapy folded into periods of expected daily activities instead of requiring separate time demands, etc. Learning to create well-ordered and adaptive environments, schedules, and plans can help any family become far more successful at caregiving and meeting developmental needs.

Meeting the emotional and developmental needs of others in the family: It is essential for caregiving parents to continue to meet other personal and family needs. This can take time, as parents may react differently to their new roles and the challenges of caregiving. Mothers may become overly focused on caregiving, fathers on employment and outside demands. Both will feel stressed when role expectations in the home must change or be further negotiated. Siblings may also feel neglected in this process. Finding ways to continue familiar and important family traditions, rituals, and activities can do much to ease

- 90 -

the demands of day-to-day care. Alone time is also important, as is respite opportunities on occasion. Single-parent families, those with special needs foster care children, and those with limited family and financial resources are likely to struggle the most. Overcoming these obstacles is crucial to successful long-term caregiving.

Handling crises and continuing stressors successfully: Regardless of how carefully caregiving is pursued, crises will occur. Medical conditions may evolve over time or move through phases of remission and recurrence or exacerbation, and new challenges will inevitably arise. These may evoke renewed feelings of grief and loss, and they may disrupt otherwise smoothly running schedules and routines. Anticipatory planning and careful consideration can minimize the impact of crises and change-based stressors. Arranging for episodic respite care, identifying ways to promptly contact medical staff in times of medical crisis, and long-term planning for future needs (such as later residential care options) are important preemptive approaches. In this way, caregiving parents can cope better with crises, and experience fewer unanticipated stressors that might otherwise occur.

Coping adequately with the emotional needs of family members: The diagnosis of chronic special needs in a child is often met with varying degrees of shock and denial in parents and extended family. However, as transitional responses, neither is necessarily indicative of ultimate poor coping. As the initial stun wears off, feelings of anger, guilt, and blaming may well arise. This is often the period of greatest trial to family cohesion and survival as an intact unit. Supportive extended family members and counselors may contribute substantially to family stability during this important time. Successful families will move forward into information gathering and developing realistic expectations and revised family plans. Assisting the family further by focusing on strengths, drawing them into collaboration, establishing normalized response patterns, and supplying ongoing encouragement are crucial contributions during this difficult period.

Teaching transiently involved individuals about the condition: Parents and other primary caregivers must obtain a comprehensive and practical understanding of the condition(s) affecting their child, not only to become quality caregivers, but quality educators as well. Extended family, friends, teachers, and others will need to be educated about the child's needs so that they can interact properly and safely. Eventually, home health nurses, respite care providers, emergency responders, and others may need similar educational input. Quality caregiving includes the capacity to ensure all involved are well informed and properly skilled for any role they may have. Further, only by way of a comprehensive understanding can parents serve as effective advocates for their child's special needs.

Developing needed resources and community supports: Becoming involved in peer support groups (also referred to as "family-to-family support") can be profoundly important for family coping and successful caregiving. These liaison organizations serve to provide valuable sources of understanding, emotional support, mentoring, friendship, problem solving, and advocacy. Professionals can provide crucial support as group moderators, resource assistants, or presenters. Support systems such as these have long been positively correlated with enhanced family coping and caregiver success. Similar support groups and opportunities for older children are also important. Group meetings, summer camps, and other activities supply important normalizing experiences for special needs children, while generating meaningful friendships and enhancing positive socialization skills.

Importance of education and development for special needs children

Children with special needs continue to need educational and other developmental experiences. Parents need knowledge of those resources available by which to advocate for their child. In 1975, Congress passed the Education for All Handicapped Children's Act (see PL 94-142), affirming the right of children aged 5-21 to a publicly funded education in the "least restrictive environment." The law was extended in 1986 to include disabled children aged 3 to 5 (see PL 99-457). Subsequently, the original Act was renamed the Individuals with Disabilities Education Act (IDEA). In 1993, the act was expanded to include infants and children from birth through age 3 (see PL 103-382, Part H). Through IDEA, children under age 3 who have or are at risk of disabilities are entitled to a comprehensive evaluation and creation of an "Individualized Family Service Plan" (IFSP). If special needs are identified, early intervention services then become available. At age 3, Part B of IDEA becomes effective, requiring evaluations and Individualized Education Plans (IEPs). IDEA was renewed in 1997 and continues today with few changes.

Home health care services

Pediatric home health care has been one of the fastest growing areas of home care in recent years. Planning for home care should be an early priority during any hospitalization of a special needs child. Planning should include not only how to meet relevant health care needs, but how to organize the home health care experience within the existing family structure. "House rules" for both family and visiting professionals should be crafted that allow for care needs to be met while still leaving the family in control of their home and reduce the potential for tension between collaborative caregivers. Woll & Arango (1993) described 5 key characteristics of collaboration, including: 1) communication, 2) dialogue, 3) active listening, 4) awareness and acceptance of difference, and 5) mutual negotiation. Applying these key features when arranging for home care benefits all involved.

Community resources and adjunctive therapeutic services: It is essential for families to seek out and advocate for all services and supports necessary for the well-being of their special needs children. Consultation with a skilled case manager familiar with local resources can be key to identifying the need for specific services, and in locating and engaging these resources. Some therapeutic and community resources of note include: 1) situation-optimized health care services (i.e., home vs. community based) and status-specific (, condition specific) health care services; 2) adjunctive health and therapeutic services (nutrition, vision, hearing, speech, language, rehabilitative, and vocational resources); 3) educational and developmental resources; 4) medication consultation and pharmaceutical services; 5) durable medical equipment, as needed; 6) financial support resources and coverage programs; 7) transportation resources; 8) parent and child support and advocacy groups; and 9) respite and daycare programs.

Financial concerns

About 8% of all children in the United States have significant disabilities. There are many expenses relative to the care of these special needs children that are frequently not covered by standard health insurance policies. These include: 1) specialty evaluations; 2) off-label or other non-standard treatments; 3) unique supplies and equipment; 4) condition-specific dietary demands; 5) frequent co-pays; 6) transportation; and 7) respite and daycare – among many others. To secure as much coverage as possible, parents may be subjected to deleterious constraints. For example, over 50% of all states are reporting an increase in parents giving up custody of their children in order for them to stay eligible for government benefits. As many as 64% of all caregiving families are turning down promotions, overtime, pay raises, and new job opportunities out of fear for losing essential benefits and coverage –

even while struggling with lost opportunities for more stable retirement and better lives for their other children. Even then, many essential services may remain uncovered. Therefore, seeking out all available benefits remains a crucially important, ongoing task.

Specific sources of financial health care and caregiving assistance for special needs children and their families include the following: 1) traditional private insurance; 2) more comprehensive health care coverage through Health Maintenance Organizations (HMOs); 3) Medicaid; 4) Supplemental Security Income (SSI); 5) age- and income-specific nutrition programs such as WIC (Women, Infants, and Children) programs and food stamps; 6) state-based "Crippled Children's Services" (CCS – known by various names depending upon the state of residence); 7) Individuals with Disabilities Education Act (IDEA), Part H; 8) social service agencies sponsored at either the state or local level; 9) local community services and resources; 10) disease-specific funding and support organizations; 11) public health departments; 12) departments of education at the state and local level; 13) religious-sponsored support services and programs; and 14) private foundations and individual contributors (including extended family).

Grief

Loss of a child

Words like "hope", "fulfillment", "future," and "continuity" come to mind at the birth of a child. Parents, grandparents, aunts, uncles, and others in the extended family find hope in the birth of a child, fulfillment for themselves and others, a sense of the future as they see children grow and mature, and a feeling of continuity as new life comes into the world. An extraordinary array of dreams come to bear, having been actively nurtured since marriage and on through the experience of pregnancy. All these feelings, perspectives, and dreams are damaged or dashed when a child is given a potentially terminal diagnosis or has died outright. The bond between parents and children is believed to be stronger than any other. Thus, even an intimation of loss is acutely painful. Coping with these difficult feelings and experiences is profoundly trying, and the associated grief is extreme.

Parental grief

The loss of a child represents the loss of some part of the parent's own person, dreams for the future, and even the hope of stability and care in his or her old age. Where factors related to the parent have contributed to a loss (i.e., genetic disease), feelings of guilt and culpability intensify and prolong all phases of coping and accommodation. Researchers describe the multiple phases of parental grieving as: 1) shock – characterized by disbelief and confusion; 2) realization – characterized by anger, guilt or blame, and sadness; 3) withdrawal – characterized by isolation and the conservation of emotional energy (typically the longest of the phases); 4) seeking meaning – characterized by efforts to find explanations or some understanding; and 5) reestablishment – characterized by reengagement in life activities. However, parental grief is represented more by accommodation and acceptance, than resolution and closure. Societal supports are few. Indeed, while the loss of parents results in an "orphan" and the loss of a spouse creates a "widow," there is not even a term for the enduring transition that marks parental loss of a child.

Piaget's theory and grief

The work of the Swiss psychologist Jean Piaget (1960) suggests 4 specific developmental stages with related cognitive developmental capacities. His insights have been widely accepted and may also be used to clarify children's ability to understand death. The stages, and general relationships to death and loss, are: 1) "sensorimotor" (ages 0-2) – infants explore the world via senses (touch, etc) and perceive relationships via attachment-based "here or not-here" constructs; 2) "preoperational" (ages 2-6) – children now gain language skills but remain incapable of logical reasoning, leaving persistent egocentric beliefs of death as temporary and reversible; 3) "concrete operational" (ages 6-12) – logic begins to emerge along with learning by observation, predisposing a greater understanding of death; 4) "formal operational" (puberty to adulthood) – abstract thinking emerges, with adult understandings and beliefs about death.

Piaget conceived of cognitive development as hierarchical (building upon itself), with sequential progression through the stages. Further, his theory was "domain general" – assuming that progress in all areas (logic, language, math, etc) occurs concurrently. Later research has identified unpredictable transitions in developmental progression, referred to as décalage. Researchers now posit that cognitive domains develop independently, with some children attaining "core knowledge" more quickly and making unexpected progress. Further, numerous "post-formal" stages have been shown to exist, with Kurt Fischer identifying 2 and Michael Commons providing evidence for 3. This appears to be in keeping with modern research that suggests that neurocognitive development continues until about age 25. Thus, although developmental guides are helpful, each child should nevertheless be evaluated independently.

Children's conceptions of death

Speece & Brent (1996) reviewed over 100 studies on children's development and understanding of death from 1934 to 1990. They found 3 essential elements that must be present before a child can meaningfully assimilate the concept of death and dying: 1) irreversibility – that something or someone who dies will not be coming back no matter what efforts are made (i.e., it is not sleep or simple absence); 2) nonfunctionality – that all functions, both those unobservable within the body and those external to the body and observable, have stopped (i.e., moving, breathing, heartbeat, thinking); 3) universality – that every living creature, plant, and insect eventually dies (i.e., that it is not just poor luck or defective thinking that brought about death); and 4) causality – the idea that death is directly caused by some event, and potentially inclusive of the idea of an afterlife. Researchers surmise that the "model age" for this level of understanding is about age 7, with approximately 60% of children accomplishing this level of insight between 5-7 years of age.

<u>When under the age of 3</u>
Under the age of 3, children do not comprehend death. They are aware a family member is missing, and they are aware of changes in routine, and that people seem to be sad. They may exhibit behavioral problems, eating and sleeping disturbances, and may become "clingy" with secure adult figures. Recommendations: 1) use proper terms (death, dead, dying) and avoid confusing euphemisms (lost, gone to heaven, sleeping, passed); 2) offer basic explanations of death, but expect ongoing questioning and confusion; 3) maintain general home and family routines (albeit flexibly); 4) keep the child with familiar adults and

environments (especially at a funeral); 5) acknowledge emotions and feelings; and 6) provide extra comfort, support, and attending touches (hugs, pats, etc).

Between the ages of 3 and 5
Children ages 3-5 are aware of death as a concept explained to them, but struggle with understanding "permanently gone." Their propensity for magical thinking may facilitate a belief in a loved one's return; it also makes them prone to fears that they may have said or done something to make them responsible for the death. Common feelings and behaviors include confusion, guilt, withdrawal, and regression. They may also use imaginative play to review scenes or experiences surrounding the loss. Recommendations: 1) review the facts of death plainly and honestly; 2) avoid abstract euphemisms; 3) preempt magical thinking and "wish fulfillment" fears (i.e., wishing another dead, gone, hurt, etc, or concerns that "being bad" caused something bad, etc) with straightforward denials of eventual return or personal culpability; 4) consistently repeat as needs and questions arise; 5) use stories to clarify; 6) provide drawing materials for children's processing of loss through art; 7) anticipate behavior problems (including regression); 8) use games applicable to death and loss to prompt questions; and 9) talk often and openly.

Between the ages of 6 and 9
Between the ages of 6 and 9 children begin to understand death more fully. This may be accompanied by fears that they may die, and that other important people in their lives may die, leaving them alone and with no one to care for them. They may also develop certain superstitions about death that need correcting. Common feelings and behaviors include using denial to cope, displaying an outward appearance of not caring, using distraction activities and play to avoid thinking of the death (often reinforcing the appearance of not caring), and behaviorally acting out. Recommendations: 1) expect questions, but often with the real question hidden within another; 2) increase physical activity as a coping measure; 3) model stress reduction behaviors; 4) encourage play and creative outlets. Use careful exploration techniques such as: 1) ask "What do you think?" when appropriate; 2) encourage them to think through possible answers to questions they ask; 3) help them identify feelings; and 4) listen carefully to find the actual information the child is after (i.e., questions within questions, etc).

Between the ages of 9 and 12
From the age of 9 forward many children are developing relatively adult views of death and loss. By 12, most will have a fairly well developed adult-level understanding (or will grasp it quickly if explained, where prior experience has been lacking). They may display a somewhat morbid interest in bones, blood, and gruesome details surrounding death. They may attempt to appear tougher than they are, and/or use humor to cope. Efforts to act very adult-like about a loss may yet end in somewhat regressive behavior and coping. Common feelings and behaviors include grief, anger, withdrawal, and some acting out. Recommendations: 1) use greater details in explaining the physical cause of death; 2) try to respond to specific questions, thereby timing explanation details to a direct measure of the child's interest and readiness to hear; 3) explore feelings, allow for spiritual questioning, and confirm family beliefs – "We don't know what happens after this life exactly, but our belief is..."; 4) create traditions to memorialize (i.e., a special Christmas tree ornament, perhaps created by the family in memory, etc); and 5) encourage creative avenues of personal expression (art, journaling, etc).

From puberty to adulthood

Adolescents are already coping with somewhat tumultuous emotions, and are seeking greater philosophical understandings of the world about them. While they conceptually have an adult understanding of death and loss, they lack considerable experience and maturity. Questions are more intense and probing, and require greater discussion. Peer supports become more important. Common feelings and reactions range from typical behavioral disturbances (sleep and eating changes, agitation, withdrawal, etc), to pronounced impulsivity, moodiness, and rebelliousness, along with risk-taking and thrill-seeking activities used as distraction and coping strategies. Recommendations: 1) allow more time for discussion and sharing; 2) treat them like adults, including shared expectations of both respect and responsibility; 3) defer to their informed choices whenever appropriate; 4) encourage peer sharing and support; 5) encourage creativity in writing, art, journaling, etc; 6) suggest memorializing ideas; and 7) recommend support groups and other social resources.

Grief unique to siblings

Issues of grief

Siblings face unique challenges when a brother or sister dies. It has been described as a double loss, because parents often become emotionally unavailable as they work out their own grief. Their emotional absence was often preceded by an extended period of caregiving absence. Siblings may resent this and the ill child at the heart of it, resulting in significant measures of guilt. Fear about contracting the same illness, guilt over the relief of not having it, etc, may haunt siblings more than others. The cause and timing of death may have been problematic as well. Deaths may be classified by the acronym NASH – natural, accidental, suicide, or homicide – with each uniquely problematic. If the illness or death was embarrassing or disfiguring in any way, siblings may have felt considerable shame, now manifested as guilt. Prior wishful thinking – "I wish he'd just die and be done with it" – may now be perceived as "wish fulfillment," with all the guilt that brings. Recognizing the many burdens that may attend siblings experiencing a loss can help others better support and sustain them.

Coping with life-threatening illness

There are a number of ways to assist siblings coping with a terminally ill brother or sister. Some recommendations include: 1) include siblings in medical update meetings with family (if they cannot attend, due to age or immaturity, specifically ask about how they are coping); 2) find time to spend alone with siblings to talk (through play or other activities if necessary); 3) have siblings join in bedside care and support activities; 4) where distance or other factors keep siblings away, include them through phone calls, e-mails, notes, etc; 5) provide medical update sessions tailored to their level of understanding and development; 6) create sibling support groups and activities for peer support; 7) praise all positive sibling coping efforts; 8) nurture parent-sibling sharing opportunities; 9) encourage siblings to maintain important peer relationships and activities, along with regular bedside visitation.

Protracted grief

Preschool and young school-aged children have been identified in studies as those finding it most difficult to cope after a sibling's death. Guilt (including "survivor's guilt") was nearly always present; irritability, attention seeking, and sleeping problems were not uncommon, and health complaints occurred over otherwise typical aches and pains. Difficulty concentrating in school was also noted. However, the longer siblings took before returning to school, the harder it became to reintegrate. About one week was identified as the optimum absence period for grieving. Reactionary symptoms were reported for up to 3 years following demise. Protracted accommodation experiences centered on siblings with changes in family roles and identity – i.e., having newly become an only child or the oldest, etc. Feeling that he or she is competing with a dead sibling's memory was also associated with prolonged recovery.

Recommended interventions
Certain interventions are associated with better coping on the part of siblings following a child's death. These include: 1) allowing them to be present at the time of death (ideally, in the arms or at the side of a loving and calm extended family member) and integrally involved in important follow-up experiences (the funeral, etc); 2) the presence of stable extended family and important adults during the initial days of parents' acute grieving; 3) role modeling expressions of feelings; 4) finding ways to properly express frustrations and anger; 5) sharing ways to release stress (exercise, sports, etc); and 6) participation in a playroom or game room, drawing, writing, or painting. Careful preparation prior to bringing a sibling into the room of a dying sibling (including allowing them to refuse) remains necessary for positive outcomes to be more fully assured.

Adolescent siblings
Although adolescents are able to cognitively conceive of death's meaning and dimensions, there are other developmental issues that may come to bear upon their responses. For example, adolescent tendencies toward emotional lability may result in impulsive reactions such as anger, risk taking, and other acting-out behaviors – or toward self-isolation and withdrawal into solo activities such as writing, music, or art. These same emotions may drive away friends at a time when they are especially needed. Normal response variations in adolescents include moodiness, moderate rebelliousness, impulsiveness, heightened sexual awareness, increased self-centeredness, and greater emphasis on peer relations. Reactions of concern include depression, academic failure (or overemphasis), drug and alcohol use, fighting, legal troubles, sexual acting out, eating disorders, severe mood disturbances, extreme isolation, and suicidal thoughts or gestures. Coping is improved via close friends and social activities, a positive personal belief system, stress-reducing activities, parental support, and family reminiscing. Specific burdens include family discord, loneliness, guilt, and others' insensitivity.

Preparing and accompanying siblings ICU visit that may include demise
Recommended steps to preparing siblings for an ICU visit or a bedside visit at the time of demise include: 1) gather information (re: siblings' current problems/concerns, past history with health and hospitalizations, immediate understanding of the situation, etc); 2) prepare support persons and materials (extended family, children's literature, medical dolls, art materials, a quiet place to talk or play in follow-up, etc); 3) offer choices (to visit or not), who to accompany them in (parent, other relative, etc); 4) meet in a quiet place to review, confirming desire to visit, immediate understanding, etc; 5) structure the actual visit (placing children with support persons, pointing out medical machinery as previously explained, modeling touching their loved one, pointing out comforting pictures and objects, allowing family any alone time desired, and observing for clues that it is time to end the visit, etc); 6) follow-up contact (sitting, talking, acknowledging feelings, rephrasing questions to clarify, etc); 7) providing support if death occurs (explaining, using proper terms, supporting spiritual beliefs offered, prompting reminiscence and sharing, etc).

Grief unique to grandparents

There are numerous issues of grief unique to grandparents when a child dies. First, they must not only cope with their own grief, but with a sense of helplessness in any effort to fully comfort and shield their own children from the pain of the loss. This can become even more acute if they are not actively included in the family grieving process. Second, feelings of "survivor's guilt" can be profound as grandparents wrestle with the fact that they continue to live on in their senior years even when a loved one has been lost. These unique stressors can be mitigated to some degree if health care professionals actively draw grandparents into updates and other family meetings and experiences. Grandparents can further escape their feelings of helplessness if they are also conscripted to assist with the caregiving of siblings while parents cope with imminent loss at the bedside and later grief work. Indeed, this can be an invaluable service for all involved.

Challenges from a long demise

The concept of "anticipatory grief" may be described as grief expressed prior to demise, when death is deemed imminent and expected. Anticipatory grief work can be engaged by both those terminally ill and by those who love them. Researchers note that skilled support by professionals can facilitate anticipatory grieving and thereby reduce the more traumatic effects and processes of grief that necessarily follow a loss. Anticipatory grief work, however, becomes less effective and valuable for parents in 2 situations: 1) when a child's illness has extended longer than 18 months – particularly if punctuated by several episodes of remission and relapse during that time (in part, this may be due to the overall "wearing" effect of such a protracted caregiving and fear-infused period); and 2) when there have been prior significant deaths. Stress and grief are both cumulative psychological components, and new stressors and grieving will often bring back the difficult emotions and burdens of prior experiences.

When demise is sudden

The sudden death of a child produces profound confusion and chaos within a family. There may well be parental issues of guilt, blame, and second-guessing that accompany such a loss (to greater or lesser degrees, depending upon the specific events preceding), all of which make grief work more complicated. Siblings, too, will have a harder time coping with sudden loss. They often respond with greater degrees of denial and/or emotion-avoidance behaviors. Where a death was violent or otherwise traumatic, successful grief work becomes even more difficult. The nature and manner of the loss itself is burdensome, grounding the loss in reality becomes more difficult, and feelings of vulnerability (especially for siblings) become more pronounced.

Jones (1978) has identified 4 major points of intervention for professionals following any sudden and unexpected demise in the hospital: 1) appropriate arrival contacts – escorting the family to a private area with staff remaining in attendance and sharing all condition updates available at that time; 2) careful death notification – completed honestly and compassionately, with contact by the physician (whether or not he or she actually broke the news) as critical to clarify what happened, that all that could be done was done, and to dispel misconceptions, blame, and guilt; 3) viewing of the body – essential to grounding the death in reality, easing into grief, etc; and 4) closure – characterized by the signing of papers, returning of belongings, early funeral discussion and preparation, etc – to ease the family toward essential matters that must very soon be managed.

Supportive interventions

Infants account for 43% of all deaths in ICUs in the United States, with rates of ICU demise for older children and adults lower at 18-26%. Because Neonatal ICUs, Pediatric ICUs, and adult ICUs are typically separate, relative rates are not widely known. There are many things that health care professionals can do to ease the trauma of a child's demise. Prior to death: 1) offering choices instead of decisions whenever possible – as parents often feel as if their lives are markedly out of control; 2) providing privacy, both at bedside and areas for contemplation, along with telephone access; 3) frequent contacts to offer support, answer questions, etc; 4) referring support staff (social work, child life, pastoral services, etc) to assist as needed. At the time of death: 1) continue to involve parents in care (holding, dressing, etc); 2) involve siblings, grandparents, and other extended family; 3) engage memory-making – gathering a lock of hair, hand and foot prints or molds, photographs, and comfort objects (stuffed toys, special blanket, etc); and 4) escorting family carefully from the facility when appropriate.

Child's preparations for demise

Waechter (1971) conducted research clarifying that children below the age of 10 actually come to be aware of their own impending demise, and can talk about it if not deflected by parents and others. Bluebond-Langner (1978) identified 5 stages in a child's increasing awareness of their own ultimate death: 1) discovering the seriousness of their illness; 2) learning the names, purposes, side-effects, etc, of their medicines; 3) better understanding about the role of involved treatments and procedures; 4) discovery that their illness has involved remissions and relapses; 5) concluding that death will occur when medicines and treatments don't work any longer. Concurrently, the child's self-concept evolves through 5 stages: 1) well until disease diagnosed; 2) seriously ill, but will recover (as told by family, etc); 3) ill all the time, but still expect to get better; 4) ill all the time and won't ever get better; 5) will die (with awareness typically arising at death of a hospitalized peer).

Research by Bluebond-Langner (1978) clarifies the ways in which hospitalized children demonstrate awareness of their own impending demise. These include: 1) avoiding using the name(s), toys, or belongings of any other deceased children; 2) increasingly interested in play or talk about their disease; 3) becoming increasingly preoccupied with play, art, and books related to death and disease; 4) singling out specific individuals for personal disclosures; 5) altered anxiety about ever becoming well enough to return home; 6) moving away from any talk of the future; 7) wanting things to be done immediately; 8) reduced cooperation with medical procedures; 9) distancing self from others by use of silence or anger.

Working with a dying child

Pearson (1999) has provided guidelines and recommendations for interacting with a dying child. These include: 1) being open to signals of a child's understanding; 2) offering to talk without pushing (listening first, giving only that information the child has requested and thus wants to know, etc); 3) making many creative opportunities available as emotional outlets; 4) letting the child guide the process; 5) being honest about the child's eventual death; 6) providing opportunities for a child to say his or her good-byes; 7) allowing the child to determine when and with whom to share grief; 8) allowing the child to protect his or her parents from their fears and feelings if he or she chooses; 9) enhance living (comfort, play, memories, friends, continuing important routines, etc); and 10) help families to give permission to a child to "let go" when it is time (as they may try to hang on longer for parents and others).

Adolescent issues

Adolescent life is filled with change. It has been noted that adolescents are: 1) acclimating to a rapidly changing body and the changes in self-image that accompany; 2) separating from family and developing independence; 3) establishing personal beliefs and values; and 4) arranging their own future vocational and family plans. Serious or life-threatening illness may undermine every one of these developing domains. Their concept of self, often centered in physical prowess and/or appearance, is threatened; they are thrust back into dependence upon others; their sense of invincibility and security is profoundly confronted; and, all future plans are disrupted and potentially altered indefinitely. Learning to cope with such stressors and change will inevitably be challenging. Because adolescents look so much to their peers for situational normalization, personal validation, and social support, including them in peer support groups can be particularly important and effective. In such groups, ill adolescents can find social acceptance, a place to openly express their unique fears, and an opportunity to learn additional coping skills and derive new perspectives on their potentially changing future.

Pearson (1999) has provided the following recommendations: 1) honestly disclose when it is known they are dying (including giving permission to talk openly, answering difficult questions, and arranging for parents and supportive others to be present); 2) frankly address issues of sadness, fear, and concern for loved ones; 3) allow time to work toward closure through personal planning; 4) if denial emerges: a) give time to adjust; b) gently reframe "will" to "wish" or "dream" (at an inappropriate expression); c) provide reassurance (they'll not be abandoned, etc); d) be available as a confidant (teens may want to protect family and others, and thus need someone else to confide in); 5) look for any underlying search for help and support (confirmation that death is coming, a desire to express last wishes, etc); 6) prompt toward completing unfinished business if necessary (seeing important others, doing important things, writing out thoughts, etc); 7) advocate if ethical issues arise; 8) endeavor to honor wishes about how, where, and with whom the adolescent wishes death to occur.

Role of hospice

Hospice combines palliative care (medical care aimed primarily at providing pain and symptom relief, in adjunct to or as a replacement for curative care if death is expected) and home health care in support of the dying. These programs utilize a multidisciplinary approach in an effort to provide a comprehensive and effective plan of care. A principal goal of hospice is to allow patients to remain in the comfort and familiar environment of their homes for as long as possible – combined with short "respite" admissions if needed to relieve caregivers, as well as terminal admissions if dying at home is not desired or possible. One of the earliest children-oriented hospice programs was begun by Martinson in 1972. Today, as many as 64% of all illness-induced children's deaths transpire in the home setting with hospice support. Follow-up studies indicate that grieving family members do better, return to work and other activities sooner, have less guilt, and can focus more on positive aspects of their child's life if hospice was involved.

Dying at home

The decision to die at home affects not only the child, but the caregiving family as well. Stevens et al (1996) note the following: Advantages: 1) the family remains intact and together, with the parents at home rather than at the hospital; 2) parents and other loved ones can provide most nursing care; 3) brothers, sisters, grandparents, and other extended family can more easily be involved; 4) familiar food is available; 5) privacy is more fully assured; 6) hospital routines are not imposed; 7) friends, possessions, pets, and other important people and things are more available. Disadvantages: 1) the family cannot avoid constant awareness of deterioration; 2) caregiving is largely without outside support at night; 3) fears about managing the death alone may be prominent; 4) medical complications must be handled first by the family (i.e., seizures, bleeding, etc); the usual demands of home life and children continue during this time. Because there are distinct advantages and disadvantages, whether or not to die at home is a family decision.

Cultural issues in dying

It is important to remain sensitive to cultural issues as related to death and dying. McGoldrick et al (1991) provide the following suggestions: 1) learn of any religious and/or cultural guidelines involving death and the management of the deceased's body; 2) ask about beliefs regarding the existence of an afterlife, if any; 3) explore norms and expectations regarding proper emotional and psychological coping with death; 4) learn of any gender-based rules and expectations; 5) find out of there is any stigma attached to certain kinds of deaths (suicide, etc) or related matters (i.e., seeking medical treatment vs. spiritually-based healing, etc). In this way, missteps and offenses can be far more easily avoided, and better patient and family support can be provided.

Ethical issues

Medical technology can unnaturally and inappropriately prolong dying. Giving up on a cure, however, involves abandoning hope. The following recommendations may be helpful: 1) consider decision making to be a partnership; 2) withdrawing a treatment may be more difficult than withholding it; 3) use "recommendations" to keep the family from feeling they must decide alone; 4) make decisions in a quiet, uninterrupted environment; 5) enhance communication by discussing family impressions, goals, and values related to suffering, disability, and death; 6) review current medical circumstances; 7) clarify misconceptions; 8) address pain and relief options; 9) ensure the family has adequate support systems in place (others do not make decisions, but bolster family strength to face decision making); 10) make a decision, recognizing that older children and teens may well have the capacity to participate (if they comprehend their diagnosis and prognosis, can reason out choices based on their goals and values, and can recognize the consequences of the various options available to them); 11) defer to best interests where actual preferences are not known.

Children and funerals

The question of whether or not children should attend funerals is common. Researchers note that children and teens that are included in funerals and other related events often cope and adjust better than those who are excluded. Careful preparation is necessary, however, including: 1) ensuring the children know in advance what they will see and hear (tears, the open casket, memorial talks, memories, etc); 2) a discussion of the meaning of death – particularly if the body will be present; 3) a child should never be forced to attend, or to view or touch the body, etc; 4) options for breaks or even absenting themselves should be secured (i.e., a supervised play area with proper materials, etc) so they need not be overwhelmed by the experience; 5) consider allowing older children and teens to actually participate in the service (reading something short, bearing the casket, etc) if they are comfortable with this, as this will ease their grief as well. Where parents feel too overwhelmed, other trusted adults may support and oversee children in their stead.

Memorializing and bereavement

After a death, families should be given written bereavement resources, including children's bereavement programs where available. In this way, if grief becomes complicated or stressful, the family knows in advance where to turn. Child life staff should remain available to answer questions and assist with referrals as needed. Families may stop by and visit the site of a loved one's death – sometimes months or even years later. Families may wish to create a "memory symbol" – lighting a candle, planting flowers, creating a quilt square – on the anniversary days important to their loved one (be it birth or death). Only over the last 100 years has a continuing role of the deceased in the lives of loved ones been denied. Renewed understanding acknowledges that life after the loss of a loved one is never the same (i.e., you do not "get over it"), and that feelings of love, grief, and the need to remember will continue throughout life. Thus, continuing bonds are important and should be nurtured.

Spirituality

At times of illness

A nationwide survey indicates that about 80% of the population believes that prayer can improve recovery from illness (Wallis, 1996). Whether from the effect of a "faith factor" or by more supernal means, numerous studies indicate that spirituality does enhance well-being and healing (Levin, 1994). Many consider spiritual orientation as significant an element as culture, ethnicity, class, or gender (Dun & Dawes, 1999). Importantly, findings suggest that people are especially desirous of spiritual care when they are hospitalized. Researchers note that even children have an innate sense of themselves as spiritual beings (Houskamp et al, 2004; Coles, 1990), and are particularly aware of this when ill (Fosarelli, 2000). Thus, it is suggested that including children in discussions of spirituality (but, importantly, following their lead and the family's), is in a child's best interest. Even so, there are also people who are not comforted by concepts of spirituality. It is therefore important for health care professionals to discover the views of patients and families, and offer appropriate support (i.e., open discussion, pastoral care referrals, etc) as needed and wanted.

Spiritual terms

Spirituality should not necessarily be equated with religiosity. To this end, the following terms are important: 1) belief – certain ideas and convictions held of significant value; 2) faith – a confidence in hopes and desires; 3) faith communities – formally organized religious entities and groups; 4) God – an omniscient (all-knowing) and omnipotent (all-powerful) being, often seen in a paternal or other familial relationship, as a source of energy or love, or force of transcendence; 5) human spirit – an element of an individual separate from his or her corporeal being; 6) religion – teachings arising from canonized literature, traditions, rituals, beliefs, etc; 7) religiosity – the strength of one's affiliation to a formally organized religion.

Further important terms related to spirituality include: 8) spiritual care – activities that nurture spirituality, such as prayer, meditation, the search for meaning, etc; 9) spiritual development – an increasing understanding and awareness of the spiritual elements of life, purpose, and being; 10) spiritual distress – a disturbing disruption of one's core spiritual beliefs; 11) spiritual health/well-being – the strength of perceived relationship with a higher power or life's meaning; 12) spiritual needs – inclusive of hope, faith, forgiveness, purpose, love, etc; 13) spiritual pain – a sense of separation or estrangement from God or formal religion, particularly when arising from personal failures; 14) spirituality – the beliefs and guiding principles that sustain an individual from day to day.

FICA

Pulchalski (2000) has provided a simple but very useful tool for taking a child's spiritual or faith history, symbolized by the acronym "FICA": F – faith or beliefs (perhaps prompted by the question, "Do you believe in God?"); I – importance or degree of influence (perhaps prompted by a question such as "How often do you think about God?"); C – community (i.e., the regularity of formal church attendance); A – address (the desire, if any, to talk about this with health care staff, perhaps prompted by the question, "Would you like us to talk about this from time to time?"). Children typically respond very readily to this approach.

BELIEF

McEvoy (2000) has provided another simple tool for taking a child's spiritual or faith history, as symbolized by the mnemonic "BELIEF": B – belief systems; E – ethics; L – lifestyle; I – involvement in a formal religious community; E – education; F – future events. Dunn and Dawes (1999) recommend constructing a "spirituality genogram," using phrases such as: 1) "Tell me about your earliest religious or spiritual experiences."; 2) "Tell me about the way that religion or spirituality influences your daily life."; 3) "Tell me about any significant or defining experiences that have shaped you spiritually."; 4) "Tell me about any times of significant crisis or difficult life transitions for you and your family."; and 5) "Tell me how religion or spirituality influenced you during those times."

Indicators of spiritual distress

McHolm (1991) has provided a list of indicators of spiritual distress, as follows: 1) self-rejection (loss of self-acceptance); 2) listing physical complaints; 3) alluding to relationship problems with others; 4) alluding to issues of guilt and needing forgiveness; 5) references to personal religious or spiritual needs; 6) demonstrating poor coping; 7) expressions of hopelessness and helplessness; 8) a focus on fears; 9) feeling overwhelmed and impotent; 10) loss of appetite; 11) withdrawal into silence; 12) persistent expressions of bitterness. *Twibell et al* (1996) have provided 9 similar indicators: 1) feeling spiritually empty; 2) unable to reconcile beliefs with current concerns; 3) feeling no reason to go on with life; 4) asking for spiritual help; 5) persistent uncertainty about the meaning of life; 6) calling beliefs into question; 7) expressing doubts about beliefs; 8) disengaging from spiritual rituals; 9) feeling absent or distant from self and from others. Marked and persistent anger, fear, self-blame, and other similar distressing feelings may also indicate spiritual distress.

Immanent justice

"Immanent justice" is a common form of spiritual distress found among children. It arises from children imagining that their illness has been visited upon them as retribution for some past misdeed. This form of distress is most common among children under the age of 7, but can occur in older children as well. Left unaddressed, the concept of immanent justice can become quite damaging spiritually. When openly discussed and with the misconceptions corrected, it can be transformed into an experience of continued learning and development. A stronger and more resilient spirituality can also emerge, once the sense of retaliation and vindictiveness has been removed from a child's understanding of spiritual matters. It has also been noted that, without proper clarification, spirituality can become a source of distress to children who may privately conceive of God as angry, fearsome, and threatening, and the afterlife as a frightening place to be. Only by introducing the idea of a truly loving God and positive images of the hereafter can children (particularly those who are dying) lose these fears and find greater peace and consolation.

Spiritual intervention

There are many ways that nonecclesiastical laypersons can nurture spirituality in hospitalized children. These include: 1) encouraging parents to invite their own religious leaders to visit and offer support; 2) combining fun with spiritual development (drawing, painting, or even making "spiritual bracelets," which are similar to friendship bracelets, but with the different colors of thread representing specific values); 3) ministering through presence (where just sharing time "spirit-to-spirit" in listening or just in quiet can become a spiritual experience offering great comfort); 4) offering therapeutic spiritual communication (i.e., simply talking about important spiritual matters – within the family's context of beliefs); 5) offering or participating in prayer (using caution, however, never to impose beliefs); 6) offering a blessing by sharing religious-congruent promises found in most scriptural texts; and 7) the comforting use of touch. These are just some of the ways to promote and share in an individual's spiritual journey.

Functions of culture

Smith (1995) cites multiple functions of "culture," which include: 1) providing a worldview and a construction to reality through culturally biased processes of perception and thought; 2) producing underlying behavioral motivations and their interpretive meanings (i.e., the same behavior may have very different meanings in different cultures); 3) shaping group identity through unique history and traditions; 4) defining and elaborating culturally relevant value systems; and 5) predisposing certain modes of communication and presentation. More than 90% of all nurses (the largest segment of the health care labor force) are of Caucasian ethnicity, yet nearly 25% of the US population is of non-white descent (mostly African-American and Hispanic, though the US Census Bureau formally recognizes more than 165 individual ethnic groups in the nation). Given this diversity, it is important for health care staff to become more culturally aware.

Cultural terms

The following definitions of cultural terms are relevant to discussing and understanding cultural issues: 1) cultural competence – academic and other skills providing an enhanced awareness of cultural concerns; 2) cultural imposition – the tendency to impose personal cultural perspectives and expectations on others, regardless of their background; 3) culture – composed of values, beliefs, traditions, etc, unique to a specific group of people; 4) ethnic – a specified group, sharing a common race and/or nationality and language; 5) language – form of speech used in a particular area or nation; 6) mainstream – typically refers to majority views; 7) nationality – a country of origin or one's "homeland"; and 8) race – a population sharing distinctive physical characteristics that are genetically inherited.

Some of the more common differences between Anglo-American culture and others include: 1) individual controls life vs. fate controls life (and health); 2) change is good vs. traditions must be honored; 3) time consciousness and punctuality vs. social niceties and sharing; 4) all people are equal vs. hierarchy based on status, rank, age, etc; 5) individual freedom and right to privacy vs. common-good perspectives; 6) self-made vs. birthright expectations; 7) competition vs. collaboration; 8) looking to the future vs. focus on the past; 9) informal vs. formal; 10) direct and blunt vs. honoring rituals of "face" and social standing; 11) efficiency vs. political and social ideals; and 12) materialistic vs. spiritualistic.

Cross-cultural interactions

Eight essential keys to more effective cross-cultural communication and interaction include: 1) be aware, attentive, and respectful of other people's traditions and values; 2) make a specific and clearly apparent effort to learn about and integrate another's views; 3) remain open to learning and following alternate approaches; 4) find innovative and flexible ways to honor another's culture while accomplishing essential goals; 5) develop a good sense of humor and self-deprecation; 6) be tolerant of variations; 7) find ways to honestly appreciate other cultures and views; and 8) maintain an ongoing desire to learn and understand people better.

Ethical treatment dilemmas

The most widely regarded approach for examining and resolving ethical dilemmas in health care has been that of "principlism." The principlist approach refers to the use of guiding ethical principles in the process of problem solving and decision making. The primary principles involved include: 1) autonomy – the right to self-determination; 2) beneficence – the obligation to do good; 3) nonmaleficence – the obligation to avoid harm; and 4) justice – implying fairness and freedom from bias and prejudice. By evaluating ethical dilemmas from the vantage points provided by each of these principles, the likelihood of ethical decisions increases substantially. Another approach that can be integrated into principlism is the "ethic of care." This approach frames ethical issues in the context of relationships and relief from burdens. Combining both approaches allows for the integration of ethical ideals with personal and culturally defined values. Casting ethical events into a "case" format for presentation and teaching is called "casuistry," and serves as a "heuristic" (i.e., self-learning) model for developing further ethical skills.

In making decisions for an adult who was once competent but who has now lost decisional capacity (whether transiently or permanently), those involved must make decisions: 1) as specifically directed by the adult in the past (if such wishes are known); 2) by "substituted judgment" (i.e., as they believe the adult would have wanted, based upon known values and past decisions the adult had made); or 3) familiarity failing, they are to act in the "best interests" of the adult as determined in consultation with a physician. However, parents of minor children, charged as they are with raising their children and inculcating their own beliefs and values, have historically been able to act entirely "paternalistically" and make those decisions they alone feel are appropriate for their child.

Making decisions for minors

In 1995 the American Academy of Pediatrics, Committee on Bioethics, issued a position statement on decision making for minors. They clarified that parents do not give "consent" for the treatment of their minor children, but rather they give their "informed permission" (i.e., with risks, benefits, burdens, expected outcomes, etc, having been properly explained to them by appropriate medical staff). They also proposed 3 levels of consent. First, for children entirely without decisional capacity (due to immaturity, illness severity, etc) the parents decide outright. Second, for children with a developing capacity that remains insufficient, the parents are to provide informed permission in combination with their child's assent. Third, where the child has sufficient decisional capacity the parents should serve as consultants but the child should make final decisions. Decisional capacity should be determined by the physician.

Establishing decisional capacity

In determining decisional capacity, Grisso and Appelbaum (1998) have proposed 4 essential elements that must be possessed by the decision-maker: 1) an understanding of relevant treatment information; 2) an appreciation for the possible impact and consequences of available treatment options; 3) a rationale or path of reasoning that demonstrates the application of personal values to the available alternatives, combined with the significance of anticipated outcomes; and 4) the ability to actually derive and express a choice or preference. Grisso and Vierling (1978) felt that children should be able to: 1) maintain attention focus on essential issues; 2) carefully consider the issues; 3) appraise both pros and cons; 4) weigh anticipated risks against expected benefits; and 5) utilize both inductive and deductive reasoning. The more serious and irreversible the decision to be made, the higher the threshold of decisional capacity should be. Age is not the final arbiter. Some children at the age of 10-12 years may be able to decide about an amputation, for example, while other children at age 17 may still lack adequate capacity.

Some professionals take exception to the American Academy of Pediatrics Position Statement, and are against allowing more mature minors to make their own decisions. They note that these same children still cannot purchase cigarettes or alcohol, nor participate in sporting programs without parental permission, etc. Hence, they contend, leaving decisions to impetuous children and adolescents is a dangerous practice. Others rebut by noting that the children involved have been pressed into these medical decisions, and will be forced to endure the treatments and live with the results. Objectors continue by noting that illness – especially chronic illness – may induce regression in children, making them even less suitable as decision makers. Further, teens may be prone to rebelliousness, and thus be poorly equipped to decide for themselves. Those in support of children's involvement in decisions counter with the concept of "dignity of risk" – i.e., allowing individuals to learn by certain lower-risk failures – as further rationale to continue to conscript older children and adolescents into decision making. Although the debate continues, formal position statements continue to be the guidelines generally followed.

The term "best interests"

Where children are too young to make their own decisions, parents are called upon to act in their stead. In doing so, they are called upon to act in the "best interests" of the children. The term has been defined as a "standard of reasonableness," the "threshold" of which is the lowest point at which this standard is achieved. The standard involved "optimizing" all of a child's interests, including a careful weighing of the expected burdens of treatments proposed and the inevitable risks involved, against the long-term benefits hoped for. Considerable burdens and risks may be tolerated when a high quality long-term result is all but assured. However, the shorter-term the benefit, the higher the burden, and the greater the risks involved, the less likely it is that a child's true best interests will be served by a given treatment.

The evolution of nurse-patient relationships in recent decades.

Historically, nurses maintained a professional detachment from their patients. The prevailing "biomedical" model of the day dictated that the patient be relegated to the status of a "biological body" in need of medical attention only, and emotional attachments were seen as unprofessional intrusions. Tactics such as close-ended and leading questioning, delivered in rapid-fire style, helped maintain distance and kept the focus on professional duties only. In more recent years, "The New Nursing" model has become paramount (Savage, 1990). Using approaches referred to as "nursing process" and "primary care nursing" (consistent nurse assignments to the same patient) the new nurse-patient relationship is now expected to be committed and mutually involved. Beyond physiological issues alone, the new nurse is now expected to address a wide variety of psychosocial variables in order to optimize healing and well-being.

Review the evolution of doctor-patient relationships in recent decades.

At the turn of the last century diploma mills abounded and churned out MD degrees at a furious pace (see the 1910 "Flexner Report"), flooding the market with many poorly skilled physicians. Even those with training had few medical treatments and options. Not until the dramatic scientific advances of the mid-1900s did the public's perception of healers improve. Media portrayals of figures such as Ben Casey, Dr Kildare, and Marcus Welby helped deepen physician-patient relationships, depicting healers who were not only medically skilled, but also served as confidants and counselors. However, while nursing has gravitated toward more involved nurse-patient relationships, physicians have recently faced increased distancing pressures. Past relationships were long standing and grounded in covenants, fiduciary principles, and benevolence. Current relationships are driven by insurers and cost, and demand skill sharing (delegating duties to nurse practitioners and other allied health staff), shorter visits, specialty care, and gate-keeping. The result has been shorter-term and less meaningful relationships between physicians and their patients.

Relationships common in medical care

It has been noted, "When a child is the patient, the patient is the [whole] family." Thus, a discussion of provider-patient relationships may need to be construed broadly in casting the role of pediatric patient. Morse (1991) described medical relationships as either "mutual" or "unilateral." Mutual relationships are characterized by degrees of involvement and intensity, and include: 1) clinical (technical, brief, relatively minor, and routine); 2) therapeutic (extends the professional view to "patient as person," with the professional serving as a primary support and resource enhancer); 3) connected (with the patient and provider seeing each other as people first, and in their roles second; trust is particularly deep); or 4) over-involved (where enmeshment overrides appropriate treatment selection and goals, and where the relationship becomes closed with essential outside resources and referrals lost). Unilateral relationships arise when one person is unwilling to adequately invest in the relationship at all (i.e., a burned out provider who keeps interactions superficial and brief).

Boundaries in relationships

It is generally agreed that the following situational factors tend to increase the degree and intensity of the provider-patient relationship, and may also increase the likelihood of boundary issues: 1) chronic illness – where necessity dictates frequent contacts over a particularly long period of time; 2) life-threatening illnesses – producing poignant feelings of attachment along with significant feelings of grief and emotional distress within the provider-patient-family relationship; and 3) home care – where the caring context and environment tends to imbue the relationship with a greater sense of "family" than would otherwise occur. As both boundary and authority issues are more complex in these situations, greater care needs to be taken to ensure balance and perspective throughout the duration of the health care experience.

The following constitute indicators of relationship power, and areas in which greater caution and care should be used: 1) time – the person who controls contact timing, duration, and scheduling wrests more power from others (be careful to honor family's time in order to better balance power); 2) touch – powerful people touch more often (i.e., bosses pat workers on the back, but not the other way around), thus use touch carefully; 3) height – standing over someone communicates power (seat yourself or move to bedside level to equalize power); 4) space – wide movements and gestures dominate a room and thus communicate power (use sparingly); 5) pointers – holding something in one's hand (a pen, eyeglasses, etc) symbolizes power when used in gestures of communication (avoid this); and 6) voice level – louder talk dominates others (use a calm and quiet speaking voice). Power strategies tend to induce conflicts. Use care to avoid unnecessary conflicts and issues.

It has been noted that boundary violations often emerge so slowly that professionals are not fully aware that they have "crossed a line" until it has already happened. The following behaviors may provide a warning before boundary violations have occurred or become severe: 1) marked feelings of inadequacy, embarrassment, or guilt; 2) feeling victimized, used, or put upon by others; 3) a sense of responsibility for things beyond control (the behavior of others, etc); 4) creating unrealistic goals or expectations; 5) being unable to accept normal human differences and mistakes; 6) feeling compelled to help when not asked or needed; and 7) meeting the needs of others to the exclusion of one's own. Regular use of a "personal inventory questionnaire" related to boundaries may be helpful, especially with complicated families and situations.

Practice Test

Practice Questions

1. A 6-year old child must receive daily painful injections and fights and screams when his mother is present but remains docile when he is alone. The mother becomes very upset during the injection and says repeatedly, "I'm so sorry this hurts so much," and begins to cry. Which of the following is the **MOST** appropriate intervention?
   a. Ask the mother to wait outside during the injection.
   b. Adjust the dosing schedule to a time the child is usually alone.
   c. Ask that a topical anesthetic be applied prior to the injection.
   d. Counsel the mother on methods to reduce her own and the child's stress.

2. All of the following are appropriate toys for a 1 to 3-month-old child **EXCEPT**:
   a. Mobile.
   b. Rattle.
   c. Crib mirror (unbreakable)
   d. Bath toys.

3. In Erikson's theory of psychosocial development, which conflict is typical of those 6 to 12 years old?
   a. Intimacy vs. isolation.
   b. Autonomy vs. shame/doubt.
   c. Industry vs. inferiority.
   d. Trust vs. mistrust.

4. Which of the following is the best approach for parents to take with the 5 and 7-year-old siblings of a critically-ill neonate?
   a. Allow the siblings to visit the neonate in the hospital.
   b. Keep the siblings sheltered from all knowledge about the ill child.
   c. Send the siblings to live with relatives until the neonate improves or dies.
   d. Keep the siblings updated about the child's condition but do not allow visits.

5. All of the following stimulate the one-month-old infant's brain growth/cognitive abilities **EXCEPT**:
   a. Providing frequent skin-to-skin physical contact.
   b. Allowing the infant to "cry it out" to avoid spoiling her.
   c. Talking to the infant during feeding.
   d. Providing adequate nutrition.

6. A 4-year-old girl is learning to write the alphabet but sometimes writes letters, such as a capital B or D, backwards and gets confused as to the difference between some letters, such as capital M and W. Which of the following is the best response?
   a. "You're not doing these letters right."
   b. "Watch me while I write the letters."
   c. "Wow! That's wonderful!"
   d. "You're learning a lot of letters!"

7. The child life specialist is planning an activity for a 30-bed pediatric department, specializing in chronic illness. Children range in age from 18 months to 17 years. Which of the following activities is **MOST** likely to engage the majority of the children?
    a. Visits from therapy dogs.
    b. Card games.
    c. Video cartoons.
    d. Guest pianist.

8. Which of the following responses to "I'm afraid of having surgery" shows reflective listening?
    a. "The surgery is very simple and everyone will take good care of you."
    b. "You don't need to be afraid. Your parents will be waiting."
    c. "Surgery is scary because you don't know what's going to happen."
    d. "You're a very brave boy, so you will do fine."

9. A 5-year old child is going to have surgery for repair of an umbilical hernia. All of the following should be included as part of the child's preparation **EXCEPT:**
    a. A real or virtual tour of the hospital.
    b. Demonstrations with a doll.
    c. A detailed explanation of the surgery.
    d. Advance preparation.

10. The child life specialist team has received a donation of $1500 to educate the public (families, the community) about the benefits of utilizing child life specialists. Which of the following is the **MOST** efficient and cost-effective utilization of funds?
    a. Create a video to play in the waiting area.
    b. Pay staff to give community presentations.
    c. Pay for radio advertisements.
    d. Print brochures about the services offered.

11. Which of the following is the primary goal of preparing children for medical procedures?
    a. Reduce the child's anxiety and fear.
    b. Assist parents in preparing the child.
    c. Reduce the burden on other medical staff.
    d. Reduce adverse effects.

12. At which stage in Piaget's theory of cognitive development do children engage in magical thinking and show egocentrism?
    a. Sensorimotor.
    b. Preoperational.
    c. Concrete operational.
    d. Formal operational.

13. All of the following are elements of family-centered care **EXCEPT:**
    a. Discussion of test results.
    b. Assistance with procedures and daily care.
    c. Restricted visitation (hours, age and relationship to the patient).
    d. Participation in plan of care.

14. An 8-year-old child is awakened at 12 AM and 4 AM for assessment and at 2 AM and 6 AM for medications. When the child life specialist reviews the records, she finds the child is sleeping only about 6 hours nightly because of these interruptions. Which of the following is the **MOST** appropriate action?
    a. Schedule 2-hour naps in the afternoons so the child gets adequate sleep.
    b. Request that the physician order a sleeping medication for the child.
    c. Teach the child relaxation techniques to help her sleep better.
    d. Work with medical staff to reschedule medications to 12 AM and 4 AM.

15. According to the CHEOPS pain scale, which of the following combinations of symptoms may indicate that a 1-year old infant is in pain after surgery?
    a. Neutral facial expression, random movements of lower extremities.
    b. Whimpering, restless movement of legs.
    c. Inactive, not touching or reaching toward incision.
    d. Not crying, inactive, random movements of lower extremities.

16. A child does not participate in team sports, and he admires older children in gangs. He fails to follow rules or understand causal relationships. He has made poor academic progress in reading, writing, math, and penmanship, and has problems throwing or catching a ball. These findings are most likely associated with developmental delays or problems for which of the following ages?
    a. 6.
    b. 8.
    c. 10.
    d. 12.

17. At what age should a toddler be able to balance on one foot and kick at objects, such as a ball, with the other foot?
    a. 15 months.
    b. 24 months.
    c. 30 months.
    d. 36 months.

18. A 4-year old child hospitalized for cancer treatment refuses to eat any foods other than bananas, milkshakes, spaghetti, and hot dogs. Which of the following is the best approach?
    a. Fortify these foods when possible and allow the child to eat what the child likes.
    b. Serve the child the same diet as other children, as the child will eventually eat when hungry.
    c. Discuss the necessity of eating a more balanced diet with the child.
    d. Withhold activities, such as watching cartoons, until the child eats other foods.

19. Which of the following is the **MOST** important to facilitate cooperation in interdisciplinary teams?
    a. Clarifying information.
    b. Responding to facts rather than feelings.
    c. Active listening.
    d. Open communication.

20. All of the following are good methods to use for distracting a young child from a procedure (such as a needle insertion) **EXCEPT**:
    a. Blowing bubbles.
    b. Singing.
    c. Self-hypnotizing.
    d. Reading.

21. An obese 15-year-old girl diagnosed with type 2 diabetes needs to change her diet and lose weight. She has 12 and 13-year-old siblings. Which of the following approaches is **MOST** likely to be successful?
    a. Referring the teenager to a weight-loss camp.
    b. Providing the teenager with intensive diet instruction.
    c. Educating the child about the negative effects of diabetes.
    d. Changing eating habits for the entire family.

22. A 12-year-old child hospitalized for treatment of AIDS is ambulatory and has started to walk in the halls. The **MOST** important consideration is:
    a. The child should have access to directly supervised activities only.
    b. The child should be advised exactly where he can and cannot go.
    c. The child should be told to avoid contact with other children.
    d. The child should ambulate only when a parent is present.

23. Therapeutic play includes all of the following **EXCEPT**:
    a. Doll reenactment play to help the child express feelings.
    b. Educational play to teach the child about medical treatments.
    c. Health based play to promote physical wellbeing.
    d. Self-chosen recreational play.

24. Which of the following is the **FIRST** step in problem solving?
    a. Define the issue.
    b. Collect data.
    c. Make a decision.
    d. Consider reasons for actions.

25. A 17-year old adolescent with asthma has started smoking, resulting in repeated hospitalizations for exacerbation of symptoms. Which is the **BEST** initial approach to convince the adolescent to consider smoking cessation?
    a. "I'd like to talk about smoking cessation with you."
    b. "You must stop smoking if you want to control your asthma."
    c. "Why are you smoking when you can see it's hurting you?"
    d. "What do you think you could do to help control your asthma?"

26. Which of the following theories includes 9 personality parameters to describe how children (beginning at about 4 weeks) respond to events?
    a. Resiliency Theory.
    b. Theory of Social Learning (Bandura).
    c. Temperament Theory (Chase & Thomas).
    d. Theory of Moral Development (Kohlberg).

27. Which of the following terms is associated with the child who tries to get information about a stressful event and remains alert to the event?
    a. Vigilant coping.
    b. Avoidant coping.
    c. Trait anxiety.
    d. State anxiety.

28. All of the following are necessary elements of clinical supervision **EXCEPT**:
    a. Reflecting.
    b. Collaborating.
    c. Criticizing.
    d. Supervising regularly.

29. A large facility has four, 5-person, child life specialist teams working 8AM to 4PM and two 5-person teams working 4PM to 12AM. All members are required to attend a monthly inservice training and are paid time-and-a-half if the training is outside of normal working hours. Which of the following is the **BEST** time to schedule training?
    a. 7 to 8 AM.
    b. 8 To 9 AM.
    c. 3 to 4 PM.
    d. 4 to 5 PM.

30. When speaking softly to soothe a 10-day old neonate, how far away from the face should the caregiver hold the infant?
    a. 2 to 4 inches.
    b. 4 to 8 inches.
    c. 8 to 12 inches.
    d. 12 to 16 inches.

31. Which of the following budget types is used for remodeling, repairing, and purchasing equipment or buildings?
    a. Operating budget.
    b. Capital budget.
    c. Cash balance budget.
    d. Master budget.

32. When positioning a toddler (1 to 3) for a procedure, which of the following positions is **MOST** likely to cause the child fear?
    a. Fetal.
    b. Side-lying.
    c. Prone.
    d. Supine.

33. Feelings of abandonment when hospitalized, exaggerated fears of people, pain, and equipment, and confusing fantasy and reality are common at what age?
    a. 3 to 5.
    b. 5 to 7.
    c. 7 to 9.
    d. 9 to 11.

34. A facility is providing orientation for new staff. The child life specialist team is asked to provide information about the child life program. Which of the following is the **MOST** effective method to ensure that new staff understands the functions and benefits of the program?
    a. Presenting a video about the child life program.
    b. Presenting a panel discussion with members of the child life program.
    c. Providing brochures and informational handouts.
    d. Providing computerized instruction regarding the program.

35. A 10-year-old girl is hospitalized for removal of a tumor from her leg. Which of the following fears should be confronted before surgery?
    a. Deformity/mutilation.
    b. Loss of independence.
    c. Lack of future ability.
    d. Change of body image.

36. Which of the following examples of medical play is the **MOST** likely to be effective in allowing a child to express fear of medical staff?
    a. Fantasy with pretend medical play.
    b. Exploration of medical equipment.
    c. Art projects (drawing and coloring).
    d. Role playing (child plays doctor/nurse).

37. All of the following categories are found in the HEADSSS psychosocial assessment tool for adolescents **EXCEPT:**
    a. Home environment.
    b. Eating.
    c. Data.
    d. Sexuality.

38. When doing procedures, such as insertion of intravenous needles or catheters, which of the following is the best environment for infants and young children?
    a. Their bed.
    b. The treatment room.
    c. The Playroom.
    d. The parent waiting area.

39. All of the following are acceptable for recertification as a child life specialist **EXCEPT:**
    a. Attending mandatory inservice training.
    b. Retaking the examination.
    c. Attending workshops related to the profession.
    d. Taking college courses related to the profession.

40. According to the Child Life Council Code of Ethical Responsibility, how much time must elapse between the conclusion of a professional role and the establishment of a personal relationship with a child or family member?
    a. 6 months.
    b. 1 year.
    c. 18 months.
    d. 2 years.

41. All of the following are part of the protocol for comfort positioning **EXCEPT**:
   a. Parent/caregiver stays with the child.
   b. Explanations provided throughout the procedure.
   c. Parent/caregiver and child taught about the procedure/treatment and their roles.
   d. Child positioned for comfort (usually sitting in hug hold).

42. A 16-year-old adolescent has been told that his cancer is not responding to treatment. Prior to this he had been very uncooperative with treatment and demanding, but he is now exhibiting a complete change in personality and is extremely cooperative, friendly, and compliant. According to Kübler-Ross's 5 stages of grief, which stage is the boy most likely experiencing?
   a. Denial.
   b. Anger
   c. Bargaining.
   d. Depression.

43. A Hispanic child requires long-term hospitalization, but the parents and 3 siblings (ages 10, 16 and 17) live 2 hours away from the hospital. The mother is not employed, and the father works as a farm laborer. They visit each Sunday and speak limited English. Which of the following is the **MOST** likely barrier to visiting their child?
   a. Socioeconomic.
   b. Geographic.
   c. Cultural.
   d. Organizational.

44. Which members of the child life specialist teams are responsible for identifying quality performance improvement projects?
   a. Administrative staff.
   b. All staff.
   c. Team leaders.
   d. Physicians.

45. All of the following are elements of outcomes evaluation as part of evidence-based practice **EXCEPT**:
   a. Monitoring and record keeping.
   b. Evaluating results.
   c. Sustaining treatment.
   d. Evaluating individual staff performance.

46. A parent stops the child life specialist and states, "Could you tell me what is wrong with the child across the hall from my son? He looks so sad." Which of the following responses is **MOST** appropriate?
   a. "The law doesn't allow me to give out any information about children in order to protect their privacy and safety."
   b. "His mother is in the lounge. You can go ask her."
   c. "Why are you asking?"
   d. "He has cancer, like your son."

47. Which of the following is an example of normalization?
   a. Painting the children's rooms in bright colors.
   b. Serving meals on trays in the room.
   c. Doing procedures in the treatment room.
   d. Allowing only parents to visit.

48. What is the purpose of a Kid Card?
   a. Identification for the child.
   b. Pay for items from the gift shop.
   c. Teach the child about his/her medications.
   d. Provide information about the child's condition.

49. Which of the following is an example of therapeutic communication?
   a. "Don't worry. Everything will be fine."
   b. "You should listen to your mother."
   c. "Is there anything you'd like to talk about?"
   d. "Why are you so upset?"

50. A 15-year-old girl who played on the tennis team at her school was involved in a traffic accident that shattered her left leg. She has been angry and depressed about her inability to participate in sports during recovery. Which of the following would be the **MOST** appropriate activity for this patient?
   a. PlayStation® video games.
   b. Nintendo Wii® sports simulation games.
   c. Watching tennis games on television.
   d. Reading books about tennis.

Answers and Explanations

1. D: The mother should receive counseling on methods to reduce her own stress because parental anxiety closely correlates with the child's anxiety. The mother's statements about pain and her crying may increase the child's stress and ability to cope. Providing options, such as distracting the child or rewarding him, may help the mother control her own anxiety. Asking the mother to leave or giving the injection when she is absent may increase the child's stress even though the child may be afraid to express anxiety and may be more cooperative. Topical anesthetics may be affective for insertion of needles, but painful injections usually result from tissue pain related to the medication, so topical anesthetics are less effective.

2. D: Bath toys are not appropriate for a 1 to 3 month-old infant, as the toys require manual dexterity and intentional play more common at 8 to 12 months. At one month, a rattle may be placed in the infant's hand, and the child will grip it but be unable to shake or lift the rattle to the mouth. By 3 months, the infant can shake the rattle and move it toward the mouth to explore. The child can reach toward mobiles and bat at them. The child's eyes can focus fairly well by 2 months, so the child may enjoy looking at his/her reflection in a mirror.

3. C: Industry vs. Inferiority.

Erikson's Theory of Psychosocial Development		
Trust vs mistrust	Birth to 1 year	Can result in mistrust or faith and optimism.
Autonomy vs shame/doubt	1-3 years	Can lead to doubt and shame or self-control and willpower.
Initiative vs guilt	3-6 years	Can lead to guilt or direction and purpose.
Industry vs inferiority	6-12 years	Can lead to inadequacy and inferiority or competence.
Identify vs role confusion	12-18 years	Can lead to role confusion or devotion and fidelity to others.
Intimacy vs isolation	Young adulthood	Can lead to lack of close relationships or love/intimacy.
Generativity vs stagnation	Middle age	Can lead to stagnation or caring and achievements.
Ego integrity vs despair	Older adulthood	Can lead to despair (failure to accept changes of aging) or wisdom (acceptance).

4. A: Parents should be encouraged to bring siblings to visit and interact, as much as possible, with the neonate. If the neonate has abnormalities, younger children may be hostile and older children ashamed. They may feel guilty about their response and neglected as parents grieve and are unable to provide the support they need. In some cases, parents may express their concern by focusing their anxiety on one of the siblings, becoming hypercritical. In these cases, the child life specialist may intervene by discussing

observations with the parents and encouraging other family members to provide support to the siblings.

5. B: Infants cannot be spoiled. Crying is a form of communication as is cooing, and the parent or caregiver should respond to both so that the infant feels secure. Physical contact is especially important for the child's physical and emotional development and may include holding, hugging, as well as skin-to-skin contact. Communicating with the infant, through singing or talking, comforts and engages the child. Adequate nutrition is necessary for children of all ages. Stressful environments with loud noises or overly bright or flashing lights should be avoided.

6. D: "You're learning a lot of letters" is the best choice because it acknowledges the child's efforts without heaping excessive praise, such as "Wow! That's wonderful!" These types of errors are common in young children and do not need correcting at this point as children should be allowed to make some errors without intervention. Pointing out errors before the child is developmentally ready or showing the child the correct form may increase the child's stress and retard the learning process.

7. A: Visits from therapy dogs are likely to engage the majority of children because all ages enjoy pets and can interact with them in different ways, depending on age. Card games are not appropriate for babies and toddlers although pre-school children may like simple games, such as Go Fish. Video cartoons must be age-appropriate and may be enjoyable, but watching a video is a passive activity. A guest pianist may be enjoyable for many, depending upon the type of music, but listening is also passive unless the pianist leads a sing-a-long; however, this leaves out the youngest children.

8. C: "Surgery is scary because you don't know what's going to happen" reflects back the feelings the child has expressed. Reflective listening includes:
- Listen actively: Turn toward the child, sit or kneel at the child's level or hold the child, and look directly at the child.
- Listen for expressions of feeling: Words such as "scared," "happy," "excited," and "sad," and "afraid." Try to identify and understand feelings rather than just words or facts.
- Reflect back: Restate the feelings the child has expressed and try to state the probable reason ("because") behind the feelings.

9. C: A detailed explanation of surgery may confuse a young child and increase anxiety. Explanations should be age-appropriate and guided by the child's questions, such as: "The doctor is going to fix the bump on your tummy." If possible, the child should receive a tour of the facility prior to the day of surgery, so the child can explore and ask questions without the immediate anxiety of surgery. Demonstrations with a doll are often effective for young children, and "surgery play" may help the child express feelings and concerns. Children should always be prepared in advance for surgery.

10. D: Brochures about the services offered are the best utilization of funds because they are relatively inexpensive and can be placed in a variety of places, such as pediatrician's offices and child-care facilities as well as given to families when children are hospitalized. Professional videos are expensive to produce and would have a limited audience if placed in waiting areas. Radio advertisements may not reach the target population and can be expensive. Paying staff would use up the money very quickly, so few people would benefit.

11. A: The primary goal of preparing children for medical procedures is to reduce the child's anxiety and fear. For all ages, the critical components of preparation include providing age and developmentally-appropriate information, allowing and encouraging the child to express feelings and concerns, and building a relationship of trust. Secondary benefits include assisting the parents, reducing the burden on other medical staff, and reducing adverse effects which may be related to anxiety.

12. B: According to Piaget's theory of cognitive development, children engage in magical thinking and show egocentrism in the preoperational stage. Stages include:

- Sensorimotor (0-24 months): Intellect begins to develop and children acquire motor and reasoning skills, begin to use language, and prepare for more complex intellectual activities.
- Preoperational (2-7 years): Children develop a beginning concept of cause and effect along with magical thinking and egocentrism.
- Concrete operations (7-11): Children develop understanding of cause and effect and concrete objects.
- Formal operational (11-adult): Children/young adults develop mature thought processes, the ability to think abstractly and evaluate different possibilities and outcomes.

13. C: Restricted visitation is not part of family centered care as the family, especially the parents, should be able to stay with the child and visit at will. Age restrictions may be appropriate in some cases, such as during flu epidemics, but generally siblings of all ages should be encouraged to visit. The extended family as well is especially important in some cultures. Family-centered care includes allowing family members to participate in discussions of test results, care of the child, and development of the plan of care.

14. D: The best approach to increasing the child's sleep is to work with medical staff to reschedule medications so they are given at the same time as the assessments, allowing the child to have longer periods of undisturbed sleep. An 8-year old child needs at least 10 hours of sleep nightly, so even a 2-hour nap will not provide adequate rest. While sleep medications are sometimes prescribed for children, the child does not suffer from insomnia but rather disturbed sleep. Relaxation techniques may benefit the child but will not ensure adequate rest if the child is awakened frequently.

15. B: Whimpering and restless movement of legs indicate pain. Pain≥4.

Children's Hospital Eastern Ontario Pain Scale (CHEOPS) (Ages 1-7)			
Characteristic	0	1	2
Crying		Not crying	Silent crying, moaning, or whimpering
Facial expression	Smiling, positive	Neutral	Grimacing, negative
Verbalization	Positive, no complaints	Not talking or complaining about other things (not pain).	Complaining about pain or pain and other things.

Torso		Inactive, at rest, relaxed	Tense, moving, shuddering, shivering, and/or sitting upright or restrained.
Upper extremities		Not touching or reaching for wound or injury.	Reaching for, touching gently, or grabbing wound or injury or arms restrained.
Lower extremities		Relaxed, random movement.	Restless or tense moving or legs flexed, kicking crouching, kneeling, or legs restrained.

16. C: Problems are associated with a 10 year-old child. Problems according to age:
- 6: Peer problems, depression, cruelty to animals, poor academic progress, speech problems, lack of fine motor skills, and inability to catch a ball or state age.
- 8: No close friends, depression, cruelty to animals, interest in fires, very poor academic progress with impaired math, reading, or writing skills, and poor coordination.
- 10: No team sports and poor choices in peers (gangs), failure to follow rules, cruelty to animals and interest in fires, depression, failure to understand causal relationships, poor academic progress in reading, writing, math, and penmanship, and problem throwing or catching.
- 12: Same as age 10 with increasing risk-taking behaviors (drinking, drugs, sex) and continued poor academic progress in reading, following directions, doing homework, and organization.

17. B: These skills should be evident by 24 months. Normal motor skills by age include:
- 4 months: Roll from the abdomen to the back.
- 8 months: Sit unsupported.
- 10 months: Pull self up to standing by holding onto furniture.
- 11 months: Walk while holding onto to somebody or something (such as a wall or coffee table).
- 15 months: Walk independently.
- 24 months: Balance on one foot and kick at objects, such as a ball, with the other foot.
- 30 months: Jump up and down in place.
- 36 months: Throw ball overhand.

18. A: These foods should be fortified when possible (such as adding protein to milkshakes) and the child allowed to eat what he/she likes. Food jags are common with preschoolers. There can be days or even weeks when they refuse all but one or two foods. Studies have indicated that children seem to suffer no ill effects from these food jags, so forcing the child to eat other foods isn't necessary, but other foods should be offered until the child resumes a more normal diet. Because the child is stressed, she may be seeking comfort in the foods she knows and likes. A 4-year-old child is probably not going to be convinced by reason, and punishing the child by serving only other foods or withholding activities will increase anxiety.

19. D: An interdisciplinary team cannot function without open communication and members encouraged to participate as a cooperative team. Other important skills include:
- Avoiding interrupting or interpreting the point another is trying to make allows for the free flow of ideas.
- Avoiding jumping to conclusions which can effectively shut off communication.
- Listening activity requires paying attention and asking questions for clarification.
- Respecting others opinions and ideas is absolutely essential.
- Reacting and responding to facts rather than feelings allows one to avoid angry confrontations.
- Clarifying information or opinions stated can help avoid misunderstandings.
- Keeping unsolicited advice out of the conversation shows respect for others.

20. C: A young child will not be able to practice self-hypnotizing, but any activity that engages the child and keeps the attention focused elsewhere can help to distract from stressful procedures. Distractions may include singing, blowing bubbles, reading, counting, taking deep breaths, coughing, watching cartoons, looking at pictures, and blowing on a toy horn or party noisemaker. Some children can benefit from relaxation techniques that involve tightening and then relaxing muscles, depending on their level of maturity.

21. D: The most successful approach includes a healthier change in eating habits for the whole family so the child does not eat differently from others. Changes should include:
- No more than 30% of nutrition should be fats.
- Carbohydrates should be complex rather than simple sugars, decreasing consumption of white flour and sugar.
- Healthy snacks, such as fruit, air-popped popcorn, and nonfat yogurt, should be provided with high-caloric snacks (chips, candy) not available.
- The child should eat 3 meals daily, served adequate but not large portions, and not be forced to "clean the plate."
- Television viewing or other sedentary activities should be progressively limited over time and exercise activities encouraged.

22. B: The staff should always know where children are, and ambulatory children must be clear about where they can go and cannot go. These limitations must be strictly enforced because access to elevators, laundry chutes, or restricted work areas could pose risks to the child or others. A hospitalized child is not a prisoner, and a 12-year old should be able to ambulate without a parent's supervision. AIDS is not contagious by contact, so avoiding other children is not necessary unless the child has some type of secondary infection that is spread by contact or is severely immunocompromised. Supervised activities should be available whenever possible.

23. D: Self-chosen recreational play is not part of therapeutic play, which is often effective in reducing children's anxiety:
- Doll reenactment play is a means to help a child express feelings and anxieties.
- Educational play teaches the child about disease, treatments, and self-care.
- Health play promotes physical wellbeing through activities to increase muscle strength, promote circulation, and prevent wasting.

Play is universal and is an important component of cognitive and psychosocial development. Guiding children in play serves an integral need for play as well as a therapeutic purpose.

24. A: The first step is to define the issue: Talk with the patient or family and staff to determine if the problem is related to a failure of communication or other issues, such as culture or religion.
- Collect data: This may mean interviewing additional staff or reviewing documentation, gaining a variety of perspectives.
- Identify important concepts: Determine if there are issues related to values or beliefs.
- Consider reasons for actions: Distinguish between motivation and intention on the part of all parties to determine the reason for the problem.
- Make a decision: A decision on how to prevent a recurrence of a problem should be based on advocacy and moral agency, reaching the best solution possible.

25. D: "What do you think you could do to help control your asthma?" shows respect for the adolescent and recognizes the need for autonomy while providing an opening to discuss smoking on the adolescent's own terms. Using words, such as "should" and "must," may result in resentment and resistance, sometimes causing the adolescent to stubbornly cling to behavior that is self-destructive. Challenging an adolescent by demanding a reason for action is rarely successful as the reasons may be quite complex or outside of the adolescent's self-awareness.

26. C: Chess and Thomas's Temperament Theory describes 9 personality parameters to describe how children (≥4 weeks) respond to events. These personality traits explain the difficult child, the child who is slow to warm up to new people and circumstances, and the child who is easy to manage and adaptable. Resiliency Theory describes the ability of children to function in healthy ways despite adverse circumstances. Bandura's Theory of Social Learning proposes that children learn from interacting with adults and their peers and through modeling behavior. Kohlberg's Theory of Moral Development outlines the progressive stages in which children develop a sense of morality.

27. A: Vigilant coping occurs when the child tries to get information about a stressful event and remains alert and vigilant to the event. Avoidant coping occurs when the child tries not to think about or deal with a stressful event, such as surgery or medical treatments, but remains detached. Trait anxiety refers to a child being constantly in a high but stable state of anxiety. State anxiety refers to anxiety in response to a specific stimulus, such as hospitalization or other stressful experience. Both the child's response to anxiety and coping style must be evaluated to determine the child's ability to cope with medical care.

28. C: Criticism is not a necessary element of clinical supervision because the focus should be on teaching and mentoring rather than finding fault and assigning blame. The 4 necessary elements of supervision include:
- Reflecting: The supervisor reflects and shares his/her own experience to help the child life specialist learn and grow in the profession.
- Collaborating: The supervisor and child life specialist work together to achieve goals.

- Supervising regularly: The supervisor must establish a regular schedule for ongoing supervision.
- Being competent: The supervisor must be current in the field and competent.

29. C: Scheduling training from 3 to 4 PM is the most cost-effective decision because only 10 people need to be paid for overtime as opposed to 20, and this time causes little disruption in normal working schedules. Early morning meetings might be convenient for those working 8 to 4, but those working the evening shift would have only 7 or 8 hours between leaving work and the meeting time. Additionally, mornings are a busy time because of physician visits, treatments, and procedures while late afternoon tends to be freer of disruptions.

30. C: Because a neonate is comforted by eye-to-eye contact and focuses the eyes at about 8-12 inches, the caregiver should try to maintain that distance while soothing the child. Neonates may comfort to rhythmic movements, such as rocking, and singing but will startle with abrupt movement. Neonates are sensitive to sounds and lights, so keeping sounds to a minimum (lower the volume on alarms) and dimming the lights may help to soothe the child. Hunger and environmental temperatures that are too high or too low may increase stress.

31. B: Capital budget: Determines which capital projects (such as remodeling, repairing, and purchasing of equipment or buildings) will be allocated funding for the year. These capital expenditures are usually based on cost-benefit analysis and prioritization of needs. Operating budget: Used for daily operations and includes general expenses such as salaries, education, insurance, maintenance, depreciation, debts, and profit. The budget has 3 elements: statistics, expenses, and revenue.
Cash balance budget: A project's cash balance for a specific future time period, including all operating and capital budget items.
Master budget: Combines operating, capital, and cash balance budgets as well as any specialized or area-specific budgets.

32. D: The supine position leaves the toddler open and exposed and is the most likely position to frighten the child. Small children tend to curl up into a fetal position or turn away in a side-lying or prone position when they are stressed or avoiding someone, so toddlers should be placed in other positions than supine whenever possible. Lack of mobility, as with restraints, is especially stressing to a toddler who usually also has stranger anxiety and is fearful of medical staff. The preferred position is usually sitting. Toddlers are normally resistive, so whenever possible, the parent should be with the child to reduce separation anxiety.

33. A: Feelings of abandonment when hospitalized, exaggerated fears of people, pain, and equipment, and reality/fantasy confusion are common from ages 3 to 5. At this age children also feel separation anxiety if parents are not present and often develop confused ideas and believe treatment is punishment. They may cope by showing regressive behavior, throwing tantrums, acting aggressively, becoming angry, or feeling guilty. Some may cope by escaping into fantasy. Preschoolers need parental support and choices and must be reminded that they are not being punished. They should be encouraged to express feelings through play.

34. B: While there are benefits to having a variety of different informational tools available, the most effective method of communicating information is usually that involving human

interaction, such as the panel discussion. This format allows for questions and answers and a more holistic overview of the program. The panel discussion should be supplemented with brochures and informational handouts for the new staff members to review. A short video is a good introduction to a panel discussion, and computerized instruction is valuable for review and for those off-site.

35. A: School-age children (6 to 12) often have very body-centric fears and are afraid of deformity/mutilation or loss of body parts resulting from surgery. They also fear loss of general control of the body and loss of bodily functions as well as general fears of pain and death. They may also be terrified of anesthesia because they feel they will have no control. They may exhibit guilt, regressive behavior and depression and may act out or withdraw. They may be very modest or shy about their bodies. The child should be educated about the surgery and what to expect after surgery and encouraged to make choices and participate in care.

36. D: Role playing is particularly effective in allowing a child to express fear of medical staff because the child often acts out those things he/she is afraid of, allowing the child life specialist to then guide the conversation and help the child deal with the fear. Fantasy with pretend medical play and exploration of medical equipment is good preparation for treatments and surgery as it helps to familiarize the child with equipment and procedures. Art projects help children to express feelings.

37. C: Data is not part of the HEADSSS psychosocial assessment tool for adolescents. Each category includes 4 to 7 specific questions.
- Home environment: Where, who, changes, living arrangements.
- Employment and education: In/out of school, grades, changes, plans, work.
- Eating: Body likes and dislikes, diet, weight management, exercise.
- Activities: friends/family activities, sports participation, church, clubs.
- Drugs/Substance use: Tobacco, alcohol, drugs (personal, family, friends).
- Sexuality: Dating, sexual relationships, romantic relationships, knowledge of safe sex, gender attraction.
- Suicide/Depression: Sad, bored, depressed, thoughts of hurting self or others.
- Safety/Savagery: Injuries, seatbelt use, risk-taking, violence (home, school, friends, neighborhood), physical or sexual abuse.

38. B: Whenever possible, infants and children should be moved to the treatment room for procedures so that they feel that their beds are safe areas or they may begin to associate their beds with fear and anxiety, and this may interfere with sleep. Other areas where families gather (waiting rooms) or children play should be off-limits for procedures so that children can feel safe in these areas. Additionally, observing some procedures may cause stress to other children or families.

39. A: A child life specialist cannot count attendance at mandatory inservice training for recertification. The following cannot be counted toward recertification: participating in patient care activities, attending routine meetings, networking or poster sessions, providing tours of the facility, making presentations, and engaging in internships and fellowships. Recertification requires either retaking of the qualifying examination or ≥50 hours of professional development, which may include taking college courses, attending inservice

programs (optional), attending workshops, participating in grand rounds, and attending local, regional, and national child life conferences.

40. D: Two years must elapse between the conclusion of a professional role and the establishment of a personal relationship with a child or family member. The Code of Ethical Responsibility outlines the goals (maximizing health and minimizing stress/trauma) of the child life specialist and to whom the specialist has responsibilities (children, family, other professions, staff, students, volunteers, and self). The Code contains 13 principles regarding professional responsibilities and obligations toward children and families.

41. B: While explanations may be provided through a procedure, this is not part of comfort positioning and often not necessary for young children. However, the parent or caregiver should remain with the child and both should be thoroughly prepared prior to the procedure so they know what will happen from education/play/manipulation of equipment and understand their roles. For example, the child's role may be to hold very still and the parent's role to hold the child. The child is positioned for comfort with small children usually sitting in a hug hold. The healthcare provider should strive to keep the atmosphere positive and non-stressful.

42. C: He is most likely in the bargaining stage. Kübler-Ross's five stages of grief include:
- Denial: People resist news and may appear confused and uncomprehending.
- Anger: As reality becomes clear, people may react with pronounced anger (directed inward or outward) and sometimes hostility.
- Bargaining: This involves if-then thinking (often directed at a deity): "If I go to cooperate with treatments, they will begin working" or "If I pray, God will answer my prayers."
- Depression: People may become withdrawn and overwhelmed with sadness.
- Acceptance: People are able to accept death/dying/incapacity.

43. A: Socioeconomic barriers are most likely. Wages for farm laborers are usually low, the mother is not working, and they have a large family. They may not be able to pay for accommodations if one or both parents want to stay. Geographic barriers, such as distance and lack of transportation, may play some part, as the parents cannot easily drive to the hospital on a daily basis. Cultural barriers, such as different health beliefs or practices, are probably not a concern because they have sought treatment for their child. Organization barriers, such as lack of adequate access or interpreters, are probably not the primary issues.

44. B: All staff members are responsible for identifying performance improvement projects. Performance improvement must be a continuous process. Continuous Quality Improvement (CQI) is a management philosophy that emphasizes the organization and systems and processes within that organization rather than individuals. Total Quality Management (TQM) is a management philosophy that espouses a commitment to meeting the needs of the customers (clients, staff) at all levels within an organization. Both management philosophies recognize that change can be made in small steps and should involve staff at all levels.

45. D: Evaluation of staff performance is not an element of outcomes evaluation, which focuses on the success of a particular intervention. Outcomes evaluation includes:

- Monitoring over the course of intervention involves careful observation and record keeping that notes progress.
- Evaluating results includes reviewing records as well as current research to determine if outcomes are within acceptable parameters.
- Sustaining involves continuing the intervention, but continuing to monitor and evaluate.
- Improving means to continue the intervention but with additions or modifications in order to improve outcomes.
- Replacing the intervention with a different one must be done if outcomes evaluation indicates that current intervention is ineffective.

46. A: "The law doesn't allow me to give out any information about children in order to protect their privacy and safety" is accurate and appropriate. The Health Insurance Portability and Accountability Act (HIPAA) addresses the privacy of health information. Child life specialists must not release any information or documentation about a patient's condition or treatment without consent. Personal information about the patient is considered protected health information (PHI), and includes any identifying or personal information about the patient, such as health history, condition, or treatments in any form, and any documentation. Failure to comply with HIPAA regulations can make a child life specialist liable for legal action.

47. A: Painting the children's rooms in bright colors is an example of normalization, a process that strives to create an environment as close to normal as possible for those in hospitals or other types of facilities. Normalization can also include communal eating areas, play areas, non-restricted visitation by family members (including siblings), planned activities, visits by therapy animals, and allowing the child to decorate his/her room. Normalization also includes allowing the child more autonomy, such as in relation to sleeping hours, treatment times, and food selection.

48. C: The purpose of a Kid Card is to teach the child about his/her medications in age-appropriate language and to encourage autonomy and participation in self-care.

Acetaminophen
This medicine is also called Tylenol®

Why am I taking Tylenol?
- You have to take this medicine so you can exercise your arm.
- It helps to keep your arm from hurting.

How do I take Tylenol?
- It is a chewable tablet (about the size of an M&M).
- You need to chew 5 tablets with breakfast and 5 with lunch and 5 with dinner for 4 or 5 days.
- You can stop taking Tylenol when your arm stops hurting.

What might happen if I take Tylenol?
- Most kids don't have any bad effects from taking Tylenol.

> - If you get a rash, start itching, or feel sick to your stomach, tell your mom or a nurse right away so she can tell the doctor.

49. C: "Is there anything you'd like to talk about?" is an open-ended question that encourages the child to share. Other examples of therapeutic communications are statements that show empathy and observations, such as "You are shaking" or "You seem worried," and statements that indicate reality, such as "That sound is an ambulance siren, not screaming." Child life specialists should avoid providing advice ("should" or "must") and avoid meaningless clichés, such as "Don't worry. Everything will be fine." Asking for explanations of behavior not directly related to patient care, such as "Why are you so upset?" should also be avoided.

50. B: While all of these activities may provide some benefit, the one that directly relates to his/her personal desire to participate in sports is the Nintendo Wii® sports simulation games. He/she can play tennis with the game and practice swinging his/her arm and hitting the ball while sitting in a chair or wheelchair. Listening to what a child is interested in and trying to match those interests in a variety of ways can help the child feel valued and encourage him/her to engage in activities.

Test Preparation Aids

Practice Test Questions

John Bowlby felt that the reluctance of a child to interact with a parent following a distressing separation indicated some measure of – 1) despair; 2) depression; 3) detachment; 4) protest. Select one and explain your answer.

Correct answer: 3 - Detachment. Although despair and protest (1 and 4) are described in the same theoretical argument, they are features of a more active scenario where the child actually still desires to reconnect with the parent. Depression, albeit common in children who feel abandoned, is not a primary feature of Bowlby's actual rejection hypothesis. Detachment is the hallmark feature, present when the child has actually emotionally given up on the relationship. It demonstrates an absence of the key attachment features that normally accompany an existing well-nurtured parent-child bond.

Four people have volunteered for child life work in a medical/surgical pediatric unit: 1) a young mother hoping work with children will help her cope with the recent death of a beloved niece; 2) a college student eager to learn but with little experience; 3) a religious person hoping to provide messages of faith and hope; 4) a pre-medical student wanting to view surgeries and treatments in a pediatric population. Select the BEST candidate and explain your answer.

Correct/best answer: 2 – a college student eager to learn but with little experience. The young mother presents a 'red flag' in that she is seeking to volunteer as a way to enhance coping, rather than after having resolved her loss issues. A candidate who wishes to focus on personal religious beliefs as a volunteer may upset and confuse children who may well have other religious beliefs. The goals of the premedical student appear more in harmony with 'shadowing' medical treatment staff than in working with children.

The value of diabetes education in a group of 10-year olds is measured following an educational intervention at one month, one year, and two years. This study would be defined as – 1) longitudinal; 2) longitudinal-sequential; 3) cross-sectional; or 4) retrospective. Select one and explain your answer.

Correct answer: 1 - longitudinal, because there is only one group being studied with measurements at multiple points in time. Longitudinal-sequential designs combine cross-sectional and longitudinal formats, requiring two or more groups of varying ages measured repeatedly over ensuing years. A cross-sectional design does not fit, as it must include research two or more groups of varying ages measured at only one point in time. A retrospective study is a 'look back' study that follows up after a specific intervention and may only require one point of measurement.

There is a stage of psychosocial development in which a child is likely to believe an illness or treatment is punishment for some "bad" thought or action. That stage is: 1) adolescence; 2) infancy; 3) preschool; 4) elementary school age. Select one and explain your answer.

Correct answer - 3. Preschool age children are most prone to thinking that illness and other negative experiences are punishment for bad thoughts or misbehavior. By contrast: infant thinking is concerned with processing sensations, seeking security through attachment, and having comfort/distress needs met and resolved; school aged children may have limited "concrete" thinking, but grasp germ theory and explanations about the workings of the body and are usually well beyond the 'magical thinking' of preschool-aged cognition; adolescents are capable of deductive reasoning and can follow disease processes and experiences, thus they will readily understand medical explanations for physiological events.

Bolig defines a child life program that focuses on a multi-modal service approach including environmental normalization, socialization, feelings expression, and family-centered care as: 1) child development oriented, 2) therapeutic, 3) diversion based, or 4) comprehensive. Select one and explain your answer.

Correct answer - 4. A comprehensive program will use a multi-modal system of care to include family-centered care, environmental normalization, socialization, and expression of the child's feelings. By contrast, child development programs emphasize activities that support and facilitate age-specific developmental accomplishments and experiences; therapeutic programs focus on children's coping with imagined fears (fantasies) and emotions related to various experiences; and, diversion-based programs are limited largely to attention management approaches that inhibit a child's anxieties related to specific events.

When a preschool-age child struggles with issues of autonomy loss, a child life specialist should respond by: 1) planning and directing specific play activities; 2) promptly imposing a planned intervention; 3) involving the child in treatment choices and activities where possible; or, 4) increasing the involvement of parents in the child's care. Select one and explain your answer.

Correct answer - 3. Only by helping the child find more control over his or her life by providing opportunities to be involved in appropriate choices and participating in treatment activities, where possible, can the child regain an important sense of personal autonomy. Planning and directing the child's activities can impose structure, but will further undermine the child's sense of autonomy. Imposing an intervention can also backfire, to the degree that it further constrains the child's behavior and environment. Increasing parental involvement typically fosters further dependence, which would be counterproductive in this situation.

Research shows that the only benefit that the use of music does NOT provide to a hospitalized child is: 1) decreased fear, anxiety and sense of pain; 2) reduced stress; 3) increased coping capacity; 4) shortened time to first post-surgical walking. Select one and explain your answer.

Correct answer - 4. The use of music has many benefits for children. Among these are lower levels of fear and anxiety, and a greater tolerance for pain; an enhanced ability to emotionally cope with the trauma of illness and difficult treatments; and, less distress overall. However, the time between surgery and post-surgical ambulation is not appreciably shortened. Even so, many of the other benefits of music may actually make early ambulation experiences tolerable and less distressing, and should improve the hospital experience in numerous other ways.

From among the following, name the greatest stressor for preschool-aged children experiencing a hospital stay: 1) the loss of daily routines; 2) treatments that cause pain; 3) the formal and sterile hospital setting; 4) being separated from parents. Select one and explain your answer.

Correct answer - 4. Daily routines are very important to a child's sense of continuity, normalcy and consequent well-being; experiences involving pain are often acutely distressing in the short term (and more so if more enduring); and, being in a foreign environment that is sterile, limiting, and filled largely only with other adults can indeed be emotionally traumatic for little children. However, when compared against these other stressors, the greatest trauma and sense of enduring distress for a preschool-aged child arises when they are separated from the security and comfort of their parents.

Among the following, what is the most fundamental to an adolescent's successful coping? 1) a supportive family; 2) personal mastery and control; 3) the use of humor; or, 4) physical capacity. Select one and explain your answer.

Correct answer - 2. Every individual benefits profoundly from a supportive and engaged family. For adolescents, the use of humor and engaging repartee is often highly valued and, without a doubt retained personal appearance and physical prowess are of great significance. However, an adolescent's positive coping capacity is enhanced most when he or she feels some sense of mastery and control over what happens with their physical self, their environment, and in the course unfolding events and circumstances. Thus, a primary goal for a child life specialist is to create situations and experiences that will support and sustain an adolescent's sense of mastery and control in the hospital setting, in process of medical treatments, and as related to changing health status.

From among the following, identify the situation of highest priority for a child life specialist: 1) a child facing impending or immediate admission to an ICU, trauma unit, or emergency department; 2) a family failing in coping capacity; 3) a child with a significant chronic illness; or, 4) a child who stops playing whenever nursing staff enter or remain in the room. Select one and explain your answer.

Correct answer - 1. The ability to prioritize services is crucial to providing high quality child life services. By way of priority: family coping is essential to adequate support of a child, and thus has considerable claim on a child life specialists' time and attention; a child coping with chronic illness is very important (although, by definition, this is not an acute or urgent situation); and, a child who is reluctant to play under any circumstances and more particularly when around medical staff is very concerning. However, a child who is acutely failing in health to the point of intensive care, trauma unit, or emergency department admission is one who is about to undergo multiple profound events and circumstances. The emotional trauma to parents and extended family will be proportionately profound. Thus, they would have highest priority claim on a child life specialist's immediate time and attention.

A child of eight is terminally ill and begins to talk about death in terms of loneliness and hopelessness during an expressive play session. In response the child life specialist should: 1) refer the child to a psychologist; 2) use another play strategy to distract the child from these feelings; 3) say that he/she isn't going to die and is safe in the hospital; or 4) support the child in ongoing play and allow further expression as feelings of trust grow. Select one and explain your answer.

Correct answer - 4. Transient feelings of despair in a terminally ill child are to be expected; expressive play is an ideal medium for sharing, and premature referral to a psychologist may unnecessarily press the child into a new and unfamiliar relationship when the current context is sufficient. Attempts to distract the child can easily make the situation worse by suggesting that such feelings cannot be tolerated by important others. Being dishonest, even in an attempt to help, will damage trust and will prevent the child from being able to seek and find emotional resolution. Only by continuing the expressive play experience and letting the child openly disclose fears (coupled with honest reassurances such as, 'we will always be here for you,' etc.) can coping and essential trust be retained and enhanced.

A child who responds to hospitalization with marked passivity may well also exhibit: 1) an extreme fear of needles; 2) constant crying; 3) long periods of sleep; or 4) an unwillingness to part from parents. Select one and explain your answer.

Correct answer - 3. An overly passive child is likely one who is also depressed, hopeless and emotionally isolated. Unremitting sleep would be an additional form of emotional escape consistent with passive disconnection from environment and circumstances. By contrast, evidence of strong fears, clinging to parents and crying are intense reactions that are more consistent with processes of increasing environmental and emotional engagement rather than disengagement. Of the two response patterns, overt passivity is usually of greater concern and more difficult to address and overcome.

Child life staff should ideally begin preparing the family for an upcoming hospitalization at the following point: 1) at the time an admission is agreed upon, while still in the physicians office; 2) in a follow-up telephone call; 3) at the time of a pre-admission medical work-up; or, 4) when the parents are brought in for a pre-admission hospital tour. Select one and explain your answer.

Correct answer - 1. After agreeing to a hospitalization, if the child and parents are immediately sent home they may well wrestle with numerous misunderstandings and apprehensions for a considerable time until they can be properly informed, oriented and have their fears put to rest. Issues of visiting hours, sibling visitation and/or daycare options, child comfort care plans, intake processes, insurance, hospital geography, parental overnight-stay options, transportation concerns, etc., along with needs for diagnostic and treatment plan review and expected outcomes confirmation, etc., would all be left unaddressed. Visits for pre-admission laboratory work-up are typically preoccupying; telephone calls may be deemed impersonal and content limited; facility tours are often large group affairs where personal questions may be inhibited. Thus, early preparation in the physician's office is typically best.

Psychiatrists Stella Cross and Alexander Thomas studied newborn infants and were able to identify nine traits that are retained throughout life. These traits are an aggregate measure of: 1) muscular tone and motor skills; 2) language fluency and communication skills; 3) temperament and personality; or 4) cognitive development and IQ. Select one and explain your answer.
Correct answer - 3. The researchers were looking for early evidence of temperament and personality traits that would persist throughout life. Beginning in 1956, they tracked 100 infants into adolescence and found measures of the following traits to be significant and enduring: activity level, "rhythmicity" (the regularity of biological functions), the tendency to approach or withdraw, adaptability, threshold responsiveness, reaction intensity and energy level, mood, distractibility/attention span, and levels of persistence. From these they described three temperamental types: easy-going, difficult, and slow-to-warm-up. The traits the researchers identified are basic to an individual's temperament and personality and are thus generally persistent and life-long in nature.

There are many play activities and strategies that are used with children in health care settings. The most beneficial and effective among them tend to be those that are: 1) high-energy and emotion-eliciting; 2) very structured and directed; 3) open-ended; or 4) quiet and passive. Select one and explain your answer.

Correct answer - 3. Researchers have discovered that open-ended activities, games, and strategies tend to be the most beneficial for children who have to cope with the limitations, interruptions, and distractions common to hospital settings. High-energy activities that evoke sharp emotional responses can be overwhelming and/or medically contra-indicated. Overly structured and directed games and activities tend to reduce children's feelings of control and competence. In addition, activities and games that are largely passive and quiet are often too disengaging and reductionist in nature for the well-being of hospitalized children.

In orienting new students and volunteers, you should limit the use of: 1) handouts; 2) question and answer periods; 3) audio-visual materials; 4) or lectures. Select one and explain your answer.

Correct answer - 4. Orientation strategies that rely heavily on lectures tend to be much less productive and engaging than those that use a variety of methods to deliver information. In part, this is because learning styles may vary greatly, with some learning more visually than others. Further, lectures can quickly become more monotone and redundant feeling. If you must lecture, at least endeavor to rotate presenters during any lengthy lecture session. Question and answer periods tend to be more engaging, as people feel far more included in such sessions.

Choose the term that most closely approximates a diagnosis of ataxia in a child: 1) dyspnea; 2) dysphagia; 3) dysarthria; or 4) dyskinesia. Select one and explain your answer.

Correct answer - 4. Ataxia is a medical term that refers to loss of voluntary muscle coordination, particularly in the extremities (arms and legs). It is seen in patients with symptoms such as staggering and frequent falls. Thus, dyskinesia, which refers to difficulty performing voluntary muscle movements, would be the most closely related term. Dyspnea, however, refers to difficult or labored breathing, dysphagia refers to difficulty swallowing, and dysarthria makes reference to speech and word-forming problems such as stammering or stuttering.

For maximum effectiveness, a child should be prepared for a medical procedure within an appropriate window of time. The ideal period for a preschool-aged child would be: 1) just prior to the procedure; 2) within a few hours; 3) within a few days; or 4) some weeks before the procedure. Select one and explain your answer.

Correct answer - 2. Research indicates that the optimum time to prepare a preschool-aged child for a medical procedure would be within a few hours of the actual event. If preparations are made a few days to some weeks before the medical procedure, a young child's memory of the effort will have faded and any rehearsal, modeling, and teaching benefits will have been lost – along with any coping skills that were presented, as well. If preparations are made too close the medical event (within minutes to an hour or so), the child is often too preoccupied and nervous to benefit fully. Thus, a few hours in advance is the optimum preparation time for a preschool-aged child.

A "qualitative" research model is: 1) rarely used because of the medical profession's bias for "quantitative" studies; 2) considered of limited value in the child life field; 3) a method that yields descriptive data; or 4) a research method incorporating statistical data analyses in its design. Select one and explain your answer.

Correct answer - 3. Qualitative research is based upon careful and systematic observation and detailed documentation and descriptions of relevant activities, behaviors or other similar outcomes. Qualitative research has been of significant value to the field of child life, and it has produced many findings of profound value. While descriptive categories may be aggregated and analyzed by quantitative statistical methods, the primary tools of qualitative research are focused on observation and are carried out by processes of recorded narrative and description.

Researchers John Bowlby and James Robertson provide a description of various responses of young children to the experience of parental separation, including all but one of the following reactions: 1) detachment; 2) despair; 3) protest; and 4) denial. Select the one not described and explain your answer.

Correct exception - 4. James Robertson (1958) and John Bowlby (1960) recognized an escalating pattern of children's reactions to imposed separation from their parents. Protest was observed to be an active attempt on the part of child to press for prompt reunion; despair was found to be associated with the trauma of early reunion failure; and, detachment was revealed to be a late-phase response wherein the child begins to abandon hope and to relinquish previous emotional attachments and reunion desires. Denial, however, is not part of the response pattern that was observed.

Identify the statement(s) that accurately describe school-age siblings: 1) hospitalized children may be more likely to play when siblings are present; 2) normally developing school-age siblings no longer use fantasy to explain the world around them; 3) hospital play settings can usually include both child patients and their school-age siblings; 4) placing siblings in separate play areas is suboptimal primarily because it separates family members. Select the correct statement(s) and then explain your answer(s).

Correct statements - 1 and 3. School-age children (whether siblings or not) continue to use fantasy to explore and describe the world around them. Indeed, the use of fantasy is a necessary and normal element in their development. Concerns about assigning school-age siblings to separate play areas go well beyond simple issues of geographical family separation. It may imply to both patients and siblings that they are unable to be in direct contact at all. Imposed separations can easily engage siblings' processes of fantasy, which may ultimately result in imagined circumstances far worse than they really are. Separate play areas also deny school-aged children access to normal processes of integration, bonding, and social exchange, and will deprive both of the benefits of enhanced play experiences that shared thought and interaction normally brings.

When orienting students and volunteers, all the areas described in the following should be covered except one: 1) review of the program's philosophy and goals; 2) outlining children and family needs and roles during a hospital stay; 3) emphasizing the problem of becoming emotionally attached to hospitalized children; 4) discussing ways that children conceive of death and how they grieve. Identify the orientation exception and explain your answer.

Correct exception - 3. Orienting students and volunteers to the goals and philosophy of the program is essential, lest they misunderstand the overall purpose and focus. Providing students and volunteers with an understanding of child and family needs and roles is a vital part of helping them serve better. Clarifying how children perceive death at different developmental stages, and how they consequently grieve (not only death, but also other losses such as loss of health, body appendage, appearance, etc.) is important information. However, describing the emotional attachments that develop between caregivers and hospitalized children as a "problem" does a disservice to all involved. Attachments are inevitable, and the presence of caring is essential to offering quality child and family support. A better approach would be to discuss ways to properly manage the attachments that naturally develop.

Identify the age-group that sees death as temporary or reversible: 1) infants (under age one); 2) toddlers (age three and under); 3) preschool aged children (ages three to under six); or 4) school-age children (ages six and above). Select and explain your answer.

Correct answer - 3. Infants are entirely unable to move beyond simplistic attachment and bonding schemas (Is a nurturing figure present?). Toddlers conceive mostly 'here and not here' and see 'moving' as alive and 'still' as dead, with peek-a-boo games working largely because of their limited understanding of 'present vs. gone'. Preschool aged children are those most prone to believing in the reversibility of death – in major part because of their concrete interpretations of the world around them, and due to their sizeable use of fantasy. By formal school age, children will begin to achieve sufficient development and vocabulary to more fully understand death, but most experts agree that they may not truly possess a mature understanding until they reach the age of about nine or ten.

Identify the best approach to enhance coping in a preschooler who is in the Pediatric ICU and is on a respirator (a breathing machine): 1) involve the child and caregivers in routine multidisciplinary rounds; 2) institute the use of 'drama play'; 3) use strategies to make the environment more familiar and predictable; 4) increase the visitation frequency of other peers and child life volunteers. Select and explain your answer.

Correct answer - 3. Generally, a preschool-aged child will have little to gain directly from multidisciplinary rounds. However, involved caregivers may obtain useful hints and ideas through such contacts. Drama play, using dolls, puppets, teddy bears, etc, and equipment (such as stethoscopes, blood pressure cuffs, tape, surgical scrubs, etc.) to reenact medical experiences to empower children, may be useful. However, a child who has been "intubated" (the respirator requires a tube pushed past the vocal cords and into the trachea - or 'windpipe') is unable to speak, and so play strategies and benefits are limited. Increased visitation should also be helpful, but has complications arising from intubation and issues of agitation, etc., as well. Therefore, the best option is to focus on strategies to make the child's environment more familiar and predictable, thereby decreasing stress, agitation, and distress stemming from loss of control.

In reading or conducting statistical research, child life specialists should know that the term "correlation" refers to: 1) measurable changes in a "dependent" variable in response to changes in other "independent" variables; 2) a matching change in the value of one variable in direct or proportional response to changes in another variable; 3) a measure of "causation" arising between two or more independent variables; 4) an unreliable statistic in statistical research compilation. Select and explain your answer.

Correct answer - 2. Simple changes between variables when manipulation occurs does not constitute a " correlation" – only when the changes observed are proportional or otherwise matching, and moving in unison (whether together or apart) to each other can a true correlation be claimed. However, the existence of a correlation can in no way be used to imply causation – where one variable explicitly "causes" change in another. Causation is a matter for inquiry beyond simple correlation confirmation. This having been said, the presence of a correlation can be a very reliable and important research finding.

Activities such as holding, rocking, massaging, stroking and hugging young children are sometimes referred to as: 1) physio-emotional interventions; 2) positive positioning; 3) vestibular rehabilitation; 4) positive touch. Select and explain your answer.

Correct answer - 4. While various touch-based comforting strategies will provide both physical and emotional benefits, the term "physio-emotional intervention" in not a formal term in common professional use and does not refer to any specific intervention paradigm. Similarly, "positive positioning" is not a formally utilized professional term. "Vestibular rehabilitation" is a professional term, but it refers to a form of physical therapy used to treat problems with balance. However, the term "positive touch" is a formal parlance in widespread professional use, and it does refer to a variety of touch-mitigated strategies to comfort, reassure, calm, and support children in distressing emotional and physical circumstances.

A passive behavioral disturbance that is common to hospitalized children is: 1) interactive problems with peers; 2) self-destructive actions; 3) angry and aggressive conduct; 4) lethargy and decreased activity. Select and explain your answer.

Correct answer - 4. A problem interacting with peers refers to "active" rather than "passive" behavioral processes. In like manner, self-destructive behaviors, angry expressions and gestures, and aggressive conduct are also active rather than passive constructs. Only lethargy and decreased activity could be defined as "passive" in nature. Behavioral withdrawal and lethargy are also common problems associated with hospitalized children, particularly when depressed and under stress. Longer-term hospital stays, burdensome conditions, and prolonged family separations make behavioral problems of all kinds more likely.

Name the research design used for a study that assigns children randomly to three different groups where each group uses a different approach to prepare children for a specific health intervention: 1) experimental; 2) cohort; 3) qualitative; 4) double-blind. Select one and explain your answer.

Correct answer - 1. This is an "experimental" study. Experimental studies are characterized by offering differing interventions or variable manipulations among multiple groups. They generally require roughly equal numbers of participants in each group, and groups large enough to be able make meaningful comparisons. The participants must be randomized into the groups to prevent any researcher bias in-group composition. Finally, a 'control' (or 'no intervention') group is needed for purposes of outcome comparisons. In this way the relative strengths of various interventions as used in a preparation process can be weighed against each other to determine 'best practices' options.

A fourth-grade girl (nine to ten years of age) has received a new diagnosis and now seems to be apathetic and withdrawn. In preparing a care plan, an initial step should be to: 1) interview the child; 2) build a supportive relationship with the child; 3) bring in a child-peer to play together; 4) talk to the parents. Select one and explain your answer.

Correct answer - 2. It is essential to first establish a relationship. An early interview with an apathetic child is unlikely to be productive without the relationship being in place; child-to-child play may well be insufficiently engaging; and, the parents most likely are not sure what is happening, either. Thus, although each of these other steps may be useful at later points, the immediate need is to build a trusting and positive relationship with the child sufficient to promote sharing and disclosure. Then in the natural course of playing and sharing, it is much more likely that her concerns will come out.

Human development researcher Erik Erikson associated one of the following with the developmental stage of infancy: 1) trust vs. mistrust; 2) initiative vs. guilt; 3) industry vs. inferiority; 4) autonomy vs. shame. Select and explain your answer.

Correct answer - 1. According to Erikson, infancy (birth to 18 months) is characterized by the "oral-sensory" phase (exploring the world by oral methods) and by the development of trust vs. mistrust. Where positive and nurturing influences are present, trust develops; where negative and abusive influences predominate, distrust may become persistent. Initiative vs. guilt is characteristic of the "play age" (three to five years); industry vs. inferiority belongs to the "school age" (six to twelve years); and, autonomy vs. shame is characteristic of "early childhood" (18 months to three years).

Evaluation of the success of a child specialist's teaching regarding coping skills for a specific procedure should be based on: 1) whether or not the child becomes tearful; 2) how quickly the child return to playing; 3) the child's use of the skills taught during the procedure; 4) how fast the procedure can be completed. Select and explain your answer.

Correct answer - 3. Different children have varying temperaments and thus differing capacities and tolerances for medical procedures and interventions. Consequently, it would be inappropriate to measure coping skills success based on the presence or absence of tears, propensity for returning to play, or the rapidity by which a given procedure was completed. The only truly accurate measure of a teaching intervention's effectiveness would be whether or not a child was able to demonstrate personal use of the materials taught – in this case coping skills for an anticipated medical procedure.

Identify which among the following principles is NOT among the Child Life Council's Code of Ethical Responsibility: 1) to remedy any personal situation that prevents effective practice; 2) show respect for other professionals; 3) acknowledge the needs of other professionals for relevant information; 4) make referrals for services beyond child life skills and competencies. Select and explain your answer.

Correct answer - 2. Specifically, the tenth principle in the Code of Ethics specifies that practitioners must assess, maintain and remedy any relationship or situation that prevents the effective practice of the profession; the ninth Principle underscores the need for respect for other professionals and their needs and involvement constraints; the eighth Principle stipulates that practitioners must make proper referrals to other professionals for services beyond their skills and competencies, with particular awareness to the competencies of other involved health care and community professionals. Nowhere does the Code stipulate a "demonstration" of respect for other professionals – rather, evidence of respect arises from adherence to other professional practices and acknowledgments.

Children use many coping strategies during a hospitalization. Select the statement that best describes coping strategies: 1) specific experiences can change, revise, extinguish, or establish them; 2) most are inborn and naturally available; 3) many are of little or no value to preschoolers; 4) most don't change as development progresses. Select and explain your answer.

Correct answer - 1. Coping strategies can definitely be taught, modified, replaced and enhanced. None however are inborn or innate. Rather, they must be identified, developed, refined and elaborated if they are ultimately to be of any applicable value. Although many coping strategies must be adapted and modified to suit the age and capacity of the children involved, most can be of great value for all ages including preschoolers. Finally, there is no question that nearly all coping strategies must be changed, revised and expanded throughout the process of development and maturation if they are to remain effective.

The primary focus of a volunteer job description should be on: 1) specific tasks, assignments, responsibilities and expectations; 2) desirable and preferred talents and background; 3) the reporting structure of the department; 4) criteria for termination. Select and explain your answer.

Correct answer - 1. A volunteer job description needs to focus most on the specific tasks, assignments, expectations and responsibilities of the job. Too great a focus on an ideal background, optimum talents or overly specific preferences can discourage and drive away otherwise high quality candidates. Among the foremost qualities truly needed are a commitment to children, eagerness and enthusiasm, a willingness to learn, dependability, and a host of other intangibles that far surpass most other formal volunteer qualifications.

When confronted with the stress of an involved medical procedure, separation anxiety can become particularly acute. The most effective way to prevent this is by: 1) ensuring the child life specialist is positioned right next to the child; 2) ensuring the parents are present; 3) having a familiar physician conducting the procedure; 4) using a 'transitional object'. Select and explain your answer.

Correct answer - 2. There is no substitute for having the parents present. The child life specialist serves best by aiding the children and parents in identifying and applying optimum coping skills. A physician who is consistent and familiar to the child can help, but cannot replace parental involvement. In like manner, a 'transitional object' (some beloved toy, doll, or other such item) is helpful, but will not supply the same measure of support that a child can derive from having his or her parents in attendance during a stressful procedure.

Child researcher John Bowlby described three sequential phases in child separation anxiety. Choose the statement that names them accurately: 1) anxiety, uncertainty, depression; 2) distress, anger, ambivalence; 3) protest, despair, disillusionment; 4) protest, despair, detachment. Select and explain your answer.

Correct answer - 4. Bowlby's description refers to protest, despair, and detachment. First a child protests (usually tearfully and loudly) the separation. This is followed by a period of despair and distress that varies in length according to other traumas involved and the temperament and coping capacities of the child. The syndrome concludes in detachment, which is a state within which the child relinquishes prior bonds and preexisting hopes for reinstatement of the desired relationship. In this phase, the eventual return of the parent does not result in immediate relief and reconnection, but instead the child may linger in a detached and even rejecting condition for some time.

The characteristics that a child life specialist can draw upon in preschool-aged children during preparation for a medical procedure includes all the following except: 1) autonomy; 2) affiliation; 3) industry; 4) verbal and expressive limitations. Select and explain your answer.

Incorrect characteristic - 2. According to Erikson's developmental stages, the strength of 'affiliation' is not predominant until young adulthood. However, desires for autonomy begin to emerge at about 18 months; a basic need for industry and personal development emerges during the period of "latency" (from six to twelve years of age); and language skills remain limited throughout children's developmental processes. Knowing the strengths and limitations inherent in preschool-aged children enables the child life specialist to design interventions that account for, support, sustain, and/or draw upon each of them.

A child's vulnerability to circumstances of trauma and distress can best be assessed by all but one of the following criteria: 1) age; 2) prior similar experiences; 3) academic success; 4) home and family stressors. Select and explain your answer.

Correct exception - 3. Academic success is not in and of itself a specific predictor of situational vulnerability to stress and trauma. Age and correlated developmental maturation are much better predictors in any assessment. Prior past experiences of a similar nature are very important, especially given research that suggests a 'pile-up' model of stress wherein stressors from past experiences accumulate when similar situations are reencountered. Home, family, and parental stressors are also meaningful contributors to any complete stress and vulnerability assessment.

- 140 -

In emotionally preparing a child for a specific health care experience, the single most significant characteristic that should be accounted for is: 1) the specific diagnosis; 2) temperament; 3) family unit status; 4) developmental maturity. Select and explain your answer.

Correct answer - 4. A child's level of development and maturity is the foremost characteristic to be considered in preparing the child for a medical procedure or treatment. However, the child's temperament and coping style are also important. Understanding the diagnosis and anticipated treatment regimen can also have significant bearing on the process. Finally, family structure (intact vs. widowed or divorced single parent home, etc.) may also be important in evaluating supportive resources and stressors as related to optimum coping skills and intervention strategies, etc.

Children who are most susceptible to distress during a hospitalization fall into one of the following age groups: 1) birth to eighteen months of age; 2) six months to four years; 3) three to six years; 4) over six years of age. Select one and explain your answer.

Correct answer - 2. Children between the ages of six months to four years are the most vulnerable to psychological and emotional trauma and distress during a hospitalization experience. Their capacity for environmental awareness, perception of threat, and consequent fear is high, while their ability to utilize compensating coping skills, to rationally judge circumstances, and to seek out help and verbally express their fears remains at a minimum. The convergence of increased cognitive perception coupled with emotional, psychological, linguistic, and coping skill limits makes them an especially vulnerable population (albeit in considerably different ways given the development breadth represented).

In preparation for surgery, identify the one group most susceptible to believing that 'bad' thoughts or behavior caused their medical condition: 1) those 1-3 years of age; 2) ages 3-7; 3) ages 7-10; 4) those ages 10-13. Select one and explain your answer.

Correct answer - 2. Children between the ages of three and seven are prone to believing that somehow 'bad' thoughts, behaviors, or things they have said may have caused or contributed to their own (or another loved one's) medical condition. Because of this, they may need specific and even repeated reassurances that related events were not of their own doing or resulting from 'fault' in any way. By so doing they can be relieved of considerable fears, guilt, and internal distress that can accompany their private assignment of blame. The problem can also be exacerbated by the fantasies and flights of fancy that are also predominant among this age group.

Some children focus on avoidance or other passive strategies in order to cope with anxiety-producing experiences such as needle sticks. These children should derive the greatest benefit from one of the following interventions: 1) a systematic review of all steps involved; 2) medical sedation; cognitive-behavioral interventions; or 4) distraction methods. Select one and explain your answer.

Correct answer - 4. When children are predisposed to avoid or use other passive strategies in coping with a distressing experience, they usually benefit the most from the application of distractions, over other approaches. Thus, use of a 'transitional object', treasure chest toy, a 'hospital friend', etc., may be particularly useful. Other children with differing coping approaches may derive greater benefit from alternative approaches. Medical sedation would be used only in the most problematic of situations, as it has medical implications, and may induce unwanted lethargy, depression, etc.

A comprehensive child life developmental assessment should include at least four domains – physical, cognitive, affective, and: 1) medical, 2) temperament; 3) social; or 4) coping skills. Select one and explain your answer.

Correct answer - 3. Assessment of the physical domain will include current health conditions, disabilities, diagnoses and prognoses, current medications, anticipated medical procedures and treatments, etc; the cognitive domain will encompass learning style and developmental level, psychiatric and academic history, etc; the affective domain will include mood, temperament, coping skills and style, etc. The social domain will include birth order and siblings, family structure (intact home vs. divorcee or widowed single parent), extended family involvement, proximity and availability to provide support, home stability, financial stability, insurance status, etc.

Select the activity which would most benefit a toddler having difficulty with issues of autonomy and separation: 1) playing house; 2) reading on the topic of separation; 3) talking about separation; or, 4) playing hide-and-go-seek together. Select one and explain your answer.

Correct answer - 4. Playing hide-and-seek brings the topic of having a loved one gone, missing them, and then seeking their return directly to the forefront. Although the symbolism is well beyond a child's capacity to comprehend, the primary issue is yet played out in some detail through the hide-and-go seek activity. When a child life specialist capitalizes on the 'finding' element of this game, it can reassure a young child that their loved ones and important others are still available to them and can and will yet return.

Activities that are based on identifying specific problems and seeking appropriate solutions are referred to as: 1) problem-focused coping; 2) situation-focused coping; 3) distress-reduction coping; or 4) solution-oriented coping. Select one and explain your answer.

Correct answer - 1. Problem-focused coping is an important tool in hospital childcare. Young children are often unable to independently carry out the steps necessary to formally identify and solve problems. By helping to inventory their environment, activities, interactions, and relationships, child life specialists can aid young children in discovering sources of stress and anxiety. Then the specialist can assist the child in seeking ways to remove, lessen, or revise those circumstances that cause them distress and thereby improve their situation. The need for such interventions is often particularly acute in the confining and frequently rigid hospital setting.

Name the researcher most responsible for using filmography to reveal the need for increased child-parent visitation hours: 1) James Robertson; 2) Mary Salter Ainsworth; 3) John Bowlby; 4) Sigmund Freud. Select one and explain your answer.

Correct answer - 1. In 1948, James Robertson was hired to observe and document the behaviors and reactions of hospitalized and institutionalized children who were separated from their parents. This led to his creation of a film in 1950 entitled: "A Two-Year-Old Goes to Hospital." The film chronicled, in part, the issues and problems related to parent-child separation and challenged the existing practice of keeping parents and children apart during a hospital stay. The movement was given further impetus after the advent of modern antibiotics that made concerns about germs and outside contamination much less compelling.

One of the primary goals of child life work is successful multidisciplinary collaboration in meeting children's needs. One of the following does not demonstrate successful collaboration: 1) joining child-related hospital committees; 2) meeting with child-family community agencies to determine how best to bring their services to children; 3) participating in daily medical rounds; 4) passing out patient care goals to other health care providers. Select one and explain your answer.

Correct answer - 4. Passing out goals to others conveys the intent that the care goals created by child life staff are the goals that everyone else must accept and implement. Better to bring sample goals to a patient care committee where input from many other participants can be obtained, and where various representatives can seek further input from their own staff, etc., and then mutually creating various care goals and guidelines. Child life programs are so new, and already require such high levels of multidisciplinary cooperation that they must be particularly careful and meticulous in adhering to collaborative and cooperative criteria.

Children hospitalized for longer periods need to continue their education if they are to successfully return to the classroom. When teachers ask how best to assist, the best response would be one of the following: 1) send homework assignments; 2) use a variety of methods to keep in touch and to offer support; 3) minimize study demands; 4) tell fellow students what has happened. Select one and explain your answer.

Correct answer - 2. Ideally, educators will be creative and use a number of ways to assist the student, depending upon the circumstances and expected length of the hospital stay. Some possibilities may include modifying homework expectations and sending in revised and shortened assignments. A child's fellow students may or may not need to know what has happened. The teacher, parents and child life specialist may want to meet together to discuss what should or should not be revealed in order to minimize embarrassment and keep the child's personal affairs as private as possible.

Many things about children can be discovered by watching them in health care play. One of the following, however, cannot be learned by health play observations alone: 1) maturity and developmental level; 2) ability to cope in new situations and with others; 3) their understanding of a proposed treatment; 4) general levels of stress and concern. Select one and explain your answer.

Correct answer - 1. Health care play is not an accurate way to assess a child's developmental level. Only by specific processes of testing and performance can appropriately accurate developmental measures be derived. However, health care play is an accurate and often ideal way to learn about a child's coping skills, understandings about treatments and procedures, and general levels of stress and anxiety. By use of medical play equipment, not only can treatments or procedures be rehearsed, but the child's understandings and quality of reactions can most often be made quite plain. Thus, it is an accurate method of evaluating many other factors important to a meaningful and comprehensive child assessment.

An eight-year-old child with leukemia is having difficulty coping with her treatments and other medical restrictions. The child life specialist recommends instituting a very consistent daily schedule. The reason is that it offers the child: 1) self-determination, consistency and routine; 2) control, independence, and predictability; 3) structure, motivation and expectations; or 4) expression, participation and requirements. Select one and explain your answer.

Correct answer - 2. Children facing serious health uncertainties need a sense of control, independence and predictability. Having a consistent and predictable daily schedule enhances the feeling that most of their life is manageable and successful. It reduces feelings of anxiety, worry and concern that may otherwise predominate when life feels unstructured, uncertain and unsettled. A consistent schedule also enhances a child's sense of independence. Although the schedule may have been created by others (though, ideally, with their input), adhering to the routines gives the child a way to clearly determine, and declare to others, what they will be doing and when. Finally, the sense of surety and destination also produces a measure of control by providing a formal mechanism by which to impose order on other activities and life uncertainties.

A high quality volunteer supervisor will have the ability to: 1) allow other volunteers to learn child interaction strategies by trial and error; 2) solve problems for staff; 3) mentor and coach others; 4) limit feedback to scheduled meetings. Select one and explain your answer.

Correct answer - 3. The best supervisors resort to rigid rules only when necessary, preferring to coach and mentor others toward success whenever possible. Leaving staff to interact with vulnerable children only by trial and error is inappropriate and potentially even dangerous. Problem solving for others, rather than coaching them as they encounter problems, limits their opportunities to explore and learn. Perhaps worse of all, withholding feedback until formally scheduled meetings leaves staff to perpetuate problems, develop erroneous habits, and miss key child support opportunities until a formally appointed time. It is far better to offer ongoing feedback and encouragement than to cast all concerns into one contact where staff may become overwhelmed and discouraged. Ongoing coaching and mentoring is a key to far greater supervisory success.

A diagnosis of "neutropenia" means that a child has the following medical symptoms: 1) arthritic joints and limited mobility; 2) poor circulation in the extremities; 3) loss of hair due to chemotherapy or other medical cause; 4) an abnormally low white blood cell count. Select one and explain your answer.

Correct answer - 4. Neutropenia actually refers to a low level of "neutrophil granulocytes" which are one specific type of white blood cell. Because neutrophil cells make up 50-70% of all white blood cells, they are our first line of defense against invading germs. When the count is abnormally low, individuals are particularly susceptible to infections. Neutropenia can be caused by cancer, autoimmune diseases, some medications, radiation therapy, vitamin deficiencies, and by certain hereditary disorders. Bone marrow biopsy (involving insertion of very long needles) may be required to confirm the diagnosis.

In medical play a child life specialist should avoid doing one of the following: 1) using realistic medical equipment or models; 2) monitoring misunderstandings revealed; 3) correcting misunderstandings revealed; 4) letting the child stop when they want to. Select one and explain your answer.

Correct answer - 2. Monitoring misunderstandings implies being aware of them and doing nothing about them. Child life specialists should routinely and promptly correct any misunderstandings they observe. This should be incorporated into the medical play process and not be negatively carried out. However, it is very important for the child's well-being that misunderstandings and misconceptions not be allowed to persist. Only through correction and clarification can the child develop an accurate understanding of the nature of the medical procedures and/or treatments they will be undergoing. Leaving misconceptions uncorrected invites surprise, fear, and distrust into the medical experience and into the child's relationship with the specialist.

Deliberate behavior focused on managing specific fears and distressing thoughts is referred to as: 1) balance-focused coping; 2) solution-focused coping; 3) emotion-focused coping; 4) feelings-focused coping. Select one and explain your answer.

Correct answer - 3. Emotion-focused coping involves the identification of specific fears and intrusive thoughts. It is followed by mapping the situations and stressors that bring the thoughts and fears to the forefront. Then specific strategies and coping mechanisms are explored, planned and tested. Finally, those strategies and interventions that appear to work are repeatedly reviewed and rehearsed until they become a natural part of the previously distressing experiences and stressors that instigated the negative emotional responses. Periodic review and rehearsal will then be a regular part of an emotion-focused coping maintenance program.

Accreditation entities require child life programs to have written policy and procedural guidelines in order to: 1) foster program quality and consistent, dependable services; 2) compare service levels against other health care programs; 3) ensure that programs offer cost-effective services; examine issues of ethics and professional conduct. Select one and explain your answer.

Correct answer - 1. Accreditation agencies are primarily concerned with monitoring program quality and ensuring that consistent and dependable services are available to patients, families, and health care providers. While service level comparisons between comparable child life services could sometimes appear in summary accreditation reports, a program's mission, goals, target populations and other services are not the point of accreditation reviews. Further, cost-benefit analyses are never used in the evaluation process. However, issues in ethics may arise where relevant to the quality of services.

Child life services are often called upon to prepare children for stressful medical events. A useful guideline would include: 1) using visual models for younger children, and lecture formats for teens; 2) preparing the youngest children 2-3 weeks in advance to allow them to practice coping skills; 3) see only children interested in child life services; or, 4) just one person should prepare any given child, obtaining support from other staff as needed. Select one and explain your answer.

Correct answer - 4. Ideally, only one person should be responsible for preparing any given child. This practice recognizes the importance of a strong and trusting relationship between the child and the child life specialist. While others may augment and support the preparation, a primary staff member that the child trusts and is open with should be the principal preparing professional. Beyond this, children of all ages (and even adults) should be offered visual depictions, pictures and models whenever possible, and lecture-only materials should always be minimized. Optimum preparation time is usually a few hours prior to a procedure, not two to three weeks in advance. In addition, all children should be seen and offered child life services, even if they or their parents initially feel that they have no particular interest in the services.

Case studies

Girl, age 9; 2 days pre-operative for chronic reflux. You are called by the urology nurse who notes in passing, "the girl had a difficult time with the exam, glad you're here." Introducing yourself to the mother and child, the girl shows interest in a Zaadi doll you are holding. Mom, however, refuses your services and prepares to leave.

Key issues: Teaching pre-surgical coping skills is "beneficent" and avoids "maleficence" by reducing stress and fear; duty includes keeping the welfare of those served the primary purpose (see Code, Principle #1); preparation is standard policy.
Conflicts: The child has shown interest (in the doll), but mother refuses – leaving respect for both persons and autonomy issues unclear.
Information Gap: Why mother refused (running late? protecting daughter? cultural issues? misunderstands purpose?).
Options: Problem solve time; explain your role, explore culture; clarify purpose.
Recommendations: Consult urology team members familiar with the family' approach mother separately; defer to the mother if she remains adamant (see AAP policy), but remain available.

Administration proposes charging for services to preserve the child life program. A six-month pilot program, limiting services to patients with insurance or Medicaid will provide data regarding which third-party payers will reimburse for services. On average, 65% of patients have some coverage. Patients without coverage will be diverted to volunteers.

Key issues: Justice demands you be fair minded, even handed, and nondiscriminatory.
Conflicts: The Code, Principle #3 specifically directs that you serve all, regardless of economic status. Code Principle #11 prohibits considerations of financial gain in providing services.
Ethical view: The pilot program is unethical.
Options: Defer to administration, or advocate for offering serving without discrimination.
Recommendations: Pursue objective service referral criteria to see those in greatest need and who will receive the most enduring benefits within cost constraint parameters. If pressures continue, consult the hospital ethics committee.

During a hospital-based group playroom session, numerous children begin sharing with each other why they are hospitalized, etc. One 6-year-old asks you to share for her because she feels it is difficult to explain. You know sharing could be helpful, but you also know her parents value their privacy and would likely not approve. How do you respond?

Key issues: Ethics Code principle #1 urges beneficence, but principle #4 requires confidentiality.
Conflicts: Beneficence vs. confidentiality and parental rights.
Ethical view: Parental privacy is also important for well-being of the child. Further, the child could share in discussion of other common experiences (feelings and fears about IV needles, taking medicines, being separated from home and family, etc.) without actually disclosing her specific diagnosis.
Options: Reveal the diagnosis for the child; avoid actual diagnosis disclosure; seek parental permission.
Recommendations: Meet with the parents; share the child's wishes; explore concerns; use the experience to learn how to handle other similar issues that may yet arise.

A 17-year-old cancer patient has had all available treatments, including radiation, chemotherapy and surgery. Only a bone marrow transplant is left, but he is a "poor candidate." His parents are "talking up" the transplant and have given their approval. The teen tells you he doesn't want the treatment. He is tired of being a "lab experiment." He says he just wants to go home, sleep in his own bed, eat home cooking, see friends, etc. He adds, "You can't tell anyone, especially not my parents." What do you do?

Key issues: Ethical Code, principle #4 requires confidentiality; fidelity requires promise keeping; beneficence requires doing "good".
Conflict: Keeping the confidence may require him to suffer unwanted treatment.
Ethical views: At 17, he may be a "mature minor". Regardless, he should be involved in decisions. Principles of Respect and Autonomy have been ignored.
Options: Reveal his concerns, explore his communication fears and work with the parents to talk more openly with him.
Recommendations: Work with the teen regarding ways to share; work with the parents to explore his thoughts about transplant and share fully with the care team so no one thwarts the process.

A 4-year-old receives physical therapy twice a day after an auto accident. She screams and objects to the therapy. In a playroom session, she treats a doll very roughly telling it, "This is good for you!" She also tells it, "Don't yell! Mind me!" You voice concerns but therapy staff insists the treatments are routine. They want you to address her "behavior problems."

Key issues: Ethical code, principle #1 requires the "welfare" of the child be your first priority; principle #9 requires respect for other professionals and their needs.
Conflict: Is the child the "problem" or are staff demands too high?
Ethical view: Seeking the child's welfare is the priority.
Options: Side with staff; enlist staff's help to mitigating the child's reactions; work with the child; press staff to change the therapy.
Recommendations: Work with the child to reduce stress, negative reactions, pain coping, and to increase tolerance. With supervisor approval, join in therapy sessions to observe and ease key issues. If rejected by therapy staff, examine issues further in a team meeting. If the situation appears abusive, pursue an Ethics Committee meeting and/or contact authorities.

You have diligently worked to develop a new relationship with the Juvenile Diabetic Clinic team, and finally received you first referral – a 10-year-old requiring insulin injections. However, both he and his mother are "needle phobic." You quickly accept the referral, only to realize that you've never dealt with this issue before. Your immediate thought is to research the literature. How do you best proceed?

Key issues: There are questions about competency to respond to the referral.
Conflicts: Beneficence requires that assistance be provided; nonmaleficence requires that no harm be done.
Ethical view: Ethics Code, principle #1 requires the "welfare" of the child be first priority; principle #5 requires practitioners to enhance the services they provide; but principle #8 requires practitioners not to engage in interventions beyond their skills and competencies.
Options: Make a 'good faith' effort; refer the patient to a colleague or other competent service (child psychiatry, etc).
Recommendations: Observe another competent professional's intervention before independently attempting to intervene.

- 148 -

A patient with spina bifida needs a brace to walk. The parents cannot afford the brace. There is a foundation that can assist them, and you present it as a "service" rather than as a "charity." The foundation provides assistance and asks to photograph the presentation to the child. The parents don't like publicity, but agree so as not to appear ungrateful. Later you learn that the family has been solicited to be filmed for a television feature and asked to attend a fundraiser. How do you respond?

Key issues: Public relations staff from the foundation are pressuring the family.
Conflicts: The family has received benefit from the foundation, but was not aware later solicitations might occur.
Ethical view: Beneficence requires presentation of relevant resources; nonmaleficence requires proper understanding and presentation of all burdens.
Options: Leave the family to cope alone; intervene.
Recommendations: Contact the foundation and clarify their policy regarding family solicitation; clarify this family's concerns; share all information with colleagues to prevent future issues.

As a child life specialist you are to be a skilled observer, recording the "comfort-providing responses" of parents to their babies during placement of an IV. One group is left to their own devices to comfort their baby; another group has been coached and provided with aides (toys, musical devices, rattles, etc). The goal is to measure parental success with and without intervention. You find it frustrating to see parents without resources struggle with babies in preventable distress. How do you respond?

Key issue: Should you violate the study to reduce genuine distress?
Conflicts: Suffering is real; long-term benefits from the study are also real.
Ethical view: Beneficence requires you "do good"; nonmaleficence requires you avoid harm; ethical Code, principle #1 requires you seek the welfare of those you serve; principle #7 requires research meet standards for ethical inquiry.
Options: Follow the study versus intervene to prevent suffering.
Recommendations: Overall beneficence is expected; participants must be voluntary and informed and risks must be minimal. If so, you must either withdraw altogether or adhere to the guidelines of the study.

A practitioner in a small hospital, your inpatient census varies widely, two to 8 patients on average. You have accepted a variety of supplemental duties – in the employee childcare center, conducting hospital tours, in the migrant farmer's children's program – to maintain services. A student calls for an internship. You describe the situation and she has no reservations.

Key issue: Should you accept the intern?
Conflicts: Build the profession versus limitations of a low census setting.
Ethical view: Ethical code, principle #5, demands practitioners provide services to diverse communities, while principle 12 states internships must provide proper learning opportunities.
Options: Accept the student; reject the student; try to augment the environment.
Recommendations: Adhering to the ethics of Veracity (truthfulness) and Justice (fairness) is key – ensure the student is well informed. While pediatric hospital experience may be limited, other diverse opportunities remain. Leaving the student unsupervised is unethical and could result in harm, thus she must accompany you in all tasks, or a divided internship with another nearby hospital may be permitted. Careful discussion and planning will be needed to ensure an ethical situation.

One of your patients has a deteriorative neurological condition and has gradually become comatose. The family values your interactions with the patient, seeing your services as hopeful and feeling you offer them crucial support. The staff, however, is confused and feels that little can be gained by your efforts. Even so, they encourage you in deference to the family. However, you now cannot keep up with services to other patients, often staying 1-2 hours late each day.

Key issues: Is your continued involvement a proper use of resources?
Conflicts: The family derives benefits; other patients may be doing without.
Ethical view: Justice and Beneficence are primary in this case.
Options: Continue the services or conclude your involvement.
Recommendations: Priorities must be reassessed. Task neglect and burnout are also of genuine concern. Allocation criteria include: 1) who will realize the greatest benefits; 2) where can quality-of-life be improved; and, 3) where are the needs most urgent. However, a careful assessment must yet take place. If benefits can accrue for this patient, it may become necessary to divide interventions among family and staff to properly use your time.

Secret Key #1 - Time is Your Greatest Enemy

Pace Yourself

Wear a watch. At the beginning of the test, check the time (or start a chronometer on your watch to count the minutes), and check the time after every few questions to make sure you are "on schedule."

If you are forced to speed up, do it efficiently. Usually one or more answer choices can be eliminated without too much difficulty. Above all, don't panic. Don't speed up and just begin guessing at random choices. By pacing yourself, and continually monitoring your progress against your watch, you will always know exactly how far ahead or behind you are with your available time. If you find that you are one minute behind on the test, don't skip one question without spending any time on it, just to catch back up. Take 15 fewer seconds on the next four questions, and after four questions you'll have caught back up. Once you catch back up, you can continue working each problem at your normal pace.

Furthermore, don't dwell on the problems that you were rushed on. If a problem was taking up too much time and you made a hurried guess, it must be difficult. The difficult questions are the ones you are most likely to miss anyway, so it isn't a big loss. It is better to end with more time than you need than to run out of time.

Lastly, sometimes it is beneficial to slow down if you are constantly getting ahead of time. You are always more likely to catch a careless mistake by working more slowly than quickly, and among very high-scoring test takers (those who are likely to have lots of time left over), careless errors affect the score more than mastery of material.

Secret Key #2 - Guessing is not Guesswork

You probably know that guessing is a good idea. Unlike other standardized tests, there is no penalty for getting a wrong answer. Even if you have no idea about a question, you still have a 20-25% chance of getting it right.

Most test takers do not understand the impact that proper guessing can have on their score. Unless you score extremely high, guessing will significantly contribute to your final score.

Monkeys Take the Test

What most test takers don't realize is that to insure that 20-25% chance, you have to guess randomly. If you put 20 monkeys in a room to take this test, assuming they answered once per question and behaved themselves, on average they would get 20-25% of the questions correct. Put 20 test takers in the room, and the average will be much lower among guessed questions. Why?
    1. The test writers intentionally write deceptive answer choices that "look" right. A test

taker has no idea about a question, so he picks the "best looking" answer, which is often wrong. The monkey has no idea what looks good and what doesn't, so it will consistently be right about 20-25% of the time.

2. Test takers will eliminate answer choices from the guessing pool based on a hunch or intuition. Simple but correct answers often get excluded, leaving a 0% chance of being correct. The monkey has no clue, and often gets lucky with the best choice.

This is why the process of elimination endorsed by most test courses is flawed and detrimental to your performance. Test takers don't guess; they make an ignorant stab in the dark that is usually worse than random.

$5 Challenge

Let me introduce one of the most valuable ideas of this course—the $5 challenge:

You only mark your "best guess" if you are willing to bet $5 on it.
You only eliminate choices from guessing if you are willing to bet $5 on it.

Why $5? Five dollars is an amount of money that is small yet not insignificant, and can really add up fast (20 questions could cost you $100). Likewise, each answer choice on one question of the test will have a small impact on your overall score, but it can really add up to a lot of points in the end.

The process of elimination IS valuable. The following shows your chance of guessing it right:

If you eliminate wrong answer choices until only this many remain:	Chance of getting it correct:
1	100%
2	50%
3	33%

However, if you accidentally eliminate the right answer or go on a hunch for an incorrect answer, your chances drop dramatically—to 0%. By guessing among all the answer choices, you are GUARANTEED to have a shot at the right answer.

That's why the $5 test is so valuable. If you give up the advantage and safety of a pure guess, it had better be worth the risk.

What we still haven't covered is how to be sure that whatever guess you make is truly random. Here's the easiest way:

Always pick the first answer choice among those remaining.

Such a technique means that you have decided, **before you see a single test question**, exactly how you are going to guess, and since the order of choices tells you nothing about which one is correct, this guessing technique is perfectly random.

This section is not meant to scare you away from making educated guesses or eliminating choices; you just need to define when a choice is worth eliminating. The $5 test, along with a pre-defined random guessing strategy, is the best way to make sure you reap all of the benefits of guessing.

Secret Key #3 - Practice Smarter, Not Harder

Many test takers delay the test preparation process because they dread the awful amounts of practice time they think necessary to succeed on the test. We have refined an effective method that will take you only a fraction of the time.

There are a number of "obstacles" in the path to success. Among these are answering questions, finishing in time, and mastering test-taking strategies. All must be executed on the day of the test at peak performance, or your score will suffer. The test is a mental marathon that has a large impact on your future.

Just like a marathon runner, it is important to work your way up to the full challenge. So first you just worry about questions, and then time, and finally strategy:

Success Strategy

1. Find a good source for practice tests.
2. If you are willing to make a larger time investment, consider using more than one study guide. Often the different approaches of multiple authors will help you "get" difficult concepts.
3. Take a practice test with no time constraints, with all study helps, "open book." Take your time with questions and focus on applying strategies.
4. Take a practice test with time constraints, with all guides, "open book."
5. Take a final practice test without open material and with time limits.

If you have time to take more practice tests, just repeat step 5. By gradually exposing yourself to the full rigors of the test environment, you will condition your mind to the stress of test day and maximize your success.

Secret Key #4 - Prepare, Don't Procrastinate

Let me state an obvious fact: if you take the test three times, you will probably get three different scores. This is due to the way you feel on test day, the level of preparedness you have, and the version of the test you see. Despite the test writers' claims to the contrary, some versions of the test WILL be easier for you than others.

Since your future depends so much on your score, you should maximize your chances of success. In order to maximize the likelihood of success, you've got to prepare in advance.

This means taking practice tests and spending time learning the information and test taking strategies you will need to succeed.

Never go take the actual test as a "practice" test, expecting that you can just take it again if you need to. Take all the practice tests you can on your own, but when you go to take the official test, be prepared, be focused, and do your best the first time!

Secret Key #5 - Test Yourself

Everyone knows that time is money. There is no need to spend too much of your time or too little of your time preparing for the test. You should only spend as much of your precious time preparing as is necessary for you to get the score you need.

Once you have taken a practice test under real conditions of time constraints, then you will know if you are ready for the test or not.

If you have scored extremely high the first time that you take the practice test, then there is not much point in spending countless hours studying. You are already there.

Benchmark your abilities by retaking practice tests and seeing how much you have improved. Once you consistently score high enough to guarantee success, then you are ready.

If you have scored well below where you need, then knuckle down and begin studying in earnest. Check your improvement regularly through the use of practice tests under real conditions. Above all, don't worry, panic, or give up. The key is perseverance!

Then, when you go to take the test, remain confident and remember how well you did on the practice tests. If you can score high enough on a practice test, then you can do the same on the real thing.

General Strategies

The most important thing you can do is to ignore your fears and jump into the test immediately. Do not be overwhelmed by any strange-sounding terms. You have to jump into the test like jumping into a pool—all at once is the easiest way.

Make Predictions

As you read and understand the question, try to guess what the answer will be. Remember that several of the answer choices are wrong, and once you begin reading them, your mind will immediately become cluttered with answer choices designed to throw you off. Your mind is typically the most focused immediately after you have read the question and digested its contents. If you can, try to predict what the correct answer will be. You may be surprised at what you can predict.

Quickly scan the choices and see if your prediction is in the listed answer choices. If it is, then you can be quite confident that you have the right answer. It still won't hurt to check the other answer choices, but most of the time, you've got it!

Answer the Question

It may seem obvious to only pick answer choices that answer the question, but the test writers can create some excellent answer choices that are wrong. Don't pick an answer just because it sounds right, or you believe it to be true. It MUST answer the question. Once you've made your selection, always go back and check it against the question and make sure that you didn't misread the question and that the answer choice does answer the question posed.

Benchmark

After you read the first answer choice, decide if you think it sounds correct or not. If it doesn't, move on to the next answer choice. If it does, mentally mark that answer choice. This doesn't mean that you've definitely selected it as your answer choice, it just means that it's the best you've seen thus far. Go ahead and read the next choice. If the next choice is worse than the one you've already selected, keep going to the next answer choice. If the next choice is better than the choice you've already selected, mentally mark the new answer choice as your best guess.

The first answer choice that you select becomes your standard. Every other answer choice must be benchmarked against that standard. That choice is correct until proven otherwise by another answer choice beating it out. Once you've decided that no other answer choice seems as good, do one final check to ensure that your answer choice answers the question posed.

Valid Information

Don't discount any of the information provided in the question. Every piece of information may be necessary to determine the correct answer. None of the information in the question is there to throw you off (while the answer choices will certainly have information to throw you off). If two seemingly unrelated topics are discussed, don't ignore either. You can be confident there is a relationship, or it wouldn't be included in the question, and you are probably going to have to determine what is that relationship to find the answer.

Avoid "Fact Traps"

Don't get distracted by a choice that is factually true. Your search is for the answer that answers the question. Stay focused and don't fall for an answer that is true but irrelevant. Always go back to the question and make sure you're choosing an answer that actually answers the question and is not just a true statement. An answer can be factually correct, but it MUST answer the question asked. Additionally, two answers can both be seemingly correct, so be sure to read all of the answer choices, and make sure that you get the one that BEST answers the question.

Milk the Question

Some of the questions may throw you completely off. They might deal with a subject you have not been exposed to, or one that you haven't reviewed in years. While your lack of knowledge about the subject will be a hindrance, the question itself can give you many clues that will help you find the correct answer. Read the question carefully and look for clues. Watch particularly for adjectives and nouns describing difficult terms or words that you don't recognize. Regardless of whether you completely understand a word or not, replacing it with a synonym, either provided or one you more familiar with, may help you to understand what the questions are asking. Rather than wracking your mind about specific detailed information concerning a difficult term or word, try to use mental substitutes that are easier to understand.

The Trap of Familiarity

Don't just choose a word because you recognize it. On difficult questions, you may not recognize a number of words in the answer choices. The test writers don't put "make-believe" words on the test, so don't think that just because you only recognize all the words in one answer choice that that answer choice must be correct. If you only recognize words in one answer choice, then focus on that one. Is it correct? Try your best to determine if it is correct. If it is, that's great. If not, eliminate it. Each word and answer choice you eliminate increases your chances of getting the question correct, even if you then have to guess among the unfamiliar choices.

Eliminate Answers

Eliminate choices as soon as you realize they are wrong. But be careful! Make sure you consider all of the possible answer choices. Just because one appears right, doesn't mean that the next one won't be even better! The test writers will usually put more than one good answer choice for every question, so read all of them. Don't worry if you are stuck between two that seem right. By getting down to just two remaining possible choices, your odds are now 50/50. Rather than wasting too much time, play the odds. You are guessing, but guessing wisely because you've been able to knock out some of the answer choices that you know are wrong. If you are eliminating choices and realize that the last answer choice you are left with is also obviously wrong, don't panic. Start over and consider each choice again. There may easily be something that you missed the first time and will realize on the second pass.

Tough Questions

If you are stumped on a problem or it appears too hard or too difficult, don't waste time. Move on! Remember though, if you can quickly check for obviously incorrect answer choices, your chances of guessing correctly are greatly improved. Before you completely give up, at least try to knock out a couple of possible answers. Eliminate what you can and then guess at the remaining answer choices before moving on.

Brainstorm

If you get stuck on a difficult question, spend a few seconds quickly brainstorming. Run through the complete list of possible answer choices. Look at each choice and ask yourself, "Could this answer the question satisfactorily?" Go through each answer choice and consider it independently of the others. By systematically going through all possibilities, you may find something that you would otherwise overlook. Remember though that when you get stuck, it's important to try to keep moving.

Read Carefully

Understand the problem. Read the question and answer choices carefully. Don't miss the question because you misread the terms. You have plenty of time to read each question thoroughly and make sure you understand what is being asked. Yet a happy medium must be attained, so don't waste too much time. You must read carefully, but efficiently.

Face Value

When in doubt, use common sense. Always accept the situation in the problem at face value. Don't read too much into it. These problems will not require you to make huge leaps of logic. The test writers aren't trying to throw you off with a cheap trick. If you have to go beyond creativity and make a leap of logic in order to have an answer choice answer the question, then you should look at the other answer choices. Don't overcomplicate the problem by creating theoretical relationships or explanations that will warp time or space. These are normal problems rooted in reality. It's just that the applicable relationship or explanation may not be readily apparent and you have to figure things out. Use your common sense to interpret anything that isn't clear.

Prefixes

If you're having trouble with a word in the question or answer choices, try dissecting it. Take advantage of every clue that the word might include. Prefixes and suffixes can be a huge help. Usually they allow you to determine a basic meaning. Pre- means before, post- means after, pro - is positive, de- is negative. From these prefixes and suffixes, you can get an idea of the general meaning of the word and try to put it into context. Beware though of any traps. Just because con- is the opposite of pro-, doesn't necessarily mean congress is the opposite of progress!

Hedge Phrases

Watch out for critical hedge phrases, led off with words such as "likely," "may," "can," "sometimes," "often," "almost," "mostly," "usually," "generally," "rarely," and "sometimes." Question writers insert these hedge phrases to cover every possibility. Often an answer choice will be wrong simply because it leaves no room for exception. Unless the situation calls for them, avoid answer choices that have definitive words like "exactly," and "always."

Switchback Words

Stay alert for "switchbacks." These are the words and phrases frequently used to alert you to shifts in thought. The most common switchback word is "but." Others include "although," "however," "nevertheless," "on the other hand," "even though," "while," "in spite of," "despite," and "regardless of."

New Information

Correct answer choices will rarely have completely new information included. Answer choices typically are straightforward reflections of the material asked about and will directly relate to the question. If a new piece of information is included in an answer choice that doesn't even seem to relate to the topic being asked about, then that answer choice is likely incorrect. All of the information needed to answer the question is usually provided for you in the question. You should not have to make guesses that are unsupported or choose answer choices that require unknown information that cannot be reasoned from what is given.

Time Management

On technical questions, don't get lost on the technical terms. Don't spend too much time on any one question. If you don't know what a term means, then odds are you aren't going to get much further since you don't have a dictionary. You should be able to immediately recognize whether or not you know a term. If you don't, work with the other clues that you have—the other answer choices and terms provided—but don't waste too much time trying to figure out a difficult term that you don't know.

Contextual Clues

Look for contextual clues. An answer can be right but not the correct answer. The contextual clues will help you find the answer that is most right and is correct. Understand the context in which a phrase or statement is made. This will help you make important distinctions.

Don't Panic

Panicking will not answer any questions for you; therefore, it isn't helpful. When you first see the question, if your mind goes blank, take a deep breath. Force yourself to mechanically go through the steps of solving the problem using the strategies you've learned.

Pace Yourself

Don't get clock fever. It's easy to be overwhelmed when you're looking at a page full of questions, your mind is full of random thoughts and feeling confused, and the clock is ticking down faster than you would like. Calm down and maintain the pace that you have set for yourself. As long as you are on track by monitoring your pace, you are guaranteed to have enough time for yourself. When you get to the last few minutes of the test, it may seem like you won't have enough time left, but if you only have as many questions as you should have left at that point, then you're right on track!

Answer Selection

The best way to pick an answer choice is to eliminate all of those that are wrong, until only one is left and confirm that is the correct answer. Sometimes though, an answer choice may immediately look right. Be careful! Take a second to make sure that the other choices are not equally obvious. Don't make a hasty mistake. There are only two times that you should stop before checking other answers. First is when you are positive that the answer choice you have selected is correct. Second is when time is almost out and you have to make a quick guess!

Check Your Work

Since you will probably not know every term listed and the answer to every question, it is important that you get credit for the ones that you do know. Don't miss any questions through careless mistakes. If at all possible, try to take a second to look back over your answer selection and make sure you've selected the correct answer choice and haven't made a costly careless mistake (such as marking an answer choice that you didn't mean to mark). The time it takes for this quick double check should more than pay for itself in caught mistakes.

Beware of Directly Quoted Answers

Sometimes an answer choice will repeat word for word a portion of the question or reference section. However, beware of such exact duplication. It may be a trap! More than likely, the correct choice will paraphrase or summarize a point, rather than being exactly the same wording.

Slang

Scientific sounding answers are better than slang ones. An answer choice that begins "To compare the outcomes..." is much more likely to be correct than one that begins "Because some people insisted..."

Extreme Statements

Avoid wild answers that throw out highly controversial ideas that are proclaimed as established fact. An answer choice that states the "process should used in certain situations, if..." is much more likely to be correct than one that states the "process should be discontinued completely." The first is a calm rational statement and doesn't even make a definitive, uncompromising stance, using a hedge word "if" to provide wiggle room, whereas the second choice is a radical idea and far more extreme.

Answer Choice Families

When you have two or more answer choices that are direct opposites or parallels, one of them is usually the correct answer. For instance, if one answer choice states "x increases" and another answer choice states "x decreases" or "y increases," then those two or three answer choices are very similar in construction and fall into the same family of answer choices. A family of answer choices consists of two or three answer choices, very similar in construction, but often with directly opposite meanings. Usually the correct answer choice will be in that family of answer choices. The "odd man out" or answer choice that doesn't seem to fit the parallel construction of the other answer choices is more likely to be incorrect.

Special Report: How to Overcome Test Anxiety

The very nature of tests caters to some level of anxiety, nervousness, or tension, just as we feel for any important event that occurs in our lives. A little bit of anxiety or nervousness can be a good thing. It helps us with motivation, and makes achievement just that much sweeter. However, too much anxiety can be a problem, especially if it hinders our ability to function and perform.

"Test anxiety," is the term that refers to the emotional reactions that some test-takers experience when faced with a test or exam. Having a fear of testing and exams is based upon a rational fear, since the test-taker's performance can shape the course of an academic career. Nevertheless, experiencing excessive fear of examinations will only interfere with the test-taker's ability to perform and chance to be successful.

There are a large variety of causes that can contribute to the development and sensation of test anxiety. These include, but are not limited to, lack of preparation and worrying about issues surrounding the test.

Lack of Preparation

Lack of preparation can be identified by the following behaviors or situations:

Not scheduling enough time to study, and therefore cramming the night before the test or exam
Managing time poorly, to create the sensation that there is not enough time to do everything
Failing to organize the text information in advance, so that the study material consists of the entire text and not simply the pertinent information
Poor overall studying habits

Worrying, on the other hand, can be related to both the test taker, or many other factors around him/her that will be affected by the results of the test. These include worrying about:

Previous performances on similar exams, or exams in general
How friends and other students are achieving
The negative consequences that will result from a poor grade or failure

There are three primary elements to test anxiety. Physical components, which involve the same typical bodily reactions as those to acute anxiety (to be discussed below). Emotional factors have to do with fear or panic. Mental or cognitive issues concerning attention spans and memory abilities.

Physical Signals

There are many different symptoms of test anxiety, and these are not limited to mental and emotional strain. Frequently there are a range of physical signals that will let a test taker know that he/she is suffering from test anxiety. These bodily changes can include the following:

Perspiring
Sweaty palms
Wet, trembling hands
Nausea
Dry mouth
A knot in the stomach
Headache
Faintness
Muscle tension
Aching shoulders, back and neck
Rapid heart beat
Feeling too hot/cold

To recognize the sensation of test anxiety, a test-taker should monitor him/herself for the following sensations:

The physical distress symptoms as listed above
Emotional sensitivity, expressing emotional feelings such as the need to cry or laugh too much, or a sensation of anger or helplessness
A decreased ability to think, causing the test-taker to blank out or have racing thoughts that are hard to organize or control.

Though most students will feel some level of anxiety when faced with a test or exam, the majority can cope with that anxiety and maintain it at a manageable level. However, those who cannot are faced with a very real and very serious condition, which can and should be controlled for the immeasurable benefit of this sufferer.

Naturally, these sensations lead to negative results for the testing experience. The most common effects of test anxiety have to do with nervousness and mental blocking.

Nervousness

Nervousness can appear in several different levels:

The test-taker's difficulty, or even inability to read and understand the questions on the test
The difficulty or inability to organize thoughts to a coherent form
The difficulty or inability to recall key words and concepts relating to the testing questions (especially essays)
The receipt of poor grades on a test, though the test material was well known by the test taker

Conversely, a person may also experience mental blocking, which involves:

Blanking out on test questions
Only remembering the correct answers to the questions when the test has already finished.

Fortunately for test anxiety sufferers, beating these feelings, to a large degree, has to do with proper preparation. When a test taker has a feeling of preparedness, then anxiety will be dramatically lessened.

The first step to resolving anxiety issues is to distinguish which of the two types of anxiety are being suffered. If the anxiety is a direct result of a lack of preparation, this should be considered a normal reaction, and the anxiety level (as opposed to the test results) shouldn't be anything to worry about. However, if, when adequately prepared, the test-taker still panics, blanks out, or seems to overreact, this is not a fully rational reaction. While this can be considered normal too, there are many ways to combat and overcome these effects.

Remember that anxiety cannot be entirely eliminated, however, there are ways to minimize it, to make the anxiety easier to manage. Preparation is one of the best ways to minimize test anxiety. Therefore the following techniques are wise in order to best fight off any anxiety that may want to build.

To begin with, try to avoid cramming before a test, whenever it is possible. By trying to memorize an entire term's worth of information in one day, you'll be shocking your system, and not giving yourself a very good chance to absorb the information. This is an easy path to anxiety, so for those who suffer from test anxiety, cramming should not even be considered an option.

Instead of cramming, work throughout the semester to combine all of the material which is presented throughout the semester, and work on it gradually as the course goes by, making sure to master the main concepts first, leaving minor details for a week or so before the test.

To study for the upcoming exam, be sure to pose questions that may be on the examination, to gauge the ability to answer them by integrating the ideas from your texts, notes and lectures, as well as any supplementary readings.

If it is truly impossible to cover all of the information that was covered in that particular term, concentrate on the most important portions, that can be covered very well. Learn these concepts as best as possible, so that when the test comes, a goal can be made to use these concepts as presentations of your knowledge.

In addition to study habits, changes in attitude are critical to beating a struggle with test anxiety. In fact, an improvement of the perspective over the entire test-taking experience can actually help a test taker to enjoy studying and therefore improve the overall experience. Be certain not to overemphasize the significance of the grade - know that the result of the test is neither a reflection of self worth, nor is it a measure of intelligence; one grade will not predict a person's future success.

To improve an overall testing outlook, the following steps should be tried:

Keeping in mind that the most reasonable expectation for taking a test is to expect to try to demonstrate as much of what you know as you possibly can.

Reminding ourselves that a test is only one test; this is not the only one, and there will be others.

The thought of thinking of oneself in an irrational, all-or-nothing term should be avoided at all costs.

A reward should be designated for after the test, so there's something to look forward to. Whether it be going to a movie, going out to eat, or simply visiting friends, schedule it in advance, and do it no matter what result is expected on the exam.

Test-takers should also keep in mind that the basics are some of the most important things, even beyond anti-anxiety techniques and studying. Never neglect the basic social, emotional and biological needs, in order to try to absorb information. In order to best achieve, these three factors must be held as just as important as the studying itself.

Study Steps

Remember the following important steps for studying:

Maintain healthy nutrition and exercise habits. Continue both your recreational activities and social pass times. These both contribute to your physical and emotional well being.

Be certain to get a good amount of sleep, especially the night before the test, because when you're overtired you are not able to perform to the best of your best ability.

Keep the studying pace to a moderate level by taking breaks when they are needed, and varying the work whenever possible, to keep the mind fresh instead of getting bored.

When enough studying has been done that all the material that can be learned has been learned, and the test taker is prepared for the test, stop studying and do something relaxing such as listening to music, watching a movie, or taking a warm bubble bath.

There are also many other techniques to minimize the uneasiness or apprehension that is experienced along with test anxiety before, during, or even after the examination. In fact, there are a great deal of things that can be done to stop anxiety from interfering with lifestyle and performance. Again, remember that anxiety will not be eliminated entirely, and it shouldn't be. Otherwise that "up" feeling for exams would not exist, and most of us depend on that sensation to perform better than usual. However, this anxiety has to be at a level that is manageable.

Of course, as we have just discussed, being prepared for the exam is half the battle right away. Attending all classes, finding out what knowledge will be expected on the exam, and knowing the exam schedules are easy steps to lowering anxiety. Keeping up with work will remove the need to cram, and efficient study habits will eliminate wasted time. Studying should be done in an ideal location for concentration, so that it is simple to become interested in the material and give it complete attention. A method such as SQ3R (Survey, Question, Read, Recite, Review) is a wonderful key to follow to make sure that the study habits are as effective as possible, especially in the case of learning from a textbook. Flashcards are great techniques for memorization. Learning to take good notes will mean that notes will be full of useful information, so that less sifting will need to be done to seek out what is pertinent for studying. Reviewing notes after class and then again on occasion will keep the information fresh in the mind. From notes that have been taken summary sheets and outlines can be made for simpler reviewing.

A study group can also be a very motivational and helpful place to study, as there will be a sharing of ideas, all of the minds can work together, to make sure that everyone understands, and the studying will be made more interesting because it will be a social occasion.

Basically, though, as long as the test-taker remains organized and self confident, with efficient study habits, less time will need to be spent studying, and higher grades will be achieved.

To become self confident, there are many useful steps. The first of these is "self talk." It has been shown through extensive research, that self-talk for students who suffer from test anxiety, should be well monitored, in order to make sure that it contributes to self confidence as opposed to sinking the student. Frequently the self talk of test-anxious students is negative or self-defeating, thinking that everyone else is smarter and faster, that they always mess up, and that if they don't do well, they'll fail the entire course. It is important to decreasing anxiety that awareness is made of self talk. Try writing any negative self thoughts and then disputing them with a positive statement instead. Begin self-encouragement as though it was a friend speaking. Repeat positive statements to help reprogram the mind to believing in successes instead of failures.

Helpful Techniques

Other extremely helpful techniques include:

Self-visualization of doing well and reaching goals
While aiming for an "A" level of understanding, don't try to "overprotect" by setting your expectations lower. This will only convince the mind to stop studying in order to meet the lower expectations.
Don't make comparisons with the results or habits of other students. These are individual factors, and different things work for different people, causing different results.
Strive to become an expert in learning what works well, and what can be done in order to improve. Consider collecting this data in a journal.
Create rewards for after studying instead of doing things before studying that will only turn into avoidance behaviors.
Make a practice of relaxing - by using methods such as progressive relaxation, self-hypnosis, guided imagery, etc - in order to make relaxation an automatic sensation.
Work on creating a state of relaxed concentration so that concentrating will take on the focus of the mind, so that none will be wasted on worrying.
Take good care of the physical self by eating well and getting enough sleep.
Plan in time for exercise and stick to this plan.

Beyond these techniques, there are other methods to be used before, during and after the test that will help the test-taker perform well in addition to overcoming anxiety.

Before the exam comes the academic preparation. This involves establishing a study schedule and beginning at least one week before the actual date of the test. By doing this, the anxiety of not having enough time to study for the test will be automatically eliminated. Moreover, this will make the studying a much more effective experience, ensuring that the learning will be an easier process. This relieves much undue pressure on the test-taker.

Summary sheets, note cards, and flash cards with the main concepts and examples of these main concepts should be prepared in advance of the actual studying time. A topic should never be eliminated from this process. By omitting a topic because it isn't expected to be on the test is only setting up the test-taker for anxiety should it actually appear on the exam. Utilize the course syllabus for laying out the topics that should be studied. Carefully go over the notes that were made in class, paying special attention to any of the issues that the professor took special care to emphasize while lecturing in class. In the textbooks, use the chapter review, or if possible, the chapter tests, to begin your review.

It may even be possible to ask the instructor what information will be covered on the exam, or what the format of the exam will be (for example, multiple choice, essay, free form, true-false). Additionally, see if it is possible to find out how many questions will be on the test. If a review sheet or sample test has been offered by the professor, make good use of it, above anything else, for the preparation for the test. Another great resource for getting to know the examination is reviewing tests from previous semesters. Use these tests to review, and aim to achieve a 100% score on each of the possible topics. With a few exceptions, the goal that you set for yourself is the highest one that you will reach.

Take all of the questions that were assigned as homework, and rework them to any other possible course material. The more problems reworked, the more skill and confidence will form as a result. When forming the solution to a problem, write out each of the steps. Don't simply do head work. By doing as many steps on paper as possible, much clarification and therefore confidence will be formed. Do this with as many homework problems as possible, before checking the answers. By checking the answer after each problem, a reinforcement will exist, that will not be on the exam. Study situations should be as exam-like as possible, to prime the test-taker's system for the experience. By waiting to check the answers at the end, a psychological advantage will be formed, to decrease the stress factor.

Another fantastic reason for not cramming is the avoidance of confusion in concepts, especially when it comes to mathematics. 8-10 hours of study will become one hundred percent more effective if it is spread out over a week or at least several days, instead of doing it all in one sitting. Recognize that the human brain requires time in order to assimilate new material, so frequent breaks and a span of study time over several days will be much more beneficial.

Additionally, don't study right up until the point of the exam. Studying should stop a minimum of one hour before the exam begins. This allows the brain to rest and put things in their proper order. This will also provide the time to become as relaxed as possible when going into the examination room. The test-taker will also have time to eat well and eat sensibly. Know that the brain needs food as much as the rest of the body. With enough food and enough sleep, as well as a relaxed attitude, the body and the mind are primed for success.

Avoid any anxious classmates who are talking about the exam. These students only spread anxiety, and are not worth sharing the anxious sentimentalities.

Before the test also involves creating a positive attitude, so mental preparation should also be a point of concentration. There are many keys to creating a positive attitude. Should fears become rushing in, make a visualization of taking the exam, doing well, and seeing an A written on the paper. Write out a list of affirmations that will bring a feeling of confidence, such as "I am doing well in my English class," "I studied well and know my material," "I enjoy this class." Even if the affirmations aren't believed at first, it sends a positive message to the subconscious which will result in an alteration of the overall belief system, which is the system that creates reality.

If a sensation of panic begins, work with the fear and imagine the very worst! Work through the entire scenario of not passing the test, failing the entire course, and dropping out of school, followed by not getting a job, and pushing a shopping cart through the dark alley where you'll live. This will place things into perspective! Then, practice deep breathing and create a visualization of the opposite situation - achieving an "A" on the exam, passing the entire course, receiving the degree at a graduation ceremony.

On the day of the test, there are many things to be done to ensure the best results, as well as the most calm outlook. The following stages are suggested in order to maximize test-taking potential:

Begin the examination day with a moderate breakfast, and avoid any coffee or beverages with caffeine if the test taker is prone to jitters. Even people who are used to managing caffeine can feel jittery or light-headed when it is taken on a test day. Attempt to do something that is relaxing before the examination begins. As last minute cramming clouds the mastering of overall concepts, it is better to use this time to create a calming outlook.
Be certain to arrive at the test location well in advance, in order to provide time to select a location that is away from doors, windows and other distractions, as well as giving enough time to relax before the test begins.
Keep away from anxiety generating classmates who will upset the sensation of stability and relaxation that is being attempted before the exam.
Should the waiting period before the exam begins cause anxiety, create a self-distraction by reading a light magazine or something else that is relaxing and simple.

During the exam itself, read the entire exam from beginning to end, and find out how much time should be allotted to each individual problem. Once writing the exam, should more time be taken for a problem, it should be abandoned, in order to begin another problem. If there is time at the end, the unfinished problem can always be returned to and completed.

Read the instructions very carefully - twice - so that unpleasant surprises won't follow during or after the exam has ended.

When writing the exam, pretend that the situation is actually simply the completion of homework within a library, or at home. This will assist in forming a relaxed atmosphere, and will allow the brain extra focus for the complex thinking function.

Begin the exam with all of the questions with which the most confidence is felt. This will build the confidence level regarding the entire exam and will begin a quality momentum. This will also create encouragement for trying the problems where uncertainty resides.

Going with the "gut instinct" is always the way to go when solving a problem. Second guessing should be avoided at all costs. Have confidence in the ability to do well.

For essay questions, create an outline in advance that will keep the mind organized and make certain that all of the points are remembered. For multiple choice, read every answer, even if the correct one has been spotted - a better one may exist.

Continue at a pace that is reasonable and not rushed, in order to be able to work carefully. Provide enough time to go over the answers at the end, to check for small errors that can be corrected.

Should a feeling of panic begin, breathe deeply, and think of the feeling of the body releasing sand through its pores. Visualize a calm, peaceful place, and include all of the sights, sounds and sensations of this image. Continue the deep breathing, and take a few minutes to continue this with closed eyes. When all is well again, return to the test.

If a "blanking" occurs for a certain question, skip it and move on to the next question. There will be time to return to the other question later. Get everything done that can be done, first, to guarantee all the grades that can be compiled, and to build all of the confidence possible. Then return to the weaker questions to build the marks from there.

Remember, one's own reality can be created, so as long as the belief is there, success will follow. And remember: anxiety can happen later, right now, there's an exam to be written!

After the examination is complete, whether there is a feeling for a good grade or a bad grade, don't dwell on the exam, and be certain to follow through on the reward that was promised...and enjoy it! Don't dwell on any mistakes that have been made, as there is nothing that can be done at this point anyway.

Additionally, don't begin to study for the next test right away. Do something relaxing for a while, and let the mind relax and prepare itself to begin absorbing information again.

From the results of the exam - both the grade and the entire experience, be certain to learn from what has gone on. Perfect studying habits and work some more on confidence in order to make the next examination experience even better than the last one.

Learn to avoid places where openings occurred for laziness, procrastination and day dreaming.

Use the time between this exam and the next one to better learn to relax, even learning to relax on cue, so that any anxiety can be controlled during the next exam. Learn how to relax the body. Slouch in your chair if that helps. Tighten and then relax all of the different muscle groups, one group at a time, beginning with the feet and then working all the way up to the neck and face. This will ultimately relax the muscles more than they were to begin with. Learn how to breathe deeply and comfortably, and focus on this breathing going in and out as a relaxing thought. With every exhale, repeat the word "relax."

As common as test anxiety is, it is very possible to overcome it. Make yourself one of the test-takers who overcome this frustrating hindrance.

Additional Bonus Material

Due to our efforts to try to keep this book to a manageable length, we've created a link that will give you access to all of your additional bonus material.

Please visit http://www.mometrix.com/bonus948/childlife to access the information.